Simon Collinson **and** Melvin Jay

From Complexity to Simplicity

Unleash Your Organization's Potential!

palgrave
macmillan

First published 2012 by
PALGRAVE MACMILLAN

Palgrave Macmillan in the UK is an imprint of Macmillan Publishers Limited,
registered in England, company number 785998, of Houndmills, Basingstoke,
Hampshire RG21 6XS.

Palgrave Macmillan in the US is a division of St Martin's Press LLC,
175 Fifth Avenue, New York, NY 10010.

Palgrave Macmillan is the global academic imprint of the above companies
and has companies and representatives throughout the world.

Palgrave® and Macmillan® are registered trademarks in the United States,
the United Kingdom, Europe and other countries.

ISBN: 978-1-137-00621-9   hardback

This book is printed on paper suitable for recycling and made from fully
managed and sustained forest sources. Logging, pulping and manufacturing
processes are expected to conform to the environmental regulations of the
country of origin.

A catalogue record for this book is available from the British Library.

A catalog record for this book is available from the Library of Congress.

10 9 8 7 6 5 4 3 2 1
21 20 19 18 17 16 15 14 13 12

Printed and bound in Great Britain by
CPI Antony Rowe, Chippenham and Eastbourne

Contents

Preface   iv

1   The Causes and Consequences of Complexity   1

2   Diagnosing Complexity and Developing a
        Simplification Strategy   37

3   How to Simplify: People Complexity   57

4   How to Simplify: Organizations   92

5   How to Simplify: Strategy   140

6   How to Simplify: Processes   173

7   How to Simplify: Products and Services   201

8   How to Simplify: Everyday   229

Appendix 1   Costly Complexity in the Pharmaceutical Sector   250

Appendix 2   Costly Complexity in the Banking Sector   265

Appendix 3   Costly Complexity in the Insurance Sector   277

References and further reading   287

Notes   292

Index   293

Preface

Complexity is one of the biggest barriers to success in big organizations, but despite this fact there is very little robust academic research into the causes and consequences of this growing problem. Similarly there are very few practical books or papers that provide actionable advice on how leaders and managers in big organizations can attack this problem.

This book combines the insights of our academic research and our practical experience with relevant examples of complexity in business from organizations around the world. It reflects our shared personal interest in the amazing complexity puzzle – and our shared professional aspiration to help improve the way that businesses are run. (Writing it also showed us that academics have no monopoly over *theory* and experienced executives have no monopoly over *practice*.)

We hope you will agree that this book adds to the sum of thinking on the complexity challenge. We also hope you find practical steps for making your organization not just more profitable, but also a better place in which to work.

Acknowledgements

Many people have contributed to this book, but we would particularly like to thank our work colleagues and our friends, Alistair, Ashley, David, Kevin, Jess and Peter, for their invaluable contributions and support. Special thanks go to Annaleena for her dazzling design work.

Chapter 1

The Causes and Consequences of Complexity

Complexity has become one of the biggest barriers to success in large global organizations. Whether you know it for a fact, or just sense it, complexity is reducing your profits, slowing you down and harming employee motivation in your organization.

Challenges like economic turbulence, understanding changes in customer needs, coping with emerging economies, successfully launching innovative new products or services, dealing with regulatory change, and finding and keeping talent are all big issues that occupy the minds of corporate leaders. In combination these amount to a complex competitive environment, which firms need to continually respond to in order to succeed.

However, today managers and leaders are increasingly preoccupied with the internal battle against the sheer complexity of effectively running their organizations on a day-to-day basis. In other words, internal complexity is now one of the big challenges preventing many organizations from reaching their true financial and human potential.

Given the size and extent of the complexity problem there is surprisingly little good academic research to help us understand it – and surprisingly little practical advice on what to do about it.

So our simple aim is to combine robust academic research with some practical experience and unique tools which will help you to understand complexity – but, more importantly, we want to show you that you can identify and remove the kinds of complexity that get in your way and cost your firm money.

Everyone knows about Nokia – so it makes a good example to kick off with. There is no question that this once-great firm missed the boat when consumer markets shifted over to the smartphone. But this was not just the result of an unlucky strategic choice; there were signs that the firm had lost its way well before taking this wrong turn. It had embarked on a series of acquisitions and was building an increasingly diverse product portfolio through investments into software, content and services, which were all adding complexity, but not value. More recently, new leadership and organizational restructuring compounded, rather than solved, the problem. Nokia became increasingly more complex and increasingly less profitable.

While Nokia has been a 'fallen star' favorite for the business media, its experience with overwhelming complexity is common to firms across all industry sectors.

We know that the competitive environment is becoming more complex, turbulent and unpredictable, and senior managers have little or no control over the underlying trends, from globalization to increasingly segmented markets to technological change. The most damaging kinds of complexity, however, come from within. More products and services, more strategic initiatives, more specialist departments, more layers of management, more processes, procedures, reports, meetings and emails – until individuals are overwhelmed. People within the business are suffering from costly complexity – but they are also (usually without knowing it) the main cause of costly complexity. This is where everyone in the organization can act and needs to help simplify – and this is what our book is about.

1. Complexity and simplicity

In business, complexity is a fact of life. Things tend to start out simply, but rapidly become more complex, for a range of reasons. When the automotive industry got underway in the early 1900s, for example, aspiring car owners could buy just one type of Ford automobile, a Model T, in any color they wanted to, so long as it was black – as Henry Ford famously commented. But such simplicity did not last long. Soon Alfred Sloan, president and CEO at General Motors (GM), had introduced a variety of differently priced auto models and brands – including Buick, Cadillac, Chevrolet and Pontiac – as well as a more complex operating structure, transforming the market in doing so.

You could say this was a natural evolution of the business model, driven by technological opportunities, new management practices and the growing diversity of customer needs. External complexity drives internal complexity.

We will come to back to this soon. First, we should try and simply define complexity and simplicity.

What do we mean by complexity?
Although we used it as starting point, the existing academic literature is remarkably weak on this topic. Despite a range of theories and studies of complexity, surprisingly few business and management academics have used this approach to understand what influences firms' performance.

For our working definition of complexity we drew from studies of 'complex adaptive systems'. This might sound a little grand, but it turned out to be quite useful for us – and senior managers that we have worked with on simplicity projects seem to get it fairly quickly.

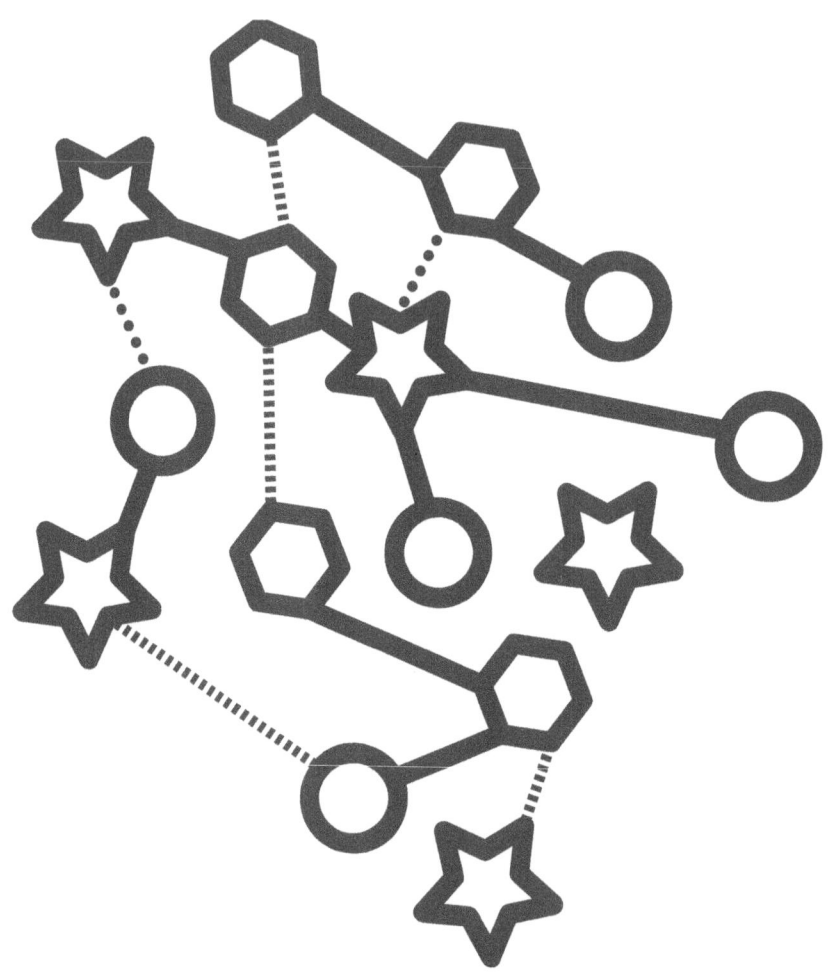

A working definition of complexity
*Complexity = the **number of components** in a system + the **variety of relationships** among these components + the **pace of change** of both the components and the relationships.*

This definition is useful as it can be applied to most business systems, at any level: from firms in a supply chain, functional departments in a firm, machines in a production line, or people in an organization. In fact you can look at any complex system and identify if the overall complexity is being driven by the number of components, the variety of different components, the number of connections, the pace of change or a combination of these factors. Once you know what type of complexity you are dealing with, the solution for the complexity problem becomes much clearer.

The number of components is obviously important. Larger systems are often more complex – but they may just be more *complicated*. To distinguish between complicated and complex, we need to understand the relationships between the components and the rate at which these are changing. An airplane is a complicated system, with many interconnected parts and interactive control systems. But there is a high level of predictability in terms of how the overall system will react, either to changes in external conditions (winds, pressure or temperature) or internal conditions (cargo, people, moving drinks trolleys) or to the controls (engine thrust, ailerons, elevators, etc.). This is good – particularly for people who regularly fly in planes.

Complex systems are characterized by diversity, ambiguity and unpredictability of outcomes relative to inputs, or changes in conditions. The interaction of three dimensions – number of components, variety of relationships and pace of change in both – means we cannot easily tell what a complex system is going to do. It also means it is more difficult to control.

As a general rule, the more a system is made up of people, the more complex it is.

We probably all know why this is the case.

As individuals, we are far from the rational, stable and predictable 'components' that would suit the average economist. In combination, in organizations, *we are the source* of the diversity, ambiguity and unpredictability of outcomes. In fact, most organizations are more like a collection of DIY mistakes than a neat pyramid.

For each of us individually and for the groups that we belong to, our need for distinctiveness, prominence and some degree of control drives 'local diversity'. Self-organization is a defining indicator of life itself. (But it can create havoc when you are trying to run a business.) When you multiply this local diversity and then take account of the huge range of interconnections and interdependences across organizations you begin to see why communication, coordination and control are so difficult. Harnessing the capabilities of all of the people in a business to fulfill a single set of goals is the key complexity challenge.

For any business, complexity may be bewildering and can become paralyzing.

What do we mean by simplicity?

Simplicity is also difficult to define, but some famous quotes provide helpful building blocks towards a definition of business simplicity:

'Things should be made as simple as possible, but not any simpler.'
Attributed to Albert Einstein

'The ability to simplify means to eliminate the unnecessary, so that the necessary may speak.'
Hans Hofmann[1]

In business, as things become more complex your organization will have more and more components, a greater variety of components, more interconnections and higher levels of change. Some of these things will create value, but others will not. Even worse, the activities that do not add value will confuse and preoccupy your time, distracting your energy from the more important activities that are essential for your success. In other words, as your organization becomes more complex it is harder to see the wood for the trees.

Our definition of simplicity: SIMPLICITY in business exists when you have exactly the right number of essential components and connections to achieve a successful result. No more, no less. Complexity is the opposite of this.

Because of this, one of the central themes of our book – and a mantra for the firms we work with – is to: SIMPLY ADD VALUE!

External and internal complexity

In this book we are less concerned with airplanes and more concerned with business enterprises. So we talk about external and internal complexity specifically in relation to firms. Firms succeed, fail, or simply survive in

Simplicity in business exists when
you have exactly the right number
of essential components and connections
to achieve a successful result.
No more, no less.

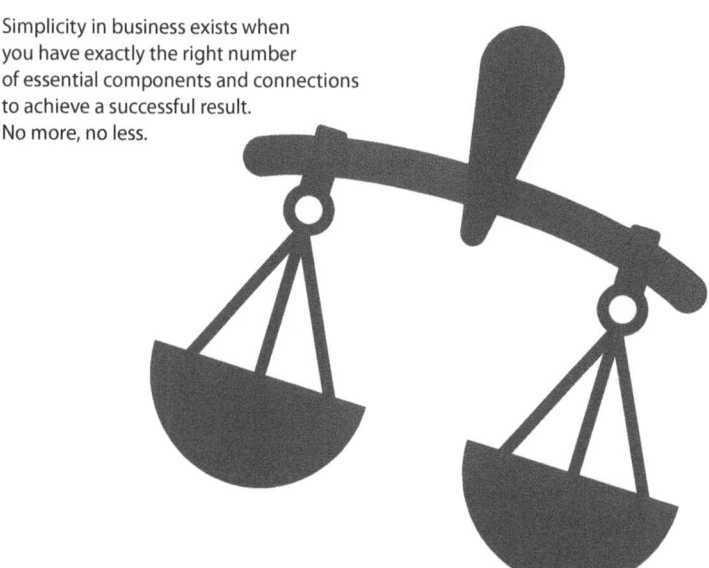

Bad complexity in business exists when you
have too many unnecessary components
and/or connections, which get in the way
of achieving a successful result.

FIGURE 1.1
Simplicity and complexity

complex competitive environments full of opportunities and threats which
they have to continually respond to.

The global economy is an increasingly complex environment in which to do
business. The diversity of customer needs and market segments is just one
dimension. Executives face numerous sources of complexity: globalization;
demographic shifts; climate and environmental change; political risks;
changes in product, process and information technologies; the pace of
innovation; new competitors; and emerging economies.

For much of the book we focus on internal complexity, for two obvious
and connected reasons: (1) managers in the companies we have worked
with tell us this is what they are interested in doing something about; (2)
there is not much we or they can do to simplify the world. It is important
to know that external and internal complexity are strongly interrelated.
Internal complexity often arises as a way of coping with external complexity.

Take, for example, the growing number of regulations, the growing
diversity of regulatory environments around the world and the rate at

which these are changing. This came top of a survey by KPMG (2010) and second in a survey by the Economist Intelligence Unit (EIU, 2011) of major causes of complexity. In response, firms have had to increase the amount of time, effort, people and money that they have to invest in compliance. Their internal structures, systems, processes and procedures related to compliance have grown more complex. This leads to more interaction, more communication, more meetings and more emails to sort out regulatory compliance issues. External change triggers internal change.

More generally, 70 per cent of respondents in the survey by the EIU (2011) saw complexity as 'one of the biggest challenges the company faces'. Ninety-four per cent stated that 'managing complexity is important to my company's success'.

The scale of complexity facing organizations alone represents a significant challenge. It drives greater uncertainty and unpredictability and makes decision-making more difficult. Firms have a broader range of options to choose from, but a more confused information picture on which to base decisions. Effective allocation of scarce resources becomes more challenging.

Industrial incidents, such as the BP oil spill in the Gulf of Mexico, and capital markets crises in the European Union are stark illustrations of the difficulties of prediction, risk management and control in complex environments. Our systems, from information and communication networks to interconnected financial portfolios, are evolving independently of any single point of control. Predicting how they are going to react to particular combinations of factors and forces now seems to be beyond us.

So, in the face of external complexity organizations often respond with an increase in their internal complexity. However, costly complexity also grows, usually unwittingly rather than by design.

We think this is where the problem starts.

2. What causes business complexity?

Two main forms of complexity relevant to business organizations are commonly discussed: strategic complexity and organizational complexity. Strategic complexity is about the positioning of the firm in a changing external competitive environment, and the senior management decision-making processes that try to navigate the best path through this environment. Studies focusing on dynamic capabilities that can help improve agility and responsiveness in the face of chaotic or turbulent environments address this kind of complexity and the firm's ability to survive.

Organizational complexity refers to internal sources of complexity stemming from the evolution of business divisions, processes, procedures and rules, and changing structural characteristics. Both forms are associated with positive (good) and negative (bad) performance effects of complexity.

Strategic change always has an impact on organizational complexity – and usually it increases it. For example, breaking into new markets means dealing with a new set of customers, suppliers, competitors, employees, business regulations and so on; this in turn means customizing products and services, adjusting the marketing approach, new contracts, a slightly different local HR management set up .... This is diversity: new components and new relationships; more coordination and control challenges – all adding to existing complexity.

A high level of merger-and-acquisition (M&A), one of the key complexity indicators in our research, tends to have a significant effect across all dimensions of organizational complexity. When Nokia expanded into multimedia content and services, it engaged in a flurry of acquisitions that added new levels of diversity in terms of the geographic markets and range of businesses the firm was involved in. New divisions and layers of management, new IT structures and multiple processes and procedures were added, which required rationalization and integration. Failure to cope effectively with these new sources of complexity left Nokia overwhelmed by costly complexity and was partly responsible for the firm's decline in fortunes.

Good and bad complexity

So, are we saying that firms should not develop new product and services, break into new markets, engage in any M&A activity – or grow at all? No. That would be irresponsible advice and a rather foolish conclusion. Like most things in life, it is about finding the right balance – between 'good' complexity and 'bad' complexity. (That may sound a bit too simple – but we have thought about this a lot ....)

The relationship between complexity and performance is not simple (see the section on our research later in this chapter), but goes something like this. As successful firms grow, they add new products and services to their portfolios, enter new markets, engage in joint-ventures and acquisitions, and add new business units and lines of management; these strategic initiatives add value and profits also grow. This is good complexity.

At some point (we predictably called it the 'tipping point') added complexity – a new line of products, one more acquisition, an extra layer of management – does not add proportionate value. The firm does more things and the number of components and/or interrelationships grows, but the added value is outweighed by the added cost of the complexity. Bad complexity is costly complexity – and if it becomes too overwhelming, it can kill not just profits but the entire business.

COSTLY COMPLEXITY AT COSTLI COFFEE

In 1987 Mario Marelli opened his first Costli coffee shop in Milan. His business proposition was simple. Good-quality coffees, freshly made, to your personal taste. All served in comfortable and authentically Italian surroundings.

Good complexity

The shop was very successful and Mario wanted to expand, so he started to open new coffee shops in nearby towns.

Then he saw the opportunity to get his customers to try new things, so he started to introduce new flavors, cold drinks, teas, etc. So Costli coffee's original product range of 12 different drinks grew steadily to over 30 different product offerings, each available in three sizes, with flavor options on top!

In the early days the business was managed by Mario and his wife, but as it grew they had to recruit new people and put more formal management structures in place. But there were just three layers of management between Mario and the baristas in the stores. He visited each store every week. All the complexity he added was good and the business grew and grew and grew. By 2001, he had 341 stores in different countries around the world. Global profits were $121m.

Bad complexity

Five years later, in 2006, Costli Coffee went bust.

Between 2001 and 2006, even more new managers had been brought in to explore further growth initiatives, like alternative blends, new recipes, coffee club membership, fair-trade sourcing alternatives, new marketing channels, social media, joint ventures, etc. All kinds of strategic initiatives proliferated across the business. The overall product portfolio now covered over 300 subtly different products. Variety and diversity had grown well beyond the simple ideas of Mario and his wife.

The simple functional organization had grown into a complex global matrix. Each additional objective, project, task, employee and network connection (internal and external) added further complexity.

Roles and responsibilities became unclear. A large number of employees were focused on things that were just vaguely related to the core strategic purpose of delivering good-quality coffee to consumers in comfortable surroundings.

Monitoring, measuring and rewarding the performance of these employees demanded an expansion of the key performance indicators (KPIs) and new central systems and processes. New kinds of strategic plans and operational reports were introduced. Each member of staff received over 80 emails each day.

Each 'improvement', each iteration, had added to the burden and complexity of support services – HR, IT, accounting and finance, central facilities, etc …

The firm had slowly evolved away from its central value proposition. Expansion had meant lots more of everything – except profits. Bad complexity had gradually replaced good complexity and this bad complexity had eaten all of Mario's profit.

Linking back to our internal and external dimensions of complexity, we think the complexity challenge is greater now than ever before. External complexity – the variety and diversity of strategic options and the pace of change – increasingly defies our individual and collective capacity to make sense of the options, plan, coordinate and execute clear-cut strategies at the top management level or down through the organization.

The increase in internal organizational forms of complexity adds further challenges for managers who are already trying to cope with this complex external competitive environment. As they invest time and effort into controlling and directing the internal 'competitive environment', they can lose sight of outside opportunities and threats, and the firm as a whole fails to respond or evolve fast enough. Bad complexity from within distracts attention from the changing external opportunities to add value.

This is critical. The very existence of firms is based on their ability to add value for clients and customers through their products and services. This means meeting or exceeding customer needs, preferences and desires in ways that customers are willing to pay for. By continually adding value, firms earn profits and live on. But to add value in competition with other firms, they must possess superior advantages (assets, resources, capabilities, agility, etc.).

Any firm's superior ability to add value for customers through better products and services depends on its people. And they need to be fully engaged, in everything they do, to value-adding actions and activities.

One of the most common problems brought about by complexity in business is the disconnect between added value in products and services and the individual who sits at the heart of the firm working away on a daily basis. In many firms that individual is becoming overwhelmed by internal complexity.

We suspected that this might be a major difference between high-performing firms and weaker firms.

So we did some research to find out.

3. Our research

Apart from our interest in better understanding good and bad forms of business complexity, we were persuaded by senior executives we work with that complexity was something they needed help with.

The challenge, then, was to distinguish between (good) organizational complexity, which adds value and contributes to superior performance, and that which adds to costs and has a negative (bad) impact on performance. We also focused on developing analytical and diagnostic tools to identify the causes of complexity in particular kinds of businesses and to suggest what managers could do to add value in simpler ways.

In 2011, we conducted two major research projects. The first led to the Global Simplicity Index (GSI) – a ranking of the top 200 global firms in terms of their complexity and their performance using corporate data (from 2005–10). The second was a survey of managers to find out what kinds of complexity had the most significant impact on their personal productivity and therefore the performance of their business. (Further details about our research can be found at www.simplicitypartnership.com.)

The Global Simplicity Index (GSI)

The GSI ranks the largest 200 firms in the Fortune Global 500 in terms of both performance and complexity. In total, 18 proxy measures were identified: nine for performance and nine for complexity. In addition to weighting the above measures in various ways we standardized the data to enable cross-firm and cross-industry comparisons. The final complexity measures are unique in that they condense a wide range of comparative indicators into a single set of proxies which represent more dimensions of complexity than in prior studies. These include both external or strategic complexity and internal, organizational complexity, as described above.

In terms of performance indicators the measures are fairly obvious, including EBITDA (earnings before interest, taxes, depreciation and amortization), profit per employee and indicators related to dividend yield. We did, however, use five-year averages where possible to ensure that we were not capturing a temporary rise or fall in firm performance.

Distilling all of the kinds of complexity we have mentioned in the chapter so far into nine individual measures was far more difficult – as you have probably guessed. We were helped by other studies that have looked at external and internal complexity, but it was the first time such detailed analysis had been done, so we had to create the best proxy (representative) measures we could. One of the nine measures, for example, is the 'transnational index', which uses asset, sales and employee data to arrive at a measure of the multinationality of a firm (the degree to which it operates in many different countries). This is a proven driver of complexity. Another, the 'portfolio measure', reflects the range and diversity of the products and services it sells. Others, for example, take account of recent M&A activity, employee turnover and the number of internal business units.

OK. So what did all this tell us?

The GSI findings

Actually, although we guessed it was important, we were a little surprised at the scale of the impact that complexity has on firm performance and shareholder value.

We estimate, through the GSI analysis, that the largest 200 firms in the Global Fortune 500 are losing an estimated 10.2 per cent of shareholder value from complexity. This amounts to losses of $1.2bn EBITDA on average per firm and over $237bn across all of our 200 firms as a result of the types of complexity that destroy value. Or to put it another way, simplifying the organization by removing bad complexity would increase the average EBITDA of each firm by 10.2 per cent, or $1.2bn.

When we plot the 200 firms on a graph of performance versus complexity, the points are scattered all over the place – and there is no *linear* relationship between complexity and performance. (Good and bad complexity partly cancel each other out.)

However (and you might have guessed this when we started talking about tipping points above), we do find that the relationship between performance and complexity is characterized best by an inverted-U-shaped curve (Figure 1.2). Initially performance appears to increase as complexity increases, then

FIGURE 1.2
Findings of the GSI study: the relationship between performance and complexity

a tipping point is reached, after which additional complexity appears to work against improved performance. (Technically this is a polynomial regression – if you are interested in these kinds of things.)

Other studies have come to a similar conclusion, although no research has looked at the effects of this range of internal and external complexity measures. Kathleen Eisenhardt at Stanford University, for example, found that if you compare firm performance and the number of rules in an organization you get the same inverted-U-shaped curve (Eisenhardt and Sull, 2001).

In Figure 1.3 some of the firms included in the GSI are mapped onto a matrix, showing the relative rankings of the 200 firms along the two dimensions, simple-to-complex (*x*-axis) and low-to-high performance (*y*-axis).

The corporate success stories, which appear to be coping well with complex internal and external environments, are located in the high-performance, high-complexity quadrant. It contains firms from a variety of industries, including high-profile names such as IBM (17, 180). The highest-performing firm is Microsoft, which is relatively simple when compared to its industry

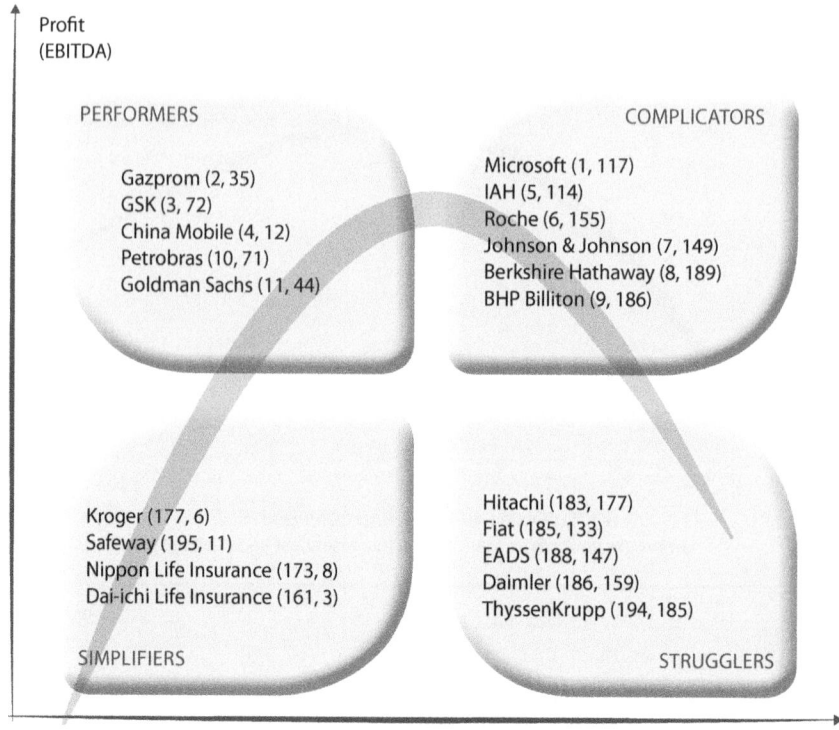

Profit
(EBITDA)

PERFORMERS

Gazprom (2, 35)
GSK (3, 72)
China Mobile (4, 12)
Petrobras (10, 71)
Goldman Sachs (11, 44)

COMPLICATORS

Microsoft (1, 117)
IAH (5, 114)
Roche (6, 155)
Johnson & Johnson (7, 149)
Berkshire Hathaway (8, 189)
BHP Billiton (9, 186)

Kroger (177, 6)
Safeway (195, 11)
Nippon Life Insurance (173, 8)
Dai-ichi Life Insurance (161, 3)

Hitachi (183, 177)
Fiat (185, 133)
EADS (188, 147)
Daimler (186, 159)
ThyssenKrupp (194, 185)

SIMPLIFIERS

STRUGGLERS

Complexity

FIGURE 1.3
The performance–simplicity matrix: some example firms (performance ranking, simplicity ranking/200 firms)

rivals. Other firms that perform well with relatively simple organizations are: GSK, Hyundai, Goldman Sachs, AT&T, Vodafone and Exxon Mobil, together with a number of simple, high performers that benefit from state ownership and/or national monopoly positions, such as China Mobile, Gazprom and Petrobras.

The high-complexity, low-profit quadrant, by contrast, contains a number of more problematic, relatively low-performing cases. The firms in this quadrant are failing to cope with complex organizational structures and business models, often in turbulent industry sectors. There are a number of banks in this quadrant of the graph, for well-known reasons. RBS, for example, is here, and the GSI analysis indicates some of the reasons as to why it became a symbol of the failure across the sector to cope with overwhelming complexity. (Also see the more detailed analysis in Appendix 2.)

SECTOR STUDY: BANKING

Banks and financial corporations, including Barclays, HSBC, Lloyds, Prudential and RBS, represent the largest industry group among the British firms in our study.

The Royal Bank of Scotland (RBS) is the worst performer among the UK firms, and one of the weakest in the sector globally, ranking 156th out of 200 in the performance league and 168th out of 200 in terms of simplicity. As many of the GSI measures for both performance and complexity are based on five-year averages, this ranking reflects embedded systemic problems, rather than temporary or one-off dips in organizational efficiency or effectiveness.

In the complexity/performance classification, RBS is a 'struggler', combining high complexity with low performance. It sits alongside a large number of firms from very different industry sectors that are all suffering the effects of costly complexity.

By comparison, Prudential, Lloyds, Barclays and HSBC are all simpler in structure and better performing. The latter two are more complex than the average firm in the GSI, but both have developed better mechanisms for coping with particular forms of complexity. In HSBC's case the firm's high level of geographic diversification is an important source of complexity, and it appears to manage this better than most.

The problems at RBS, and in the wider banking crisis, were partly due to the failure of due diligence practices, risk analysis and stress testing to take account of the real levels of complexity in the global banking system. Andrew Haldane, executive director for financial stability at the Bank of England, noted this in 2009, describing how these approaches were based on models that simplified the complex realities of the industry and the economy, and as a result were (reflecting Keynesian analysis) 'very precise and very wrong' (Haldane, 2009).

The global banking system is one of the most complex systems in the global economy. It has evolved well beyond the design parameters of any architect and beyond the plans of any regulator. Unpredictability and risk grow with complexity. One of the major causes of this (and the on-going crisis in the Euro-zone) is network externalities: the connectivity and interdependence (in value terms) of asset portfolios around the world making them susceptible to spill-over or contagion effects. Failure in one part of the network, such as the collapse of Lehman Brothers, has knock-on effects elsewhere that may be far greater than the original catalyst. Instability can become endemic.

These are, however, industry forces that all banks must cope with. So why did RBS cope less well than other banks? As indicated by the GSI analysis, RBS faced other forms of costly, self-inflicted complexity – an over-stretched global network of subsidiaries, and a large and complex portfolio of products and services compared to other banks. It faced the dual problems of external and internal complexity: operating in multiple markets, with many regulatory agencies and a diverse range of customers, along with multiple business units, expanding compliance functions, complex layers of management and coordination problems.

The UK government's Independent Commission on Banking (ICB), established in June 2010 'to consider structural and related non-structural reforms to the UK banking sector to promote financial stability and competition', came to a similar conclusion. It recommended a massive disposal and rationalization program, which began to affect RBS's performance in 2010. Ultimately it was complexity, from multiple sources, and the inability to deal with it, that caused RBS's relatively poor performance.

Those firms that score relatively low on both performance and complexity are found in the bottom-left quadrant. The findings place a number of American retailers in this quadrant including Lowes, Walgreens, Target and Home Depot, along with several Japanese life insurance companies, such as Meiji Yasuda and Sumitomo. These firms have simple business models and customer propositions and a limited product portfolio, and are domestic-market based rather than multinational. Lowes and Walgreens, for example, are ranked first and second in the simplicity ranking respectively and show average levels of performance. They are, however, operating in stable, predictable and simple competitive environments which suit uncomplicated structures and strategies.

SECTOR STUDY: RETAIL

Four complex challenges face large retailers at present:

The Customer Relationship challenge: This stems from the complexities of the cost–benefit trade-off involved in providing customized rather than standard mass market products and treating customers as co-developers in product innovation. Creating a range of customer relationships to match the diversity of customers is part of this challenge.

The Service Innovation challenge: Product and service innovation has become increasingly complex, partly because of the customer relationship challenge, but also because of the drive towards service provision. As retailers try to leverage their location and brand advantages to expand into services, they need to cope with the complexities of managing product and service innovation simultaneously.

The Supply Chain challenge: The growing diversity of global procurement networks is pushing retailers to become much more agile and intelligent in their management of global supply chains. Integrating multiple materials and products inputs from around the world, and switching suppliers in response to changes in pricing and availability, lies at the heart of their cost competitiveness, and is becoming increasingly complex.

The Internationalization challenge: As Western markets plateau, retailers are looking to expand internationally to access growing foreign markets (such as China and India). A key question is whether existing competitive strengths and business models can be leveraged to gain access to these markets. The experiences of Walmart, Carrefour and Tesco show that 'local responsiveness' is necessary, but also that it creates diversity across the group, adding coordination and communication costs as the firm becomes more multinational.

Retail firms are trying to cope with these complexity challenges, with varying levels of success. Metro AG, the fourth largest global retailer, operates in the same competitive environment as its larger competitors, Walmart, Carrefour and Tesco. The GSI analysis ranks Metro as a low-performing, high-complexity firm, and shows that it copes with sources of complexity the least well of the four retail firms.

It is Metro's diversity that underlies the costly complexity undermining the firm's performance relative to its competitors. It is one of the most global and diversified of the four retailers, with 61 per cent of sales from overseas markets, and organized into five sales brands: Metro Cash & Carry, Real, Media Markt, Saturn and Galeria Kaufhof GmbH.

Finally, among high-performance, low-complexity firms, a less dominant pattern emerged. In this quadrant the research placed a large proportion of state-owned, emerging economy enterprises, which benefit from monopoly positions in large, asset-based businesses. There were also firms in very different industry sectors (such as GSK and Goldman Sachs) whose simple business models relative to competitors in their industry sectors appear to underpin part of their superior performance.

Simplifiers, performers, complicators and strugglers

The simplicity index allows us to divide the sample of firms into four types of firm, based on their relative performance and complexity scores. So firms are classified as performers, complicators, simplifiers and strugglers, as shown in Figure 1.4. We can take a closer look at these categories by examining a firm in each quadrant.

The simplifiers

One company placed in the low-performance, low-complexity quadrant – or 'simplifiers' category – is Renault, the French automotive company. Renault's problem is that it fails to capitalize on 'good' complexity.

Renault fails to match its better-performing competitors in terms of their portfolio of designs and ability to target a wide range of market segments. The car firm is relatively dependent on one nation – France – for both manufacturing inputs and sales, for example. Other firms have invested in manufacturing capacity in China and other emerging economies to tap into cheaper local inputs and growing markets. The firm's strategy may make for a simpler corporate structure, but it means that the company has failed to respond to the significant internationalization driving the automotive industry.

In recent years, Renault has struggled to maintain profitability; in 2009, the firm recorded a $4.3bn net loss. Toyota, by way of contrast, is larger and more diverse in terms of its product portfolio and geographic spread, but manages the inherent complexities of the automotive sector better than Renault. In 2010 it achieved almost double Renault's revenue per employee.

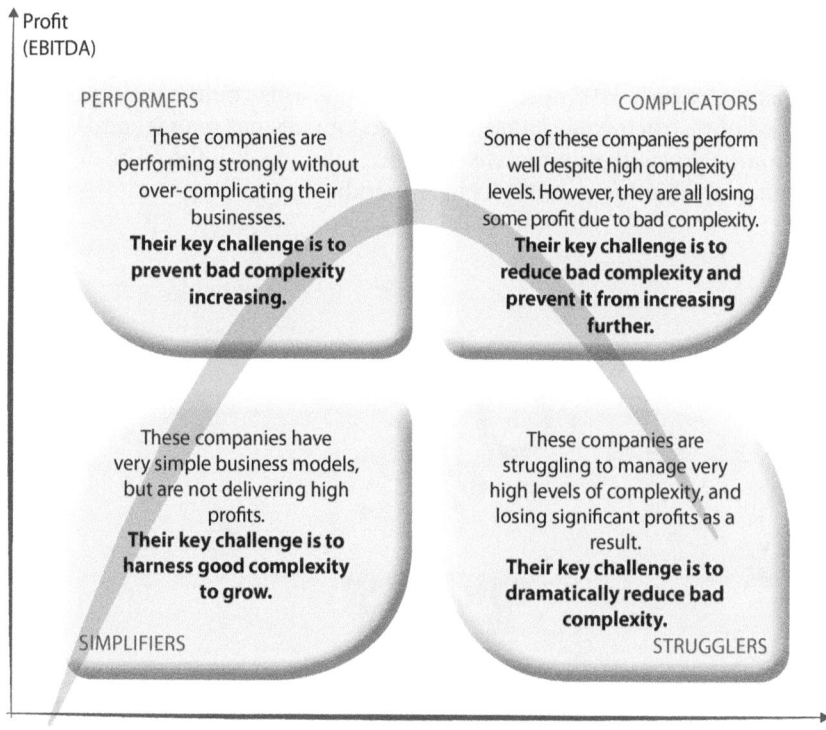

Profit
(EBITDA)

PERFORMERS

These companies are performing strongly without over-complicating their businesses. **Their key challenge is to prevent bad complexity increasing.**

COMPLICATORS

Some of these companies perform well despite high complexity levels. However, they are all losing some profit due to bad complexity. **Their key challenge is to reduce bad complexity and prevent it from increasing further.**

These companies have very simple business models, but are not delivering high profits. **Their key challenge is to harness good complexity to grow.**

These companies are struggling to manage very high levels of complexity, and losing significant profits as a result. **Their key challenge is to dramatically reduce bad complexity.**

SIMPLIFIERS

STRUGGLERS

Complexity

FIGURE 1.4
Four firm types

The performers

In the high-performance, low-complexity quadrant, pharmaceutical giant GlaxoSmithKline (GSK) outperforms rivals such as such as Pfizer, Roche and Novartis, and achieved an impressive profit level of 19.5 per cent of sales in 2009, well ahead of more complex competitors.

An important factor in GSK's success is how it copes strategically and operationally across two dimensions that can create bad complexity for companies operating in the pharmaceutical industry in particular – the research and development (R&D) pipeline, and M&As. A pharmaceutical company that over-extends itself along either dimension could create harmful complexity, reducing its strategic focus, the efficiency of its coordination, and the careful balancing act orchestrated by senior management between too few and too many strategic options.

GSK spends over $4.6bn on R&D each year, but manages a tightly focused product development strategy and has developed an efficient structure for its research organization. GSK frequently acquires partners and competitors, as it did with Stiefel Laboratories, which specializes in skin health, and Pfizer's HIV business, for example. This could easily create an overload of restructuring initiatives, but so far GSK has managed to derive maximum value with minimal disruption. (Take a look at the more detailed pharmaceutical industry analysis in Appendix 1.)

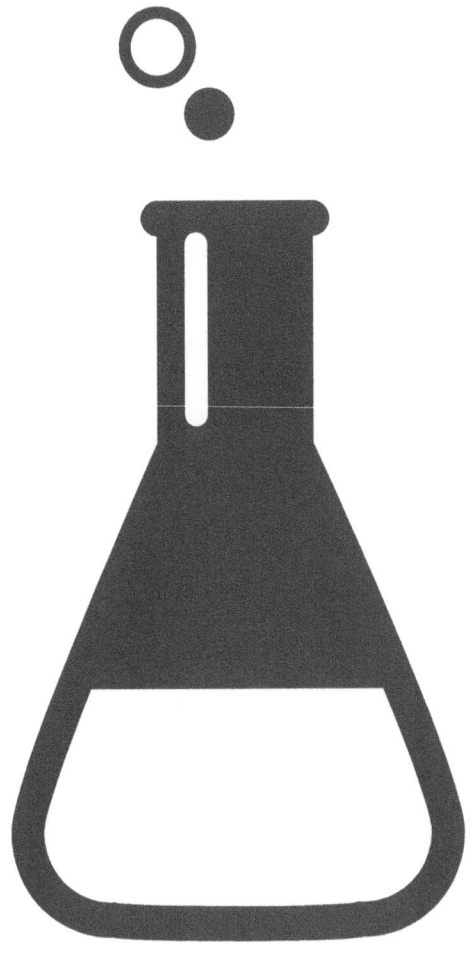

SECTOR STUDY: PHARMACEUTICALS

Increasing patient and physician demands, stronger regulation and the growing diversity of regulatory regimes, dramatic changes in government funding, growing competition from Asia, declining R&D productivity and new technologies all combine to make the pharmaceuticals industry an increasingly turbulent place to operate. Coping with these challenges will require pharmaceutical firms to be more agile: able to navigate in and adapt to their changing operating environment and to do so better than their competitors.

Our study shows that some pharmaceutical giants, such as GSK and Sanofi-Aventis, manage this complexity more effectively than others. Their long-run performance is superior to that of Novartis, Pfizer, Roche, and Johnson & Johnson, who have reacted to external complexity less effectively than their competitors. Additionally, the GSI identified Bayer as the company within the industry that struggles most with excessive complexity.

Pressures for consolidation in the pharmaceuticals industry have driven up the number of M&As. This reduces the number of competitors in the sector but presents additional complexity challenges for the remaining firms.

The Novartis acquisition of Alcon in the spring of 2011 provides lessons for others. This was one in a long line of acquisitions in the pharmaceuticals industry which left the acquirer with the challenge of integrating another equally complex firm into its operations. With a presence in over 140 countries Novartis was already a massive business, and merging with Alcon added further complexity to the firm. In a drive to overcome the declining productivity of R&D pipelines and achieve even greater economies of scale from R&D to marketing, firms like Novartis are multiplying their strategic and operational complexity, rather than simplifying down to their core competences.

The GSI categorizes Novartis as a 'complicator'. Our study suggests that much of Novartis' costly complexity had already been driven by previous acquisitions, as well as high R&D intensity, over-engineering of processes, and a wide portfolio of operations, across a large number of therapeutic areas. Such acquisitions may initially appear to add value, but often result in increased complexity, strategic misalignment and poor organizational coordination between sub-divisions.

In order to improve profits, complexity reduction needs to take center stage within the pharmaceutical industry and companies like Novartis need to learn from their competitors. It is vitally important for pharmaceutical firms to view complexity more holistically. Although closing factories and R&D centers will reduce operating costs, it will not be enough to reduce the stifling levels of complexity within the industry. This requires complexity to be reduced in strategy, organizational structure, process and many other areas of the business. Additionally, it requires a change in management behaviors to ensure that complexity does not creep back into the organization.

The complicators

A firm that has managed to couple high complexity with high performance is IBM. The company, which in 2010 had over 400,000 staff and earned $96bn in revenues, has a turbulent history of reinvention – from mainframes to PCs to services – undertaken in order to remain in step with its changing competitive environment.

From 1991 to 1993, IBM suffered cumulative losses of $20bn before a radical restructuring rid the firm of its overcomplicated manufacturing model. Following this overhaul, revenues for the Global Services Division grew from $7bn to over $35bn in the 1990s, culminating in the 2002 purchase of PwC Consulting. In recent years IBM has performed well, but now, almost 20 years on, IBM has once more become highly complex, and a radical push towards strategic focus and structural simplification is likely to be needed.

Key sources of strategic and organizational complexity include IBM's wide range of client partnerships and the global network of R&D centers and collaborations through which it channels $6bn of R&D expenditure each year.

The strugglers

The fourth quadrant contains the strugglers – those firms that are among the most complex firms but also the weaker performers. Nokia, our favorite mobile phone company, is here.

Remember (as if we haven't picked on it enough already), Nokia was the world's leading mobile phone maker in the last decade, enjoying a fivefold increase in turnover between 1996 and 2001. From 2006, however, Nokia shares lost two-thirds of their value because of the firm's inability to respond to smartphone competition and the 2007 launch of Apple's iPhone. Internationalization, product diversification, overstretching of the brand (Loudeye, Twango, Enpocket, NAVTEQ, Novarra and MetaCarta are examples of acquisitions by Nokia as it tried to extend its business model into new media), new divisions and new CEOs have all added complexity. While still a leading handset maker by volume and sales, profits at Nokia fell by 21 per cent in 2009–10 and it lost its market lead to Apple.

Time will tell whether new partnerships (e.g. with Microsoft) will add value for Nokia or just more costly complexity.

SECTOR STUDY: TELECOMS

At the heart of the innovation efforts of many firms is the continuous process of connecting new technological opportunities with changing customer needs. In the telecoms industry the rapid rate of progress across both of these dimensions is a source of significant complexity. Firms must cope with the multiple opportunities presented by new combinations of hardware, software, applications, services and content in different regulatory environments to suit a variety of customers.

Mobile telecoms ecosystems can evolve into virtuous cycles through positive network externalities, where better applications attract more subscribers, making a particular platform more attractive to developers who then produce more applications for it. But value chains involving platform operators, applications and content developers, as well as users themselves, are complex and unpredictable.

The telecoms industry overall has evolved rapidly. In the past, a simpler business model existed, consisting of separate firms with the distinctive roles of network providers, hardware, software and content developers. Companies now increasingly span all of these roles. They have either grown to become multi-divisional (often through M&A activity) or they have established myriad joint ventures and alliances and maintain interrelated innovation activities across all of these fields.

Two firms in the GSI provide very different lessons about coping with complexity in this environment: China Mobile and Nokia.

China Mobile occupies an unassailable market position in the largest mobile telecoms market in the world; China has over 860 million mobile subscribers, and most are customers of China Mobile. The firm has a near-monopoly supported by the Chinese government. Through this it co-develops the technologies, infrastructure platforms and regulations that become the de-facto national standards. Despite its large R&D program China Mobile has a relatively simple portfolio of products and services and geographic markets, focusing almost exclusively on mainland China. So it emerges as one of the simplest and highest performing telecoms firms in our study, yet its business model is impossible to emulate.

Contrast this with Nokia. Once a stock-market star and product innovation leader, Nokia has floundered in recent years, experiencing weak performance and thousands of job losses.

Added complexity has been detrimental to Nokia in two ways. First, it added coordination and administration costs, making it more difficult to compete against its cheaper rivals. Second, complexity caused employees to lose their focus on the things that add value for customers and clients. They lost sight of the strategic priorities or became distracted from these priorities by procedures, reports, personnel issues and myriad peripheral issues. This makes decision-making and resource allocation highly inefficient and has a particularly strong impact on the innovation capabilities of firms. As a result Nokia is surrounded by competitors who are either cheaper or, in the case of Apple and Research In Motion, more innovative.

Nokia is identified as a 'struggler' in the GSI, and is the fifth most complex firm across all industry sectors. Strugglers fail to cope with complexity, directly and heavily impacting their profit levels. The combined pressures of external market turbulence and internal upheaval significantly constrain an organization's ability to adapt simply and quickly. Nokia are not alone: technology firms such as Hitachi, Panasonic, Sony and Toshiba are also classified as strugglers.

The problems for all these firms are not caused by individual products or software platforms; they are systemic. If Nokia is to regain its position within the mobile industry, focusing its product development processes is a start, but reducing complexity across the business is essential for Nokia's long-term survival. Moreover, a concerted effort to change management behaviors will provide a longer-term solution to the issue, helping Nokia to avoid the current levels of complexity it battles with on a daily basis.

Our management survey

Our second research project involved a survey of managers to find out what kinds of complexity have the most significant impact on firm performance. Six hundred executives were interviewed in 300 firms (with over 5000 employees) across Europe, spanning a wide range of business sectors. (Since then we have had responses to this survey from over 1200 managers, supporting the same set of findings.)

We asked them how much of their productivity losses were the result of complexity-related problems. Almost two-thirds of managers (63 per cent) put the figure at over 5 per cent; a third (33 per cent) said over 10 per cent; and 10 per cent of managers said that it was over 30 per cent. (A particularly stressed-out 2 per cent reported that over 50 per cent of productivity losses were due to complexity.)

Our survey asked managers about the causes of complexity – but (because we know that most people like to complain about most things most of the time) we specifically asked them to rank these according to the impact they have on their business performance. Their responses allowed us to capture a wide range of sources of costly complexity. These include:

- changes in strategy or multiple project demands (it turns out that one in three managers are dealing with six or more strategic initiatives at any one time);
- convoluted management hierarchies (28 per cent of managers have over 16 levels of management in their firm!);
- monitoring, control and planning procedures (one in ten have over 11 stages for capital expenditure sign-off procedures);
- a diversity of processes and systems (38 per cent of managers are grappling with six or more specialist IT systems); and
- overwhelming communication and coordination mechanisms (dealing with emails takes up over 30 per cent of the time for a sad 15 per cent of managers).

A range of this data is distributed in the appropriate chapters through this book. We had to make sense of the variety of complexity sources – so we came up with a framework.

The dimensions, drivers and impact of complexity

As a result of the senior management survey we were able to confirm the key dimensions and drivers of complexity. There are six main dimensions in all, as shown in Figure 1.5.

This has become something of a symbol, not just for our research or the contents of this book – but also for all the firms we have worked with to identify and help remove costly complexity.

As we said earlier, we will focus mainly on the internal sources of complexity throughout this book – and this framework is used as a signpost in each chapter. As described above, the external environment is comprised of a range of interrelated drivers of complexity including social, political, economic and technological change, globalization, competitor activity and regulatory change. These have an obvious, direct impact on the strategic choices that managers have to make to maintain their corporate competiveness in the face of external change. These choices in turn affect the firm's product and service portfolio, how it is organized, the management processes and procedures in place, and the behavior of people (i.e. the other internal dimensions of complexity). So strategy affects structure and the way people behave, but in a circular way

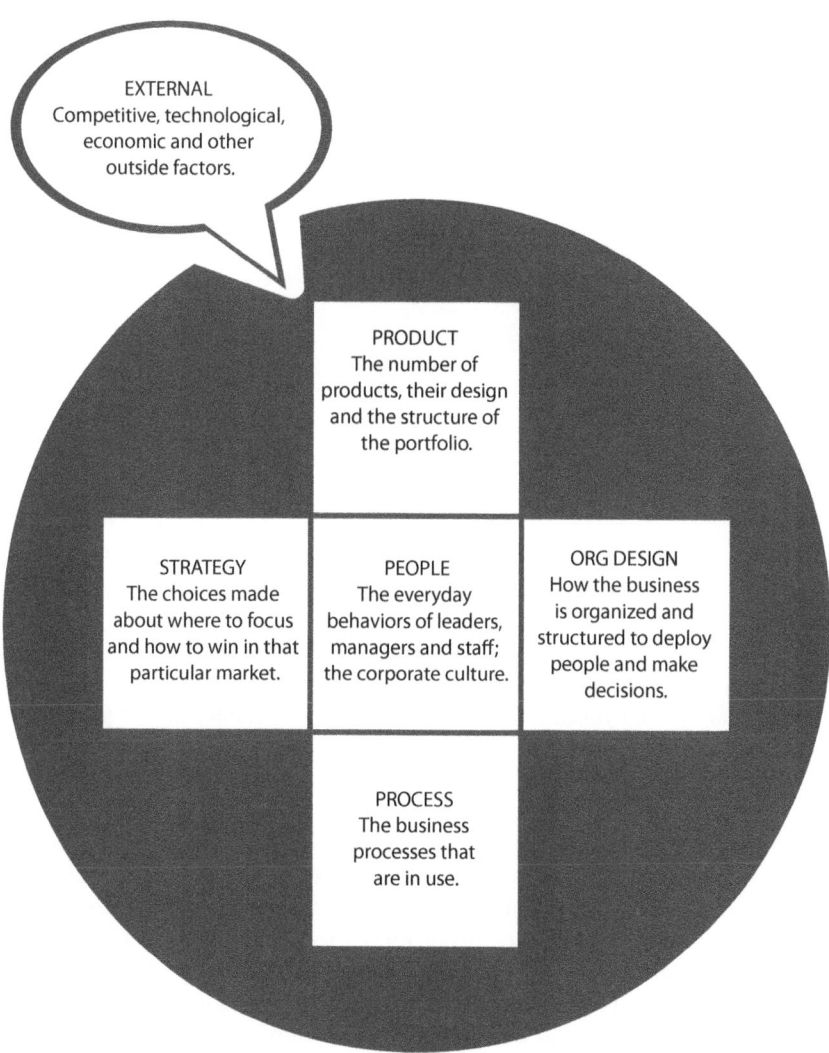

FIGURE 1.5
The six dimensions of complexity

the firm's structure and the behavior of its people affect the strategic options open to managers. In this way the complexity dimensions are interrelated.

Over 100 sources of complexity were examined across these six dimensions – one external, five internal. Respondents ranked each of these different kinds of complexity sources in terms of the impact on their businesses. We then looked at the overall, average responses for the different dimensions shown in Figure 1.5. The results are shown in Figure 1.6.

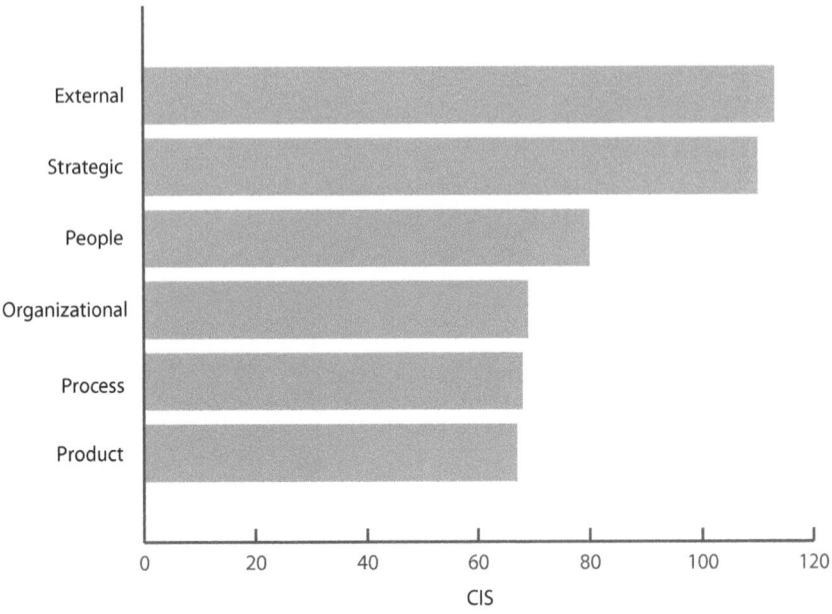

FIGURE 1.6
Survey ranking of the impact of different dimensions of complexity on firms
Note: Complexity Impact Score (CIS) is a product of the level of complexity caused
by a driver multiplied by the impact it has on performance.

The **external** drivers of complexity have, on average, the most significant harmful impact on businesses. These are related to the strategic challenges outlined above, but stem from sources beyond a company's direct control. It is easy perhaps to blame external forces for a firm's complexity woes, but all competitors in a given market are subject to the same external complexity forces. However, our study proves that some companies are much better than others at managing the complexity that external drivers exert on them.

Among the wide range of external drivers we tested, the top three were: 'fluctuations in the performance of the economy', 'the number of competitors' and 'social changes in the customer base'.

The **strategy** challenge stems from the proliferation of opportunities and strategic options facing managers, alongside the growing unpredictability and uncertainty of competitive environments.

Strategic decision-making requires managers to allocate scarce resources to the most promising of these opportunities, but the set of choices of where to focus and how to win in particular markets is increasingly complex. Respondents say the speed and complexity of strategic decision-making has a significant impact on their operations. Trying to do too many things and operate in too many markets or geographies, having unclear strategic boundaries, or making frequent changes in strategy, are all sources of disruptive and costly complexity. The strategic planning and reporting process itself can also be a significant contributor to organizational complexity and may take a year or even longer.

The third most important dimension of complexity is the way **people** behave in organizations. In particular the research highlighted management behaviors that lead to work becoming over-complicated and embellished. Communication overload was another issue, whether it be a proliferation of emails or lengthy reports. Plus, internal politics was flagged up as a people-related issue that increases complexity.

Next comes **organizational** complexity, where high-impact sources include: 'measuring and/or reporting KPIs and/or scorecard objectives' and 'levels of management and/or the organizational structure' as a whole, followed by: 'clarification of roles and responsibilities' and 'decision-making processes' in general.

Process complexity is clearly linked to both organization design and the people issues. 'Customer support processes', 'major project processes' and 'core business processes' were put at the top of the ranking of process-related sources of costly complexity by survey respondents.

Finally, **products and services** had the least impact when taken as a category average, but specific sources of complexity within this category (particularly 'launching new products and services') were rated very highly as key sources of costly complexity.

We examine these five internal forms of complexity further in Chapters 3–7. If we look at how respondents in our survey ranked all of the sources of internal complexity, in terms of the impact of these on their performance, we get an interesting insight into the overall problem (see the top ten in Figure 1.7). The organization, its people, their strategic choices, and the processes which underpin the products and services a firm produces, all combine to create good and bad complexity. We are conducting further research at the firm level and this is beginning to show how particular combinations and 'clusters' of these sources work in tandem to kill profitability.

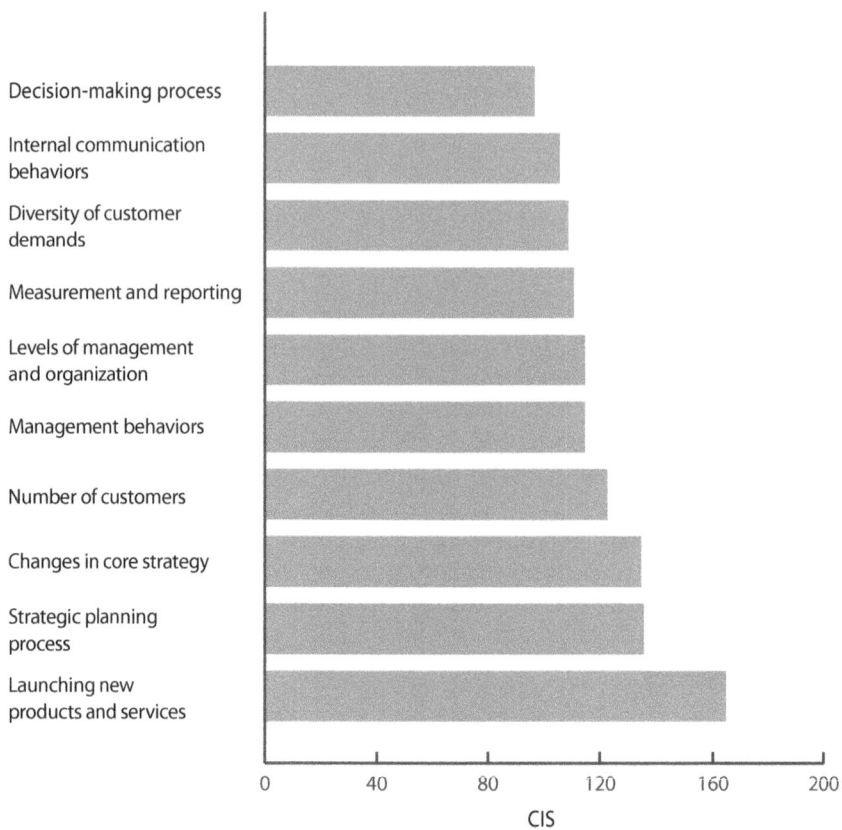

FIGURE 1.7
The top ten biggest drivers of internal complexity
Note: Complexity Impact Score (CIS) is a product of the level of complexity caused
by a driver multiplied by the impact it has on performance.

High performers versus low performers

Finally, we separated the high-performing firms and the low-performing firms in the management survey to see if there was a difference in the kinds of complexity affecting their managers. Again, we were initially surprised – but this result began to make real sense when we thought it through.

It turns out that lower-performing firms suffer more (relative to the high performers) from internal complexity drivers, particularly the people-related, organization design and process kinds of complexity. Contrasting this, respondents in high-performing firms are relatively more concerned about external sources of complexity. So there is one simple, major difference. Managers in low performers are 'introverted' and inward-looking, distracted or overwhelmed by costly internal complexity. High performers are external-facing, rightly concerned about the competitive environment and focused on the kinds of opportunities and threats that their firm needs to respond to in order to succeed.

4. Why should you care about complexity?

You should care about business complexity because it has a negative impact on the performance of your organization. This happens in a variety of ways, for a variety of reasons. Some of the most obvious impacts are shown in Figure 1.8.

Complexity wastes resources

It wastes resources because you and your people are doing things that do not add value. Managers are either distracted from adding value, or cannot see the connection between what they do and added value for customers. They are lost in the complexity.

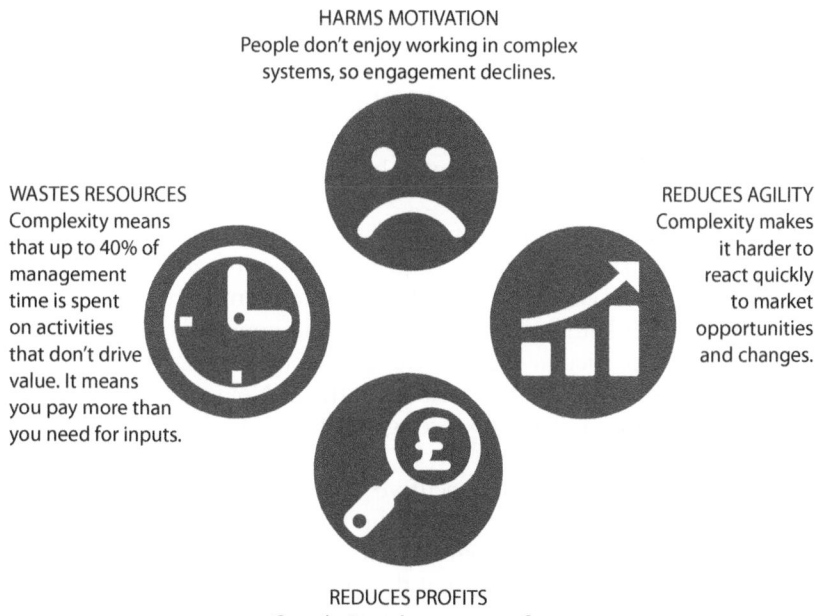

FIGURE 1.8
The impacts of complexity

In complex organizations significant amounts of valuable management time and other resources are wasted either on doing the wrong things, or on doing the right things but doing them in a manner which is unnecessarily complex. This is usually referred to as bureaucracy or in more modern terms as 'corporate treacle'. Whatever we call it, the result is the same: valuable time being spent on the wrong activities.

Complexity harms motivation

We are often called in to help people because of falling scores on their employee engagement surveys. It is well known that the majority of people prefer to work in simpler systems. In a simpler system our actions and behaviors have a direct and visible impact on outputs/results. Things can be easily influenced by an individual or team to achieve the business and personal goals we have. As complexity increases it is harder to get simple things done. People spend less time on the content or enjoyable aspects of their work and more time on processes, politics and organizational alignment. In addition, frustration and conflict between different parts of the organization increase in complex systems as people struggle to find the best way to get difficult things done.

Complexity reduces agility

In fast-moving global markets with rising levels of external complexity, agility – the ability to react quickly and decisively to market changes – is becoming more and more important to both performance and survival.

Complex organizations find it difficult to act on new information and move decisively in the right direction. Overly complex organizations become very internally focused, so they are less able to identify relevant external change and respond quickly to it. Organizational complexity can also 'lock' managers into a particular view of the world, which means they tend to 'deny' that some external forces will affect them (Nokia is a good example of this – but we don't need to go through that again).

We recently spoke to a senior executive at one of the big pharmaceutical companies. This company has one of the most complex business models within the pharmaceutical industry, but long-term profit performance had been good, so it was no surprise that they had come out as a 'complicator' in the GSI study and wanted to know why. The fact that excess complexity was probably costing the company ten per cent of its profit was not of immediate concern, because profits were growing strongly each year. Would its shareholders have the same view?

The executive in question argued that they had made a strategic choice to be more complex, by choosing to play in multiple disease areas, rather than focusing on fewer disease areas. He agreed that this created complexity, but countered that it also creates diversification which acts as a safety net against uncertainty. They have also been highly engaged in M&A, another proven driver of complexity.

We are sure Nokia executives would have made the same argument at one point in time when they were busy buying software companies.

The choice to be more complex is theirs to make, and is not wrong per se, but you need to be really great at managing this complexity; otherwise it will affect your future performance. At the time we wondered whether the loss of agility associated with complexity would become a problem to this particular pharmaceutical company one day. At the time of writing, we heard that it is having some major difficulties with the management of its core manufacturing systems. Is this a complexity problem?

5. Can the complexity problem be solved?

If you knew that your business was wasting 10 per cent of its R&D spend or 15 per cent of its marketing budget, you would do something about it. Very quickly.

Many leaders and managers intuitively know that they are wasting profit and harming motivation because of complexity, but only an enlightened few organizations are doing anything substantial to attack the problem. To us it seems that complexity has been placed on the 'too difficult to deal with' pile of challenges. A variety of reasons are put forward to explain why it is impossible to do anything about complexity. There are bigger problems for us to solve, people are resistant to change, it's hard to quantify the financial benefits. Yes, we have heard them all.

And to some extent we agree, the problem is big and systemic, but from real life experience we know that complexity can be systematically pinpointed and removed. In the rest of this book we hope to inspire you with a variety of ways in which you can pinpoint and then attack complexity in your organization.

In our view we all have a duty to fight back against complexity. We owe it to our shareholders, taxpayers and other stakeholders to take concerted action and give them back the money that is being wasted by complexity. We also owe it to our employees to make work a more enjoyable, motivating and productive place.

So, please, even if you do not read the rest of this book, make it a priority to reduce harmful complexity in your organization.

6. What next? How to use this book

The rest of this book is organized into a further seven chapters plus three appendices – and focuses on how you can identify specific types of harmful complexity and then systematically remove them from your organization.

We start with the all-important diagnosis. Chapter 2 helps you pinpoint the most harmful types of bad complexity and develop a simplification strategy.

After that a series of chapters focus on each of our five internal complexity drivers, following our framework: How to simplify… people complexity (Chapter 3), organizations (4), strategy (5), processes (6) and products and services (7). These are the building blocks of a simplification strategy.

We would hate you to be reading stuff that is not of interest to you or your firm. So, starting with the diagnosis in Chapter 2 you can jump to any of the five core chapters to focus on the most important dimensions of complexity for you.

Finally, we have put some longer industry-sector studies in the appendices – taking a good look at key sources of complexity and simplification approaches in the pharmaceuticals, banking and insurance sectors. We have also provided details of references and further reading (in case you really want more after reading all our stuff …).

Chapter 2

Diagnosing Complexity and Developing a Simplification Strategy

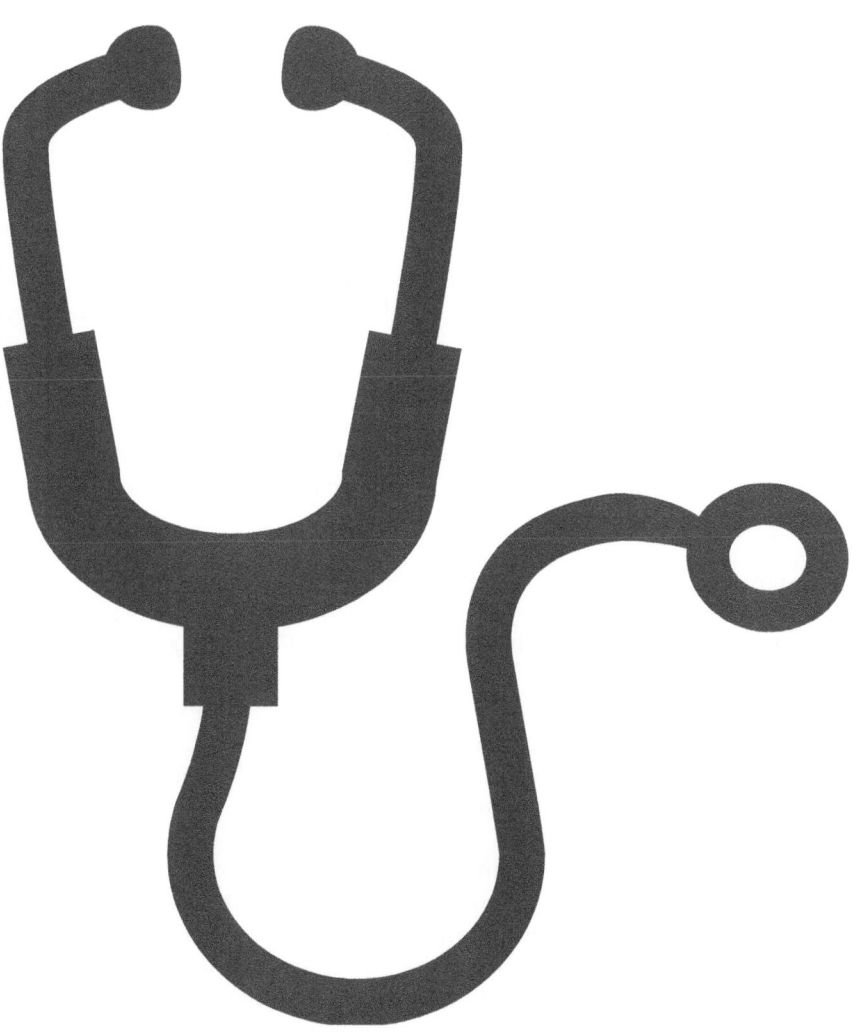

Attacking complexity in a big company can be a daunting problem, because complexity takes so many different forms, is affected by so many people and hides in every corner of your company. This can make it feel like a 'boiling the ocean' kind of problem, so big and impossible that we shouldn't even try. In many cases we find people treating complexity as if it is an inevitable consequence of business and feeling powerless to deal with it. Sometimes they even decide that the best way to deal with complexity is to create a complex way of managing it better!

Let's be clear: complexity is not an unsolvable problem. Difficult yes, but not like putting a man on the moon!

In our work we have proven that it is possible to identify the major complexity problems in your organization, to prioritize them and then to solve them. We have yet to discover a complexity problem that cannot be identified and solved with the right skills, experience and behaviors.

1. How to conduct a detailed complexity diagnosis for your organization

The first step in tackling complexity is to pinpoint the most harmful sources or types of complexity in your organization. Taking a systematic and rigorous approach is essential, as there will be thousands of complexity problems in most organizations. You need to ensure that you focus on the biggest problems and solve these first.

Break it down: You should aim to conduct a **detailed** diagnosis of the biggest complexity problems that fall within each of the six forms of complexity shown in the 'Complexity Cross' diagram (Figure 2.1), i.e. you should identify the sources of external complexity, process complexity, organization, people, product/service and strategic complexity. This structure will help organize and prioritize the information. You can look at the organization as a whole, but you should also consider diagnosing complexity within individual teams/functions/countries.

Talk to different levels of management/staff: In many cases the only people who can see and/or solve complexity problems are the ones who live with them each day, so you should involve all levels of management and staff in the diagnosis. Looking from the top of an organization it is very difficult to see the real complexity problems you have. Most senior managers delegate complex issues to the people below them, so the people who will really understand complexity are usually the middle management and staff.

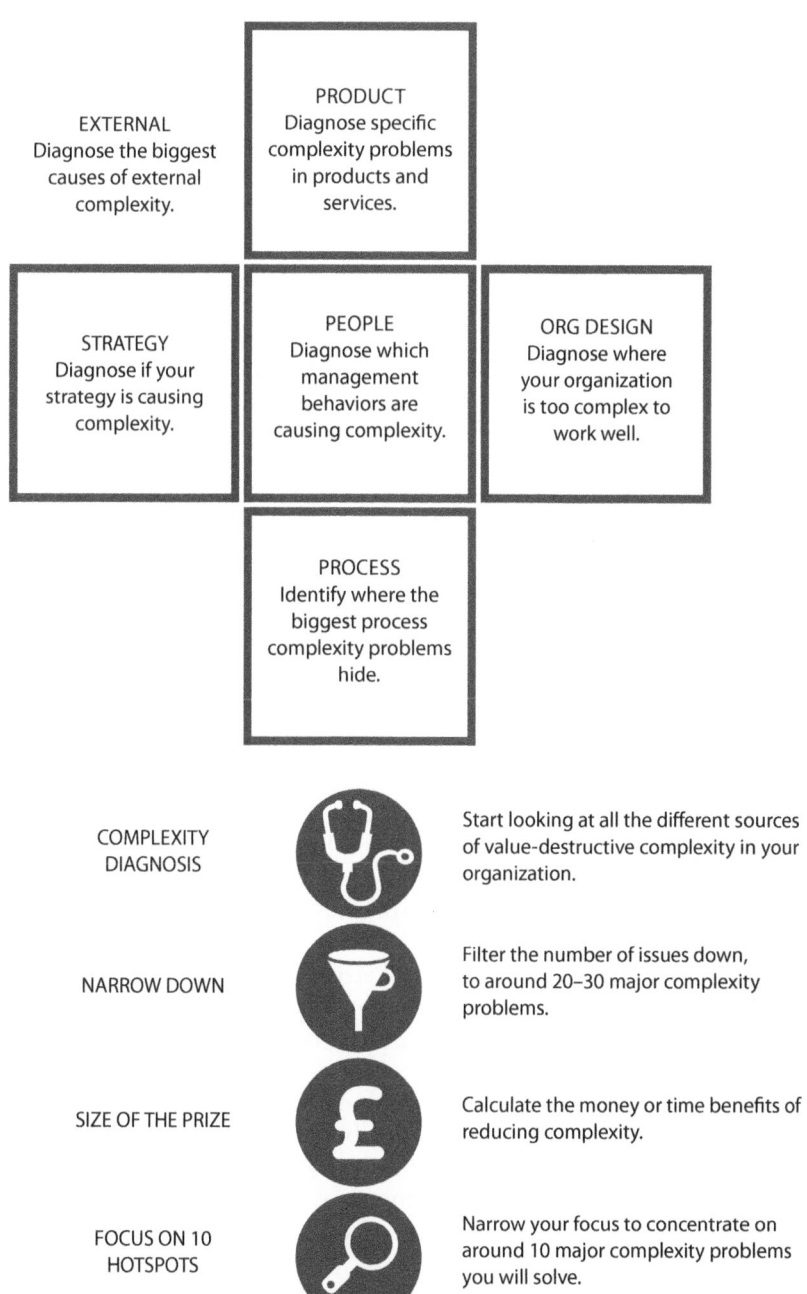

FIGURE 2.1
An overview of the complexity diagnosis approach

We recently joined a project after the diagnosis had been completed. The company, a retailer, was struggling to get middle management to buy in to the program. When we explored the reasons for this we discovered that the executive committee and board members had done the diagnosis without any input or involvement of the middle managers who dealt with the complexity on a day-to-day basis. As far as the staff and middle managers were concerned, the complexity reduction program was focusing on the wrong problems.

Often we find senior management are causing added unnecessary complexity without realizing it: for example, a manager may ask someone in their department to provide a quick report highlighting a certain issue – a seemingly simple task which will just provide a bit of extra background for the management meeting. What they may not realize is the true level of complexity required to produce this report. However, not wanting to disappoint the boss, the next person down the chain will often do whatever is needed to achieve the request – even if this means spending half a day extracting data from multiple systems. This may be happening on a daily basis and the manager may be totally unaware. If they knew how long each task was taking, they would probably conclude that the value in some cases was not worth the effort.

Understand root causes: Make sure your diagnosis gets to the root cause rather than just the symptoms of complexity. Spending time understanding why the problem exists will give you an early indication of how to solve the problem. One of our clients came to us because they thought their antiquated systems were causing complexity in their roles. However, when we dug down into what the real complexity issues were, we found that much of the complexity they were blaming on the systems was being driven by their rigid siloed organizational structure, and that if they fixed this, which was a much cheaper solution than implementing new systems, they would get a good part of the way towards reducing their complexity.

Benchmark yourselves: Big companies are complex, so complexity may be high in your company, but it might not be at abnormal levels. So it is advisable to compare your level of complexity with competitors, peers and/or 'best in class' complexity performers, i.e. companies that are better at managing high complexity levels than you.

Prioritize and focus: Do not try and tackle every single complexity problem you find. Prioritize ruthlessly (the Pain/Gain matrix in Figure 2.2 is a great tool for this). Make sure you are clear on your overall objectives (e.g. to save time, save money, increase employee engagement, make it simpler for your customers to interact with you) so that you can prioritize based on 'Gain' in the right area. Your prioritization criteria should reflect your overall objectives. You should try and end up with around 10–20 major complexity problems to focus on in the first wave of complexity reduction. It is useful to do the following as part of this prioritization:

- Identify some low-hanging fruit or 'Simplicity 101' ideas that everyone can start to implement quickly (e.g. simplifying communications, clarifying RACIs, which describe who is Responsible, Accountable, Consulted and Involved in each major decision, project or activity); this gets the whole company engaged and allows you to bank some confidence-building quick wins.
- Identify some 'high impact' or 'big win' complexity problems that will have a very big positive impact if you can solve them first.

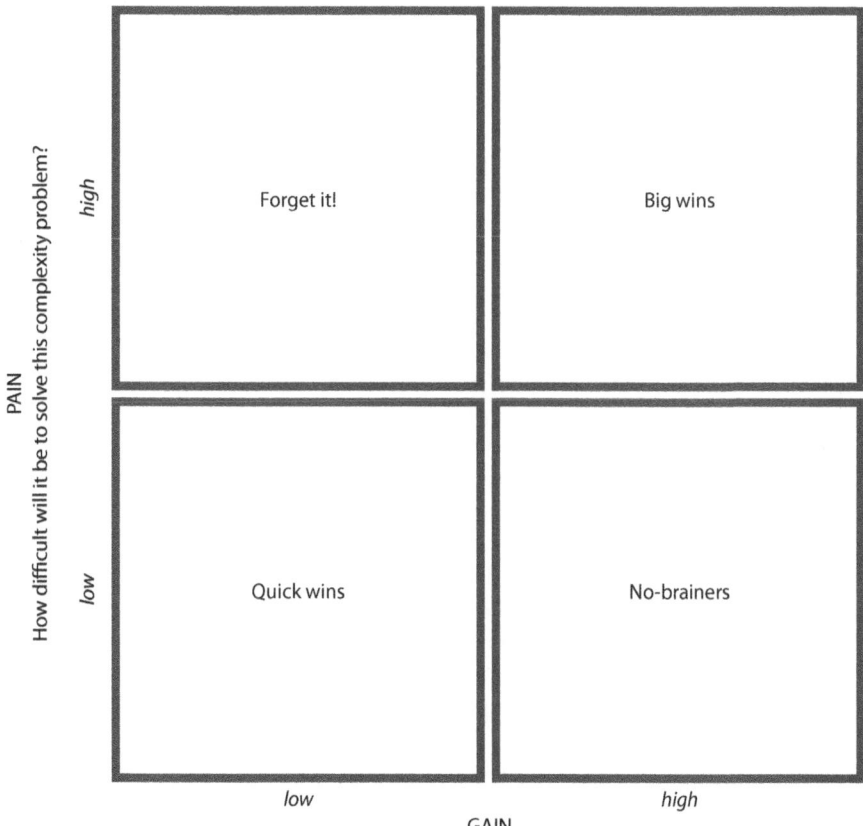

FIGURE 2.2
The Pain/Gain matrix: this can help to prioritize the complexity problems you want to focus on

Identify complexity behaviors: Make sure you diagnose the management and leadership behaviors that are driving complexity. Each company has a different culture, so the complexity behaviors that your organization tends to exhibit will be different from those of other organizations (see Chapter 3).

Quantify the size of the prize: Identify the profit/time/motivation impact of the complexity problems you are going to focus on, so you can calculate the size of the prize. Unless you know how much gain is available it is hard to gain commitment to a complexity reduction project and it is hard to justify the resources you might need for the program.

2. Different tools for complexity diagnosis

Every company is different and has different complexity challenges, so it is useful to have a variety of different diagnosis tools you can use. The following complexity diagnosis tools and techniques will be useful:

Complexity diagnosis survey: Creating a short (10–20 minute) management/staff questionnaire is a good way to collect in-depth data on the complexity issues that are having the biggest impact on your performance. This diagnosis tool can be used by a whole organization, or by an individual country, function or department. This will quickly identify where your biggest problems are so you can focus on them.

We use a standard questionnaire that is derived from our academic research and covers the 100 (or so) types of complexity that have been proven to be most harmful to performance. Using a standard questionnaire allows you to compare different functions/departments/countries within your organization and also allows you to benchmark your organization against competitors, peers and best-in-class complexity managers (for an example, see Figure 2.3). The survey should cover all six drivers of complexity in considerable detail, in order to get under the skin of your company's complexity problems. Many complexity problems are intertwined with other ones, so if you only look at organization complexity, for example, you will miss the interconnections to process complexity, strategic complexity and management behaviors.

Complexity diaries: Managers/staff are asked to keep a diary of anything which creates complexity or is done in an unnecessarily complex way. This includes organizational complexity, products, key processes, systems, etc. Their findings are then downloaded at workshops or interviews, clustered into similar themes and then ranked according to the level of impact they are believed to have on performance. This is less scientific and quantitative than a complexity diagnosis survey, but it can be still generate useful results.

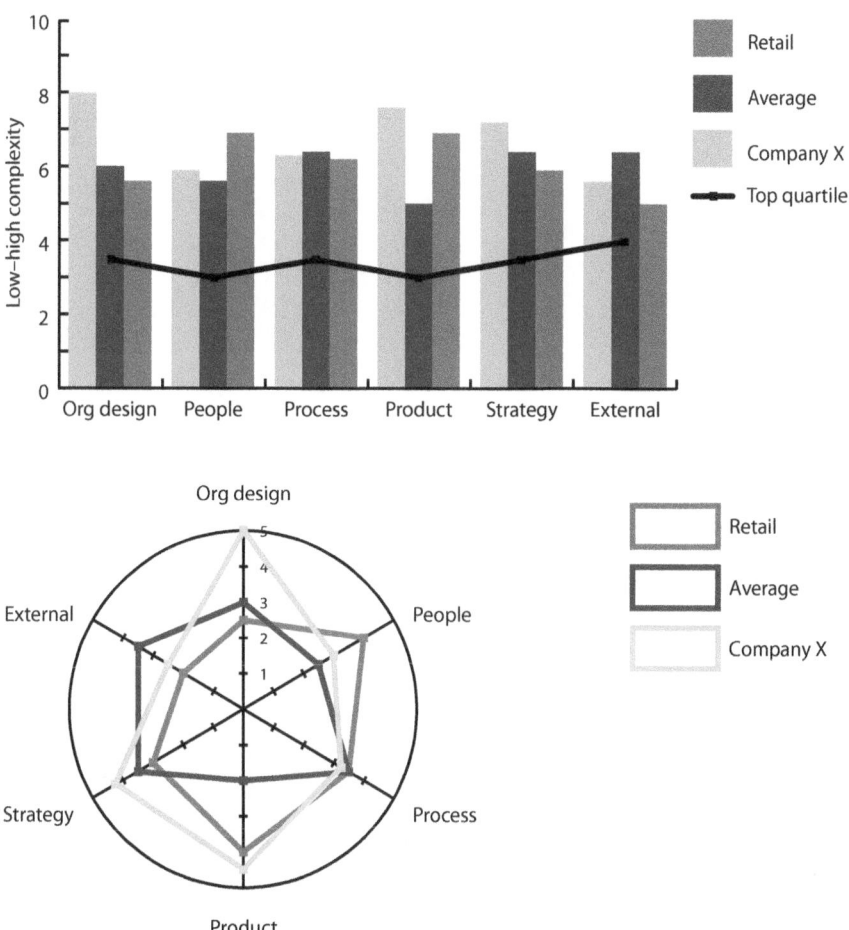

FIGURE 2.3
Company X: summary of key complexity drivers versus benchmarks

Personal and leadership complexity: All complexity comes from the decisions that people make and the behaviors they exhibit on a day-to-day basis (see Chapter 3 for more detail on this point). Do you create complexity yourself? Are you good at communicating simply? Do you encourage others to keep things simple? You can use a simple 360° feedback tool to identify whether your own personal behaviors/activities are creating complexity. By running this on the whole leadership team or department you can identify which complexity-creating behaviors your team should try and work on. If you are trying to build a culture of simplicity, understanding the management behaviors that are holding you back will be essential.

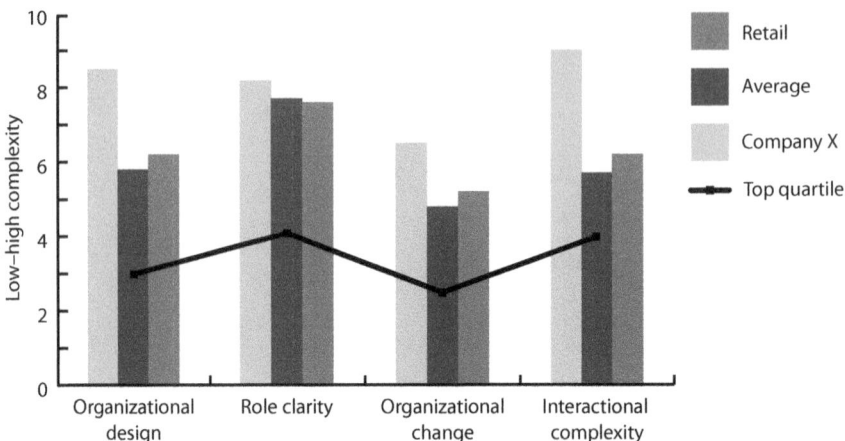

FIGURE 2.4
Company X: breakdown of key drivers within organizational benchmark

Complexity deep dives: These are used to dig deeper into the issues identified in the surveys or diaries. They take the form of structured one-to-one interviews with managers using a set list of questions. The purpose of these is to understand more about why a specific complexity problem exists and what impact it is having on performance. It also allows you to brainstorm some early ideas on how to solve the complexity problem.

Value driver analysis: This looks at how much time is spent on value-adding activity and identifies why more time is not being spent on value generative activities.

- All the activities that the individuals in a function/department regularly complete are listed and put into a time-sheet system.
- The staff and managers keep time sheets for 1–4 weeks, recording roughly how much time they spend on each activity.
- Identify what the key drivers of value creation are for the company overall.
- Look at how each specific function/department contributes to delivering these value drivers.
- Each activity is then allocated against a value driver if possible, to indicate that this activity is useful to the overall success of the company.
- This allows for you to see what percentage of your department's time is spent directly on value-driving activities. Usually it's about 60 per cent of time, the other 40 per cent being spent on non-value-driving activities.
- Are we doing the right things? This process immediately identifies things that you can stop doing.

- Are we doing things in the right way? For the remaining activity you will then look more detail at how the work is done to see if it can be simplified to make it easier for people to create value for your business.

Management report use analysis: One of the major drivers of complexity in companies is management information and reporting. Vast quantities of information are collected at great expense and turned into long and complex reports that are not actually used by anyone or are not central to making important decisions! This diagnosis tool simply looks at all the major reports that are produced by a function/department.

- First, identify how much time and cost goes into producing the information and each major report.
- Then follow the report to its recipients, who are interviewed in depth to understand what they do with the information and how it is used to make important decisions. You may also wish to work out how long each recipient spends reading the report, and multiply this by the total number of recipients. Added to the amount of time taken to produce the report, this is the true cost (in time) that needs to be justified by the benefit it is driving.
- Where the report, or parts of it, is redundant or overly complex, go back to the author and brief them to improve and reduce the report accordingly.
- If the report contains the same information as another report, decide if both are necessary – too often a new report gets added each time a stakeholder has a slightly new requirement, without taking an existing report away. This can lead to situations where four different stakeholders are receiving the same information in slightly different ways.
- Also analyze each report for clarity and simplicity of communication. Where necessary, reduce and reshape reports to be simpler and easier to read.
- If you are still having trouble identifying where your reporting can be reduced, try listing all the reports produced in order of how long they take. Then list reports in the order of how essential or useful they are to the recipients. If you find any reports on the top of the first list and the bottom of the second, these are candidates for stopping or simplifying.

3. Complexity diagnosis questions

Below are some of the key questions you might want to gather data on during the diagnosis phase. Under each of these headings we use a more detailed list of specific sub-questions. However, listing all the questions here would be overwhelming, so we have only included a few here for each topic. Make sure you gather data (not just opinions) on as many of these topics as possible. Figures 2.5 and 2.6 show the complexity priorities that two client firms – one from the food industry and one from the pharmaceutical industry – came up with following this exercise.

Strategic complexity diagnosis questions
- How many strategic initiatives are you pursuing? How complex will each one be to deliver?
- Are you trying to play in too many markets/segments/countries, or do too many things?
- How many weeks does your strategic planning process take, how many people are involved and what percentage of their time is spent on strategic planning?
- How frequently does your strategy change?
- How simple is your strategy to understand? Is your strategy clear to everyone?

People complexity diagnosis questions
- Is simplicity one of your company values?
- Do your leaders encourage, model and reward simplicity?
- Do you have a culture of making things complex/over-engineering? Or do people tend to keep it simple? Do your managers demonstrate any of the major complexity behaviors shown in Chapter 3?
- Do people communicate simply in your company?
- Are everyday things, like meetings, decision-making, reporting and emails, making everyday life complex in your company? What percentage of time do your managers spend on email, in meetings or on conference calls, etc.?

Product/service complexity diagnosis questions
- How many products/services do you have?
- Which products/services account for 80 per cent of your profit? How regularly do you review and retire poor-performing products/services?
- Are the products/services standard where they can be, i.e. do you use the same components/ingredients in your products wherever possible?
- Are you simple for your customers to do business with?
- Supplier interaction: How many suppliers do you have? How many new suppliers do you use each month/year? What are the volume and frequency of purchases?
- How frequently do product/service specifications change?
- How many different channels and/or distribution networks do you supply to?
- How many different customers do you have? How many are unprofitable?

- How much are customer requirements changing?

Process complexity diagnosis questions
- How many major processes are there in your company/department?
- On average how many different processes does each employee need to manage each day? What percentage of people's time is spent managing or complying with company processes each day?
- How many steps/stages are there in each of your major processes?
- How easy is it to find and follow your process guidelines?
- How many existing IT systems are there? How many new IT systems are introduced each year? How complex are the IT systems that support core processes? Are old IT systems decommissioned regularly?
- Are processes standard across business units/departments/countries? For example, do you have several different enterprise resource planning (ERP) systems, or several different payroll systems?
- How many different management reports are written each month/year? How long are the key reports? How long do they take to create? Are they used by the people that receive them?
- Measuring and reporting on KPIs: how many are measured and with what frequency are they reported?
- How complex are pricing lists/systems and promotions?

Organizational complexity diagnosis questions
- To what degree has there been recent/current organizational change?
- Interaction complexity: how many different internal and external connections are you trying to manage and co-ordinate across your team/department/country?
- How many layers are there from the CEO to the shop floor? How wide are spans of control?
- How many different functions/departments/divisions do you have?
- How many different measures/objectives do managers have on average?
- How many people have matrix roles? How many different matrix connections do they have on average? Are matrix decision-making processes and roles clear? Are objectives aligned across the matrix? Are your desired matrix behaviors clearly stated?
- Is decision-making simple?
- Do you have clear RACIs with one person who has 'final accountability' for each major task/decision?
- Role clarity: are people's roles and responsibilities clear? Does everyone know what the key value drivers are for your business? Does everyone have a job description that shows how their role creates value for the company?

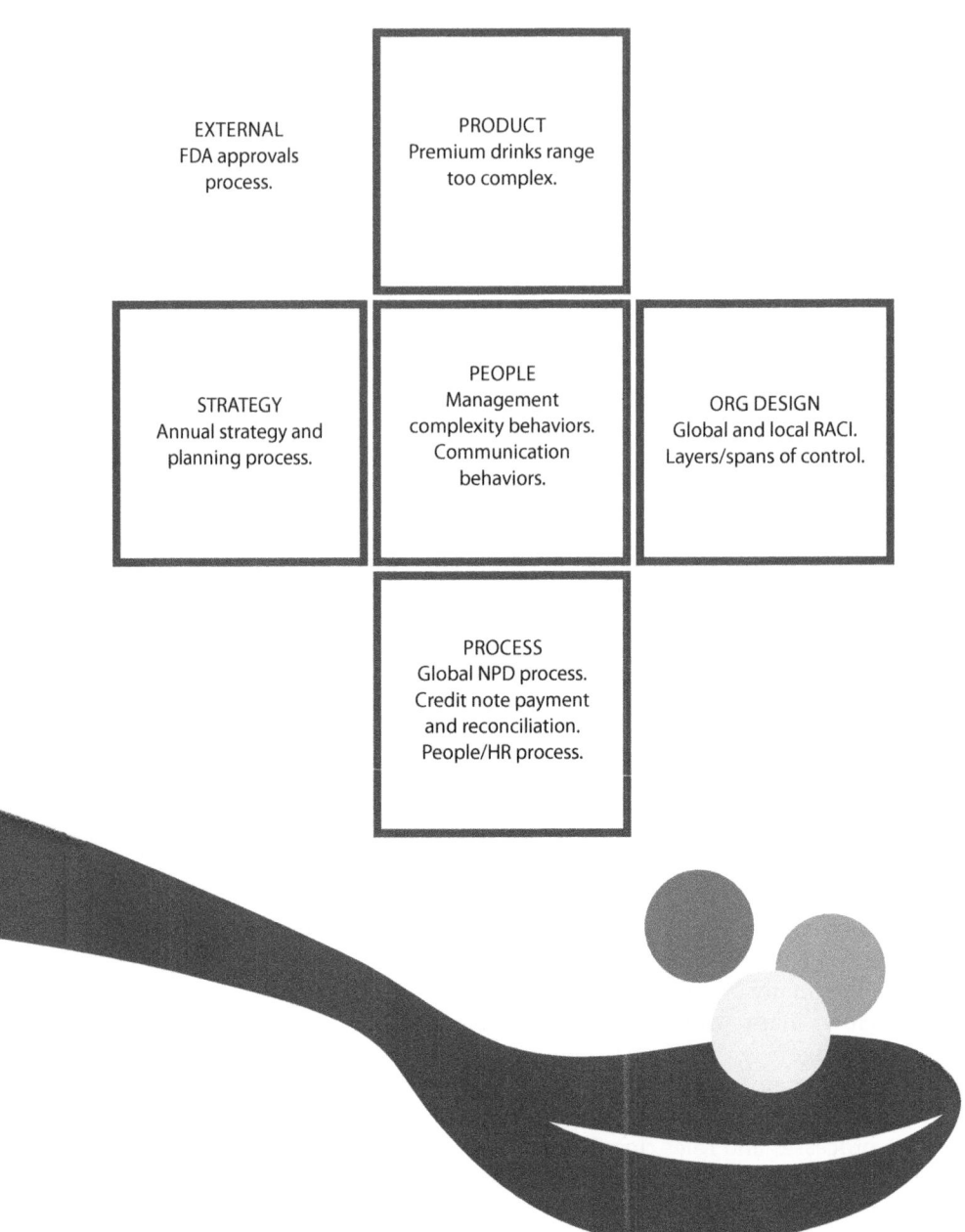

FIGURE 2.5
Complexity hotspots diagnosis: a summary of the top ten complexity drivers for a global food company

EXTERNAL
Compliance training
process.

PRODUCT
Duplication in non-
strategic products
portfolio.
Generics pack formats.

STRATEGY
Annual strategy and
planning process.

PEOPLE
Management
complexity behaviors.
Meetings and
communication culture.

ORG DESIGN
Matrix design, too many
connections.
Layers of management
in generics.

PROCESS
Eight different ERP
systems.
Redundant
management reports.

FIGURE 2.6
Complexity hotspots diagnosis: a summary of the top ten complexity drivers for a
European pharmaceutical company

4. The size of the prize: putting a value on harmful complexity

Once the diagnosis is complete, focus on quantifying the cost of complexity. Reducing complexity is not free. It will require significant management time, consulting fees and sometimes capital investment. So it is important to have a clear understanding of how much money is on the table. Without this, there is no financial rationale to justify the investment you will need to make in reducing complexity.

It would be difficult to get an accurate number for harmful complexity across the whole company. We know from the Global Simplicity Index that on average it's costing you between 10 per cent and 40 per cent of your profits, but this is not an actionable number it is a high-level average that would need to be broken down into specific projects in order to be actionable.

So the key is again focus. At the end of the diagnosis work, you should have identified around 10–20 major complexity reduction projects for your company. You should now calculate how much complexity is costing for each of these projects. Once you have calculated the 'size of the prize' for each complexity reduction project, you can make a final decision on which major complexity hotspots you will attack and remove.

Use the roughly right principle: When calculating the size of the prize, be pragmatic and use the 'roughly right principle'. The roughly right principle states that often your rough calculation will be quite close to the more detailed 'precisely wrong' calculation that you spend hours working on. So it's often better to calculate a roughly right number than trying to get to a precisely wrong figure. Sometimes you may conclude that a higher level of detail is needed, but you should only try to make a more detailed calculation if you have identified that further accuracy is mission critical. A roughly right calculation for a moon rocket launch could be catastrophic, but roughly right 'size of prize' calculations will be fine for many management activities.

There are many ways to calculate the size of the prize; the approach will depend on the type of complexity you are trying to quantify. Below we outline some 'size of the prize' calculation methods that have worked well for us in the past. We do not go into great detail here – you will no doubt have access to good analysts and accountants who can provide the in-depth expertise you may need.

Activity based costing: This uses work diaries or observations to identify how long it takes to complete an activity or individual steps in a whole process. Redundant or non-value-adding steps or activities are then identified. The cost of or time taken on non-value-adding or redundant activities can then be added together to identify how much money and time can be saved by simplifying the process or activity.

Cost vs. value creation method: This approach can be useful for calculating the cost of knowledge-based processes (e.g. the innovation process) where the outputs/results maybe long term or less tangible. First calculate how much the current process/activity costs: e.g. the employee's time spent on working on this process/activity, plus any direct input costs (such as raw materials, data, IT costs).

Then calculate how much value the activity/process creates for your organization. This can usually be done by calculating the value of all the outputs created by the process. The difference between the process cost and the value created show how much this process/activity costs you. If the process cost is greater than the value created you clearly have a problem! You have no choice: you must find a cheaper way. The cheaper way will often be a simpler way. In the example of the innovation process we often discover that the true cost of the process is higher than the value created by new product launches.

Zero based method: If you started from scratch and created the simplest process possible how much would this cost or how much time do you think you could save? The current process cost minus zero based cost gives you an alternative size of the prize calculation, indicating how much you could save if you simplified the process.

The cost of organizational complexity: Work diaries are also a good way to calculate the cost of organizational complexity. First, the value drivers for the function/department in question are identified: e.g. speed of customer response, number of orders processed in less than one hour. Each person then keeps a record of all their activities over a 2–4 week period. At the end of the measurement period the data is summarized and each individual is asked to identify which value driver each activity contributed to.

Doing the wrong things: Many activities completed during the diary period will be hard to allocate against one of your department value drivers. This would suggest that these activities are not generating value for you. You can now calculate the cost of non-value-adding activities by attributing salary costs and overheads to the non-value-adding activities you have identified, e.g. senior managers spending half an hour a day signing off purchase orders they don't even read!

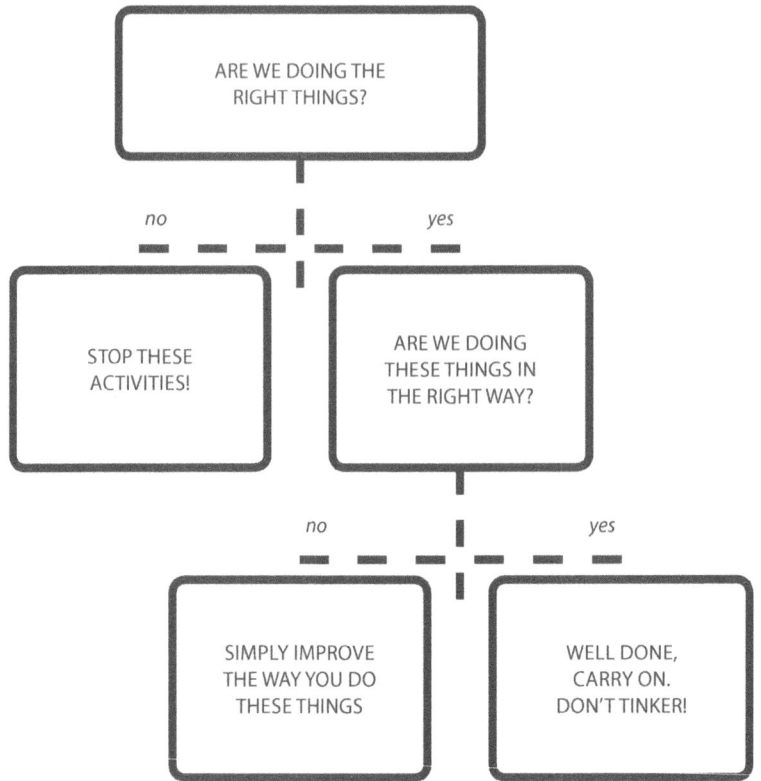

FIGURE 2.7
Are we doing the right things, in the right way?

Doing the right things, but in the wrong way: Some activities will be value generative, but will be done in a complex or inefficient way. So where this is the case (too complex), the individual is asked to identify how much quicker they could complete this activity if it was made simpler for them. The flaw in this subjective approach is clear, but there is no better way that we are aware of. So the calculation is done at a 'roughly right, not precisely wrong' level. We ask people to be conservative when estimating how much time would be saved by making things simpler. They can only chose a time saving of 10 per cent, 20 per cent, 30 per cent or 40 per cent. We don't let them go higher.

The cost of major projects: Many companies fail to adequately account for the management time that is invested into major projects. They calculate all the other project costs very diligently, but they miss this one massive line called people costs. List all the major strategic projects that you are driving through the business, then identify how much value you expect to generate from each of these projects. Then estimate the cost – be realistic, not optimistic.

Time costs: Use work diaries to identify how much time each manager/employee is spending on these strategic projects. Now estimate how much time it will take to complete the project.

Other costs: Identify the other costs and how much it will cost you to complete each strategic project (capital costs, external fees, materials, etc.).

Then compare the total project cost (including management time) with the expected return. Often you'll stop doing three or four projects straight away!

The cost of meetings: People are often blissfully unaware of the costs of a meeting. We recommend that each meeting that lasts more than 30 minutes has a cost associated with it and that the participants are told how much it is costing for them all to be there. (We have created a simple MS Excel ready reckoner for this that you can get from our website).

Calculate the number of hours the meeting will take, the number of people in the meeting and then multiply by the average hourly cost of the people in the room. For simplicity, we use one departmental average cost per person/hour (i.e. we use the roughly right principle). Now add travel costs for getting everyone in the meeting. We recently attended a two-day meeting with 15 people that cost £75,818. Throughout the meeting we reminded everyone that we needed to find £75,000 in complexity reduction savings just to pay for the meeting itself.

The cost of management reports: List the 10–20 most time-consuming reports that you produce each month. Calculate the total cost of producing the report, again including all management/employee time. This is how much value that report would need to create (or cost it would need to save) in order to break even. Now see if you can quantify the value of the report in terms of how it contributes to growing sales or reducing cost. Can you prove the report is worth the investment? If you can't prove that, why are you still doing it?

5. Develop a complexity reduction strategy for your organization

If you are still reading by now I can assume that you agree that complexity is a big issue for your organization. It is reducing your profits by at least 10 per cent, so as a leader you have a responsibility to your stakeholders to act. Our view is that every big organization should have a clear strategy for taking complexity out of the company. By now you understand precisely where your biggest and most expensive complexity problems are. It is time to start a simplicity revolution in your business. But how can you enroll the engagement and energy of your whole organization to eradicate complexity? How can you make simplicity a core value or operating principle of your company? The answer is to have a clear strategy that is clearly communicated across your organization.

Your simplification strategy should consist of:

- **Diagnosis results:** a summary of your diagnosis identifying where you will focus your attention and the size of the prize when you are successful at reducing complexity.
- **Measurable complexity reduction objectives:** Your strategy should set clear and measurable objectives for how much time and money you expect to save through the complexity reduction project. You should also measure employee engagement to understand how much complexity reduction is improving staff motivation.
- **Core simplicity principles:** Introduce some simple principles that everyone in your company can easily live by day to day. These create a general set of high-level complexity reduction rules that can be broadly applied by all your people every day (see Figure 2.8).
- **A simplicity people program:** As you will learn in Chapter 3, all complexity is created by people, so you will need a program for changing the way your people work. You will have to create a leadership program. You will also need to train/coach people in the new skills, so they can learn how to reduce complexity. Very few people know how to make the complex simple. It's hard, so training in complexity reduction skills is essential.
- **Everyday simplification:** These are easy-to-execute simplification ideas that everyone can quickly start to implement (e.g. rules about simpler presentations, simpler decision-making processes etc.). See Chapter 8.
- **Major simplification projects:** These are the big areas of complexity identified in the diagnostic that, once removed or reduced, will significantly reduce your overall complexity footprint. These are often very hard, but they have to be done.

PRIORITIZE AND REDUCE
Work out what's really important. Focus only on that and
reduce the rest. You should cull the number, variety and
frequency of everything you can. Words, pages, projects,
number of people involved, stages …

STANDARDIZE
Find consistent ways of doing things,
naming things, defining things, etc. so that
the whole team is on the same page.

CLARIFY
Make roles, decision-making,
matrix design and concepts
as clear as possible.

what you need to do

how you can do it

ENABLE
Give your employees the
tools and training they need
to simplify things.

INCREASE AWARENESS
Point out management behaviors
that create complexity as soon as
you spot them.

REINFORCE
Stress the importance of simplicity as a value through
reward, review and recruitment processes.

FIGURE 2.8
Examples of general simplicity principles

6. Where next? Navigating through the rest of the book

As we said at the end of the last chapter – we would hate you to be reading useless stuff.

From here the simplest way to navigate through this book is to go directly to the complexity drivers, in the respective chapters, that interest you the most (Figure 2.9).

People complexity comes next – and sits at the heart of our five-part internal complexity framework.

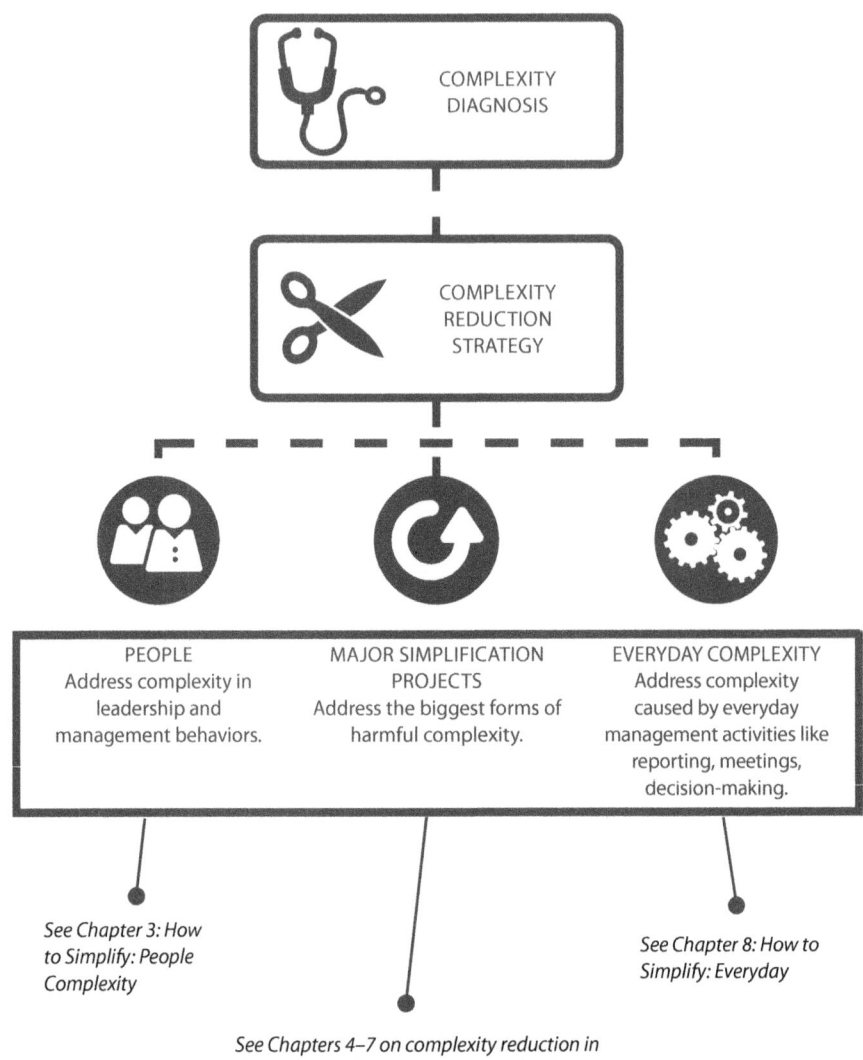

FIGURE 2.9
Where next? Navigating through the rest of the book

Chapter 3
How to Simplify: People Complexity

COPING WITH COMPLEXITY: STORIES FROM THE FRONT

We had a manager once who was very hot on the Microsoft Project software package. He used it for all his project plans, and he also made everyone reporting to him create their project plans in it as well. From his point of view, it made it easier to see everything in the same format, but he didn't realize the impact this was having – many people in the team weren't used to using MS Project, and the fact of having to translate their plans from Excel, PowerPoint or other mediums was taking an inordinate amount of time without really adding any value.

The plans weren't complicated enough to warrant all this extra effort, and the additional functions of MS project, such as resourcing and dependencies, weren't being used as no one understood them.

We thought this was a process problem, but it was a people problem. The manager thought that he was simplifying work by having all the plans in the same format, but what he didn't see was the increased complexity and higher workload he was creating for other people. Looking back, we also think that he liked to be the expert on the one tool that everyone was forced to use (and got a little bit of a kick from the fact that everyone had to fit in with his preferences).

Individual preferences, diverse desires, a need for control, a problem with power.

Organizations are complex because people are complex.

64% of our sample lose more than 5% of their productivity to complexity (33% lose more than 10%).

1. The simple truth: business complexity does not create itself, it is created by people

Edward De Bono in his great book *Simplicity* observes that things never evolve over time to become simpler, they evolve to be more complex.

He's right of course, but the harder truth is that this evolution is driven by people. An organization design, product or process does not wake up in the morning, go to work and make itself more complex! Business complexity is created by the decisions and behaviors of people. So people are both the creators of complexity and the victims of it as well.

It follows that we can't understand complexity unless we understand why people make business more complex than it needs to be. In this chapter we focus on the people side of the complexity problem.

Why and how are the people in a business a major source of costly complexity?

If you remember our definition of complexity, it stems from the number and variety of components in a system, the relationships between these components and the pace at which these are changing. Change in one component or relationship has a knock-on effect for others and the cumulative effect can be overwhelming.

We can relate this to the people dimension. Complexity results from the sheer number of different kinds of individual employees in a firm. These are the 'components' of our system. Their variety, including different levels of knowledge, specialist capabilities and their individual agendas and motivations, underpin the complexity of the organization.

On top of this mix we have to consider the variety of relationships, links and connections between people, including:

- up and down the organizational hierarchy, from CEO down to trainee
- across divisions and functions: marketing versus production; back office versus customer-facing; business group A versus business group B, etc.
- international: HQ versus regional HQ versus Subsidiary.

To add value people have to connect, communicate and cooperate across these boundaries. This is in addition to overcoming cultural, age, gender and other differences that add to the differences in their motivations, roles, responsibilities, specialist skills or geographic location.

Finally, people change, their roles change and their value-adding relationships with others change – continually. Individuals, their interrelationships and the organization as a whole adapt and evolve all the time.

The behavior of these people – their actions across all of these dimensions – is at the heart of the organization and is the fundamental driver of all its complexity.

> For 54% of our sample, more than 5% of their workforce were new hires in 2011 (for 27% more than 10%).
>
> For 64% of our sample, more than 5% of their workforce left last year (for 32%, more than 10% left).

2. Why do we make things more complicated than they need to be?

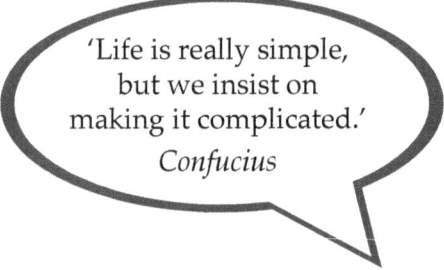

'Life is really simple, but we insist on making it complicated.'
Confucius

Let's start with the individual manager. Why does our behavior add complexity?

It's in our programming

We create complexity because it's in our nature. Humans are successful because of our creativity and our desire to progress and to survive. This means that we just can't resist developing and improving ourselves and our surroundings, even if this 'progress' is eventually harmful to ourselves and others. Add to this the collective effects of many individuals in a firm, all seeking personal progress, and we can see that companies quickly become highly complex, adaptive systems. So complexity increases largely unconsciously as we seek to improve things, to learn and progress and to satisfy our own needs. It seems that, sometimes, we humans just cannot help making things too complicated.

A quick look at Maslow's hierarchy of human needs illustrates our point.

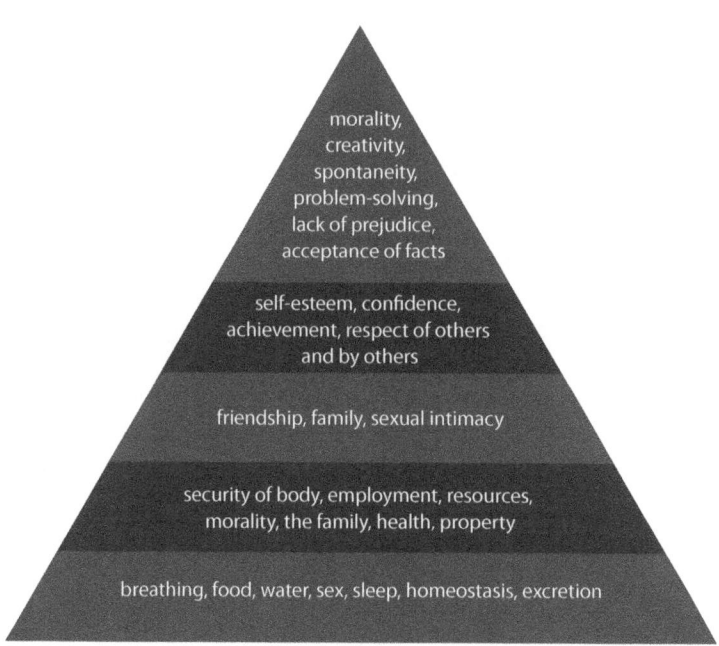

FIGURE 3.1
Maslow's hierarchy of human needs

Safety needs

- Security of employment: In a modern organization (especially in turbulent economic conditions) tenure of employment is far from guaranteed. In order to survive we have to show that we are doing great things. So we look for projects and initiatives that prove our value to our organization. Many of these initiatives are great, but just as many add complexity without adding value.
- Anxiety: In a similar way if we are anxious about our chances of survival we will create organizations and systems to defend us from predators. We will also hide behind complexity as an excuse; you won't dare to get rid of me if you fear the consequences!

Esteem needs

- Self-esteem, confidence and respect from others: By doing clever things and achieving great results we gain the respect and recognition of others and we feel better about ourselves. The search for this self-esteem and recognition by others will again drive us to look for new and 'better' ways of doing things, some of which will create unnecessary complexity.

Self-actualization needs

- Creativity: Humans are creative, we love to invent and improve our surroundings. This means we will take something that works well and try to improve it, even if it does not need to be improved! Sometimes things are best left alone, or cut down. But that goes against our creative nature.
- Problem solving: We find it intellectually stimulating and challenging to solve difficult problems and master the complex subjects that others find difficult. This again creates complexity as we seek understanding and truth and experiment with new ways of doing things.

These human needs are difficult to address, because they are intangible and innate. It's hard to see self-esteem, safety and self-actualization on people's faces! However, these needs do manifest themselves in a number of more observable management habits and behaviors in big companies.

How many of these do you see each day in your organization, and which ones are you guilty of yourself?

- *Over-intellectualizing or over-engineering:* Making something more intellectual or more complex than it needs to be for the situation or the audience in question. This is a form of self-actualization.
- *Reinventing:* Creating a new way of doing the same thing we already do. Giving something a new name when it already has a good name. This is driven by our need to be creative, but reinvention is not creativity, it is tinkering!
- *Mistrust:* This stems from our need for safety and leads to us creating new organizations, reporting systems and control systems ostensibly to control people or protect ourselves. We should invest more in enabling people to do their jobs effectively… and then trust them to deliver.
- *Tinkering:* Making changes that reflect your personal preference or desire to stamp your mark, rather than making changes because the result will be substantially better, is again linked to self-actualization and creativity.
- *Avoidance:* Focusing on the process or the politics rather than the real problem or issue in hand. This creates a distraction that confuses people about the real issue/problem.
- *Lack of focus:* Focusing on too many small things, failing to look for and/or prioritize the bigger opportunities that create real value in your company.
- *Aimlessness:* Failing to set a clear and/or correct destination from the very start. This leads to wandering aimlessly in lots of wrong directions!

- *Adding without taking away:* Adding to something without taking something less important away first.
- *Perfecting:* Trying to make things 100 per cent perfect, when roughly right now is plenty good enough!

As mentioned, it is very difficult to see the intangible needs that are causing complexity. However, these behaviors are the physical manifestation of the intangible needs and can be observed and measured in your organization. This will allow you to identify the complexity behaviors most common in your organization. Once you know what they are, you can start to work on changing them. By improving these behaviors you can start to attack complexity by getting people to think and work in different ways.

There's no way of knowing we have gone too far

A more philosophical take on this might be that humans also have a tendency to push things until they break, e.g. global warming, the credit crunch. This also seems to be the case with complexity, and in this sense the Complexity Curve (Figure 1.2, discussed in Chapter 1) can be seen as a human behavior curve as well.

As a business grows it adds good complexity, and we get rewarded for this with improved business results, self-esteem, recognition, promotion. etc. Because we are rewarded we keep doing more of these things and get better and better at adding complexity. At some point the returns on adding more complexity start to diminish and soon the returns became negative. Complexity is now eating your profits.

This is completely understandable, as we have no way of seeing whether our decisions will increase complexity too far, pushing us up the Complexity Curve and beyond the tipping point. There is no red light or warning signal that tells us that we are over-engineering a process, organization or product. This means that over time, more or less everything at work eventually evolves to become too complex.

So what?! In the same way we are trained to consider the financial impact of our decisions and the environmental impacts, we also need to learn how to identify the 'complexity impact' of our decisions and to see when more complexity will limit our success.

Corporate leaders and leadership is a good place to start.

3. Good leaders keep things simple

'Simplicity, simplicity, simplicity!
I say, let your affairs be as two or three, and not
a hundred or a thousand; instead of a million
count half a dozen, and keep your accounts on
your thumb-nail.'
Henry David Thoreau

As the competitive environment has become more complex, turbulent and unpredictable, the role of business leaders has changed. The strategic imperative has shifted from efficiency to adaptability; the top-down, command-and-control structures of the past have given way to 'enabling leadership' styles that promote learning, knowledge and innovation (at least for some firms).

The rules-based, bureaucratic organizations of the past survived because leaders were able to cope with the pace of change and tell others what to do. But gone are the days when the top team, however bright it is, can understand and strategically respond to the multitude of threats and opportunities facing firms. Its role now is to create the organizational context where others can take responsibility, have the capability and are accountable for strategic decision-making.

The problem is, when you remove the rules, people-driven complexity grows; hence the need for self-discipline, self-awareness and strategic clarity at all levels of the organization. The role of leaders is to set clear, simple strategic boundaries and encourage others to set the direction of the firm within these boundaries.

Micro-management and over-intervention by senior management is a common problem. Command-and-control hierarchies and autocratic bosses often increase complexity by driving their people to disengage with team approaches and maintain their distinctiveness and differences.

To improve the constructive engagement of others, senior managers must invite discussion and disagreement, but also focus the agenda, and place boundaries around the discussion and the acceptable outcomes.

APPLE: A CULTURE OF FOCUS AND SIMPLICITY

What was the complexity problem?
By the time co-founder Steve Jobs returned to Apple in 1996, the computer company had lost its edge and fallen behind its competitors. Some went as far as writing it off as one of the failure stories of Wall Street. Shortly before returning to the reins, even Jobs admitted that the company, previously a decade ahead of everybody else, had been standing still for ten years. Things looked bleak.

How did the power of simplicity help?
Steve Jobs's homecoming ushered in the era of 'focus and simplicity'. This mantra led to a slashing of the number of R&D projects Apple was running in 1997. Instead, it concentrated only on the high-value ones. One of those projects went on to become the iMac, a record-breaking product for the company. Apple has maintained a focused portfolio ever since and it has clearly paid off to downsize: for the full fiscal year 2011, Apple earned $108bn in revenue and was the largest publicly traded company in the world.

Today, the mantra of focus and simplicity is present throughout the company. Apple products radiate simplicity both in design and usability. More complex devices such as the Microsoft Zune never stood a chance next to the iconic iPod.

But the philosophy of simplicity is also followed in many of the other areas of Apple. As a brand, it is highly distinctive, its strong identity setting it apart from its rivals in the technology industry. Having a boldly simple brand allows Apple to keep branding consistent globally. Unlike many other companies who adapt their brand offering to different countries and cultures, Apple remains uniform, unfazed even by seasonal holidays (famously, there are no Christmas deals or spring sales in Apple stores).

Jobs was good at stopping doing the wrong things. He famously took the same approach to people management, keeping only those that were clearly adding value. For a company this size, Apple is a very flat organization. This allows it to make decisions quickly and to disseminate ideas and concepts through the organizational hierarchy with speed and ease.

What was the impact?
During Steve Jobs's tenure as CEO, Apple's market capitalization increased on average by 42 per cent every year. In 2011, Apple became the most

valuable firm in the world, overtaking Exxon. Just a decade earlier they ranked no. 287 on the S&P 500 index.

Apple's simple products, strategies, processes and organization structure have helped them to get to the top. But at the heart of the company, employees that have been inspired by Jobs are dedicated to the simple goal of adding value through cool designs and great technology.

Leaders should create order through simple rules

Simplicity and complexity are related to, but not the same as, order and chaos. Things can be complicated but well-ordered and (relatively) predictable – like the controls of an airplane or the operations of an army.

One of the well-known actions of new CEOs is to lead wholesale restructuring exercises to change the way that firms operate. They orchestrate disorder and then create a new order across complex businesses. In this and other ways – like picking the core values, focusing the strategy and selecting where to invest – leaders simplify and clarify.

One of the benefits of this is that it shakes up the organization. Managerial routines may still be relevant and useful; if so, they will be kept. Those that have become redundant habits that no one has stopped will be culled.

At least they should. Too often leaders fail to set clear boundaries. In Chapter 5 we talk about 'strategy as simple rules' – suggesting that the key challenge for leaders is to clarify, through simple rules, where the firm 'plays'. What are the limits: to the range of products we develop and sell? To the number of markets in which we compete? To the kinds of customers we target? To the number of suppliers we partner with? 'Borderline' rules, 'priority' rules and 'stop' rules are discussed in Chapter 5. These can all help managers throughout an organization decide on their own strategic trade-offs and those of others.

The very business of business is about strategic trade-offs. Managers at every level have to make decisions all the time about their time, their budget and the resources of other staff that they manage: where to focus these limited amounts of assets, funding and capabilities and, more significantly, how to guide the allocation of the limited time, energy and enthusiasm of the people you lead. The answer lies in simple rules. Place clear boundaries and let others decide the detail. That is what simple leadership is about.

Leaders should not be the source of costly complexity

One of the leading causes of frustration for respondents to our Management Survey of Complexity is the reporting requirements of senior management. The planning cycle, budget reports, monthly personnel reports, details of key performance indicators (KPIs), and so on, all weigh managers down with routine requirements.

Much of this information exchange is necessary to monitor, control and guide a business. But much of it is useless and time-consuming. It is not read, it is out of date by the time it reaches the decision-maker, or it is ignored while the politics of senior management relationships dictate the strategy.

Leaders have a responsibility to minimize this and other sources of unnecessary complexity.

Across the three most common areas of leadership complexity – strategy and planning, goal setting, follow-up and communications – you need to decide how much detail is enough. A simple request from a senior manager can lead to cascading workloads for others down the organization.

Teams should overcome, not create, costly complexity

Cross-functional and cross-business teams are an essential part of the modern corporation. In theory, they provide the platform for a temporary coalition of specialists to integrate their knowledge and experience to add more value, more rapidly, than individuals locked into departmental routines.

Sony, for example, is fantastic at bringing together a variety of engineering specialists with a manufacturing manager, plus software and content experts and one or two design and marketing people to create new consumer electronics products. They come together in 'skunk works' or 'NPD (new product development) hit-squads'. Project teams develop an energy and a focus that overcomes individual differences in their knowledge, experience, interests and incentives. Their creativity is harnessed and focused within clear strategic boundaries regarding costs, product types that are acceptable within the portfolio, target market segments and technology platforms that the firm has standardized around (like Blu-ray).

Without clear strategic boundaries and a strong team culture, firms like Sony would be less effective at using multi-divisional teams to reduce the complexities of work together across the inevitable territories and silos of large organizations.

Defensive and dysfunctional teams spring up where the boundaries are unclear, where resources or rewards are up for territorial 'land grabs' and where any unifying team culture is over-ridden by the individual divisional cultures from the members home departments. These teams will tend to exaggerate and accentuate the complexities of working together, rather than reduce them. They will fail more often than they succeed and will cost the business money.

4. What does our research show?

In Chapter 1 we provided an overview of the various research studies and surveys we have conducted to develop our understanding of complexity and performance. Our management survey in particular highlights some of the leading sources of people-related complexity that harm efficiency and profitability. Again, the irony is that these kinds of complexity also demotivate people, making working lives far less rewarding, and yet people, usually unwittingly, are the source of the problem.

Table 3.1 shows some examples of people-related sources of complexity, ranked by managers in our survey in terms how much they impact on productivity.

The top three drivers of people complexity are: general management behavior, internal communications behavior, and the content and politics of meetings. These are clearly sources of frustration for most managers. But we find something even more interesting when we re-work the responses according the relative performance of the firms surveyed. It turns out that 'people factors' are *the leading category of complexity factors* (out of our six categories) cited by managers working in poor-performing firms.

Moreover, when we examine which complexity factors have the strongest correlation with poor performance we find that 'time spent dealing with email' comes at the top of our list of over 100 sources. Yet this gets an average ranking in the overall survey: 43rd in our list of sources of complexity impact.

> 43% of our sample spend more than 10% of their time dealing with email (16% spent more than 30% of their time).

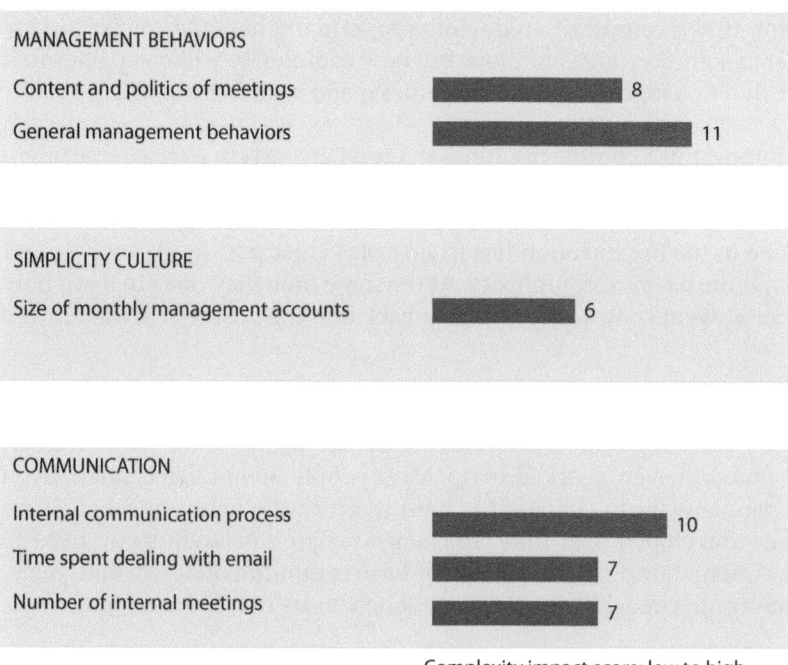

MANAGEMENT BEHAVIORS

Content and politics of meetings — 8

General management behaviors — 11

SIMPLICITY CULTURE

Size of monthly management accounts — 6

COMMUNICATION

Internal communication process — 10

Time spent dealing with email — 7

Number of internal meetings — 7

Complexity impact score: low to high

TABLE 3.1
The impact of people-related sources of complexity on the business
Note: this is a relative measure that combines the frequency with which this source of complexity was cited by managers in our survey and their rating of the impact it has on performance.

It is intriguing to think that one of the best indicators of costly complexity – the strongest proxy measure for all of the others representing a whole range of complexity sources – is 'time spent dealing with emails'! Managers in the weakest firms in our study highlighted this as their top problem. Rather than thinking that this is a causal relationship (i.e. email overload causes a drop in profits – or do falls in profitability lead to email overload?), we see this indicator as one of the strongest *symptoms* of overwhelming complexity. It is perhaps the most important alarm bell, telling you that you are well past the tipping point!

5. How to attack the people side of complexity

By now it must be clear to you that in large multinational organizations, you can't attack complexity unless you change the decision-making processes and behaviors of the many people that cause it in the first place.

A big top-down complexity reduction program might make your company simpler in some key areas for now, but new complexity will creep back in if people don't change their ways of thinking and working as well.

More importantly, complexity hides everywhere, across every department and every function. So you can't solve complexity with a small project team of people, however well equipped and motivated they are. To win, everyone in the organization has to first play their part in identifying and removing the harmful complexity. At the same time they have to learn how they can prevent complexity creeping back into the business in the future.

Take a systematic approach

Changing the deep-seated behaviors of people is one of the most difficult things you will ever be asked to do. Most people do not like change. Even when people want to change it is hard to break the habits and behaviors that have developed over time. To change people's behaviors you need to have a systematic approach and a long-term commitment. It will take years, not months, to change the management behaviors that cause complexity.

There are many different theories about change management and supporting models you can use. It is beyond the scope of this book to tell you about them all. Many companies will already have a preferred change model or approach that they will use. In the rest of this chapter we describe the change model we use and then specific tools that you can try. Most of these tools and ideas can be fitted into your own organization's change model, so you do not need to slavishly follow ours. It is usually very important to consider a range of interventions. Some people will just want to be told what to do, some will want to discuss the barriers they perceive and some will just want to be given new tools or approaches to experiment with. All of these reactions need to be catered for and be effectively managed through the change.

Changing complexity behavior is much like changing general behaviors like giving up smoking or losing weight. First, you have to raise awareness of the issue and the current situation. Next you have to create a pull and/or a push to change. This is often referred to as creating a 'need for change' by showing the personal and collective benefits of change and/or the risk or danger of not changing.

In Beckhard's Change Equation:

$$C = [A+B+D] > X$$
i.e. change can only occur when factors ABD are stronger than the cost of change (X)

C = Change
A = Level of dissatisfaction with the status quo
B = Desirability of the proposed change
D = Practicality of the change (minimal risk and disruption)
X = 'Cost' of changing

This equation states that the case for change (factors A, B and D) must be greater than the cost of changing (X) before any meaningful change can occur. It follows that to reach a 'tipping point' then the case for change (A, B and D) must be convincing and compelling, but it must also be possible for people to change. For example, many people want to stop smoking, but often it is physically impossible for them to quit their addiction. If the change equation is not satisfied, then you will find resistance from people. Your change plan will have to be designed to overcome this resistance. Considering this equation for each group will at least allow you to foresee where major resistance may occur so you can cater for this in your plans.

For our weight-loss example a change equation might look like:

C = Losing some weight
A = I cannot get into a favorite pair of jeans and I am not attractive to others.
B = If I lose weight, I could get into my favorite jeans and I will feel more attractive.
D = How will I change my eating habits and get some exercise?
X = Need to make a packed lunch and cook a fresh meal in the evening rather than a ready meal, which means losing weight is more work than sticking with my current habits. The food I love is bad for me, so I don't know if I can stop eating my favorite things.

Once you have established the need for change, you will then need to plan your change approach using a variety of different tools. Finally you will need to practice the new behaviors and continually reinforce them. Our change approach has been developed to encompass all of these elements.

To change complexity behaviors, we take people (as individuals, as teams and as a culture) through these stages of change via a four-stage process (Figure 3.2):

- **Engage:** This is about starting a dialogue with your leaders/influencers and managers about the need for change and its benefits to them as individuals and the company as a whole.
- **Enable:** This stage focuses on ensuring that people have the skills and support they will need to change complexity behaviors.

1. ENGAGE

Engage your leaders and then the whole company by demonstrating the need for change and benefits of change, both at company and individual level.

2. ENABLE

Establish change agent teams. Give the leadership team and your managers the enabling tools, so that they can change their behaviors and learn how to reduce complexity.

3. ACT

Set measurable objectives. Get your leaders and managers actively working on complexity reduction projects to create a 'learning by doing' and 'changing by doing' effect.

4. REINFORCE

Recognize and reward teams and individuals for success. Keep communicating. Build simplicity into your feedback, objective-setting and recruitment process.

FIGURE 3.2
Engage, enable, act and reinforce

- **Act:** This stage focuses on setting measurable objectives and learning by doing. Getting people to identify and then work on their own personal, company and team complexity challenges means you can attack complexity with the full might of your organization. Your people will learn new skills and start to change their behaviors through the practical process of doing things.
- **Reinforce:** The final stage is about making sure the momentum to change is maintained by embedding the behaviors you need at every opportunity.

In the next four sections we will give you some ideas of tangible things you can do at each of the four stages shown above.

We urge you to see this as a toolkit, not as a step-by-step process. Each company will have different circumstances, needs and resources for this, so the exact approach and tools should be tailored to your company using a combination of the ideas shown below. If you have a toolkit at home you will know that you don't use all the tools for every job you do. This toolkit is no different.

There are many different theoretical tools and approaches for change that you can consider; we believe that they all have a role to play. So our complexity behaviors toolkit uses a number of different approaches: psychodynamic approaches for raising awareness; cognitive approaches for goal setting and feedback; humanist tools for development; and behavioral approaches for practice and reinforcing change.

You can address people complexity at a company, team/department or individual level

The tools we use are designed to work in several different situations where you might need to change the behaviors that create complexity within your organization:

- Whole company: creating a culture of simplicity across your whole organization
- Team: changing the complexity behaviors of individual teams/functions/departments
- Individual: changing individual complexity behaviors (for leaders, influencers, managers)

A summary of how the toolkit works in these different situations follows.

Whole company: creating a culture of simplicity across your whole organization

What can you do at the Engage stage?

Make simplicity one of your values

As you know, your company values define how you want people to work and think within your organization. An effective way of changing people's behaviors is to ensure that simplicity is valued as a way of working in your firm, and that people have the permission and skills to make business simpler and are rewarded for it. Individuals who are motivated and enabled to simplify things can help you remove complexity and are less likely to introduce complexity into a firm. If you truly want to attack complexity, simplicity has to be one of your values. If you don't want to attack complexity you should leave it out of your value statement.

The CEO of a retailer said to me, 'we already have five values; we don't have room for another one.' My response was this: one of your values is integrity. Tell me how many genuinely dishonest cheats make it through your 13-step recruitment process? Answer: 'none'. Okay, so how many people come to work every day and deal with complexity? How many come to work and create more of it? Answer: thousands. Let's drop 'integrity', and put 'simplicity' in its place.

Many of the values we see on company websites are, in our view, just hygiene factors or 'givens' in modern business:

- Teamwork: in a modern company who still thinks they'll do anything without this?
- Quality and service: do we still need to tell people that this is important?
- Innovation: also a given.

The difference is clear. In highly complex modern organizations, simplicity is not a given. If it was, complexity would not be endemic. Your people have been rewarded in the past for making things more complex. So your managers and staff need to be told that your organization values simplicity and that they will be rewarded both financially and emotionally for being good at this.

Align your leaders/influencers behind the simplicity cause

This is a whole-business problem, so the revolution has to start with your leaders and the key influencers[1] within the organization demonstrating that they are deeply committed to reducing complexity wherever it hides. Ultimately simplicity needs to be a core value of your business and this will only happen if your leaders and influencers make it a central operating principle.

Create a team of leaders and influencers

This is a critical aspect of a successful program like this. Many of our more successful clients (in tackling this issue) have first aligned the top leaders, but then also set up dedicated program teams to drive the simplicity program forward. These are senior managers and leaders, with a direct line to the CEO or main board sponsors. Bayer, Zurich and Vodafone are all examples of companies where this has been a major feature of their success in attacking complexity.

In addition to having a dedicated team of senior leaders focused on the problem, some companies have also created teams of internal simplicity experts or 'change agents'. Their role is to promote the value of simplicity on a day-to-day basis at a local, functional or departmental level. In addition, they provide expert advice, tools, facilitation skills and resources to assist specific teams on local complexity reduction projects. We regularly train these teams so they have the skills and case examples to perform these roles with the great skills required.

Show people how to lead simplicity

The good news. In any change-management program or initiative you have one very big and effective lever – it's called leadership. Everyone watches what the leaders do and take their lead from your example and actions – literally taking your lead! They also listen to what you say and interpret the meaning and implications of each sentence. At the coffee machine people analyze what the leaders are doing, are thinking and want.

As a leader you may not always be aware of the power that your words, actions and behaviors have. But as soon as you are aware of this you have a great opportunity. You can start using your words and actions to influence large numbers of people. Start modeling the behaviors you want others to follow. Start talking about and constantly reinforcing the importance of simplicity. If you live the value of simplicity, you will have an immediate impact on the rest of your organization.

The opposite is even more true: 'a fish always rots from the head'. If the leadership team is exhibiting the complexity behaviors above, or making work more complicated, then the people below it will copy its (misguided) behavior.

Almost certainly your very talented leaders are creators of some of the complexity in your company, so you have to change their behaviors first.

This can be done by observing whether they exhibit the above behaviors and giving them feedback so they can build self-awareness of these complexity behaviors. A simple action plan for personal development of simplicity behaviors is an imperative for all your leaders.

The Personal Simplicity 360 Survey is used by many companies to measure an individual's simplicity/complexity behaviors, so they can see if they are creators of complexity or leaders of simplicity. This gives timely feedback and direction for self-awareness and improvement through continual feedback and coaching.

Some of your leadership team may not believe that simplicity is a good thing or necessary. If this is the case you will need to align the leadership team and get everyone to agree that a simpler organization is a great idea. We use the simplicity beliefs shown in Figure 3.3 to clarify what we mean by simplicity and to check that people believe in simplicity (or not).

Once everyone is in agreement that this is the right thing for your organization and you know how good your leaders are at leading simplicity, the next step is to integrate 'leading simplicity' into your existing leadership training, tools and approaches to get your leaders using the leadership lever to start the simplicity revolution from the top.

If your leaders are living the value of simplicity this will soon be copied, so your leaders need to model the simplicity behaviors you want to encourage. Here's a simplicity leadership model that your leaders can adopt:

- **Model the way:** Demonstrate your commitment by showing that you are always making things simpler yourself and improving your own complexity behaviors.
- **Inspire:** Communicate the personal and business benefits of simplicity.
- **Challenge:** Continually challenge anything that is not simple. Keep asking 'Will this add complexity?' and 'Is this the simplest way to do this?'
- **Feed the heart:** Openly recognize and reward teams and individuals who are successfully simplifying things.
- **Enable change:** Constantly coach, support and train your teams. Make sure they have the skills and support they need to simplify your business.

If you already have an existing leadership development program, 'Leading Simplicity' should be built into it as a core module, tailored to fit the learning from your company and leadership diagnosis. If you don't already have a leadership development program then creating a 'Leading Simplicity' program is a great way to start.

SIMPLICITY BELIEFS

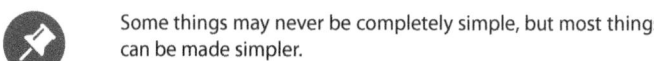

Some things may never be completely simple, but most things can be made simpler.

Complexity is fine, as long as it does not reduce quality, speed or performance. Unfortunately, it usually does.

It's difficult to make things simpler but the effort is always rewarded with better and more predictable results.

Simple is different from simplistic. Most things can be made simpler without becoming simplistic.

Things can be made simpler and at the same time better, faster and safer. These concepts are not at odds.

Always try to reduce complexity first. In the unlikely event that complexity cannot be reduced, only then look for a way to manage it better.

FIGURE 3.3
Simplicity beliefs

Communicate your strategy for complexity reduction
Once you have done your diagnosis you will have the information and
data you need to create an overall complexity reduction strategy and
detailed plans to attack complexity in your organization. Complexity is a
major source of value destruction in your company, so you need to have a
detailed and coherent strategy to tackle the problems – see Chapter 2. Make
sure the strategy is clearly communicated as part of the Engage stage.

Engage managers and staff across the whole company
Now you have communicated your strategy and your leaders are role
modeling and communicating the importance of simplicity, the next step is
to engage and enable the masses.

As we mentioned before, the majority of your complexity problems lie
beneath the surface. Only the managers who deal with these complexity
problems on a day-to-day basis can see them and in most cases only they
can remove them. But they are also the people who cause complexity. You
can't address this problem from the top down alone. So you have to engage
thousands of people from the bottom up as well and enlist their help.

It is well known that people prefer to work in simpler systems. Complexity
is frustrating. Many of your people are demotivated by the difficulty
of getting simple things done in a big company. A senior manager in a
technology company once said to me, 'I can see where we are and I know
exactly where we want to get to, it's just that the sheer complexity of this
company stops me getting there.' This problem may be indicative of the
reality of modern business. We have all become very good at vision and
mission strategy thinking, but getting to the destinations identified in
your vision, mission and strategy is very hard. The barrier to getting to the
desired place is often the sheer complexity of making things happen in big
organizations.

In our work the majority of people are happy with the idea of simplification
from the start, and the ones who are not quickly come around to the idea
once they see the personal benefits and the company/collective gains that
are possible. Giving them permission and rewarding them for simplifying
the company is a classic win-win. It makes work more enjoyable for them
and makes the company more successful.

In our workshops we always run a 'What's in it for Me?' session with the
participants. The idea of this is to get people to create a personal vision
of what it will feel like to work in a simpler company. What we quickly
see is that there are lots of personal benefits of simplicity and people soon
connect the idea of simplicity with individual benefits. Once people see

what's in it for them, you immediately release a massive amount of human energy towards helping deliver the desired outcome.

Some examples of the personal benefits of simplicity are:

- more time to focus on the enjoyable aspects of your job, less on reporting, justifying, process and politics;
- it is easier to get important things done quickly and well;
- a more successful company creates more promotion opportunities and can pay higher salaries;
- better work–life balance – I can meet my objectives within a normal/ acceptable work day; and
- better relationships – working with other people and functions in a simpler way creates less conflict.

There are many different ways to engage people in this subject and get them to see the benefits of change: we encourage you to be creative and not to underestimate the importance of engaging people in a two-way dialogue on this issue, not a lecture!

- Company, department or team newsletters.
- Posters, videos, screen savers etc., to show a vision of how it will feel to work in a simpler organization.
- Discussions at town-hall and regular team meetings.
- Communicate the results of the complexity diagnostic (see Chapter 2) to raise awareness of the issues.

Using simplicity to reduce headcount
The only time you will definitely encounter resistance is when the sole purpose of simplification is to reduce head count. The survival instinct in people is strong, so you will encounter both tacit and explicit resistance from people when their jobs are at risk. But complexity reduction can help you achieve this goal as well. By focusing your diagnosis on the areas of non-value-adding complexity, you can quickly identify where there is room to reduce headcount without affecting the quality of outcomes. Once these areas are identified you need to reduce headcount in these areas as fast as you can.

The remaining people will by now be worried about how all this work can be done with fewer people. This is where complexity reduction becomes liberating for them as well. Here's the message: we are going to let you redesign how work gets done in your area, to remove non-value-adding activities, making work simpler and more productive. By doing this you will be able to achieve better results with fewer resources. You will spend more time on the content of your work and less on the politics and process. What's more, we are not going to send in hundreds of consultants to do this to you. Instead we are going to train you in simplification tools and techniques so you can diagnose and solve the complexity problem in your own work teams. Great, where do I sign?

GENERAL ELECTRIC: THE ETERNAL PRAGMATIST

'You can't believe how hard it is for people to be simple, how much they fear being simple.'

Attributed to Jack Welch

What was the complexity problem?

At a company as large as General Electric (GE), a high level of complexity is only to be expected. Just look at the sheer size and diversity of its product portfolio!

How did the power of simplicity help?

It was GE's CEO Jack Welch who made it his mission to reduce complexity. He undertook a series of simplification projects across the firm, arguing that 'for a large organization to be effective, it must be simple'.

Welch first simplified the structure of the conglomerate, combining many business units, in order to create a simpler, more unified structure. However, despite the organizational structure being improved and simplified, the people inside it went about their business pretty much the same way as before, continuing to add complexity and being burdened by it. 'Insecure managers,' Welch noted, 'create complexity.'

This led to a decision to embed simplicity into the culture of the organization. Through workshops and exercises, GE managers were gradually made aware of the cost of complexity, which empowered them to take action.

He also clarified and toughened up the penalties for failure, regularly firing the bottom 10 per cent of his managers. But at the same time he extended stock options from top executives to almost one-third of GE's employees. This clarified the link between individual and firm performance, through the rewards structure.

What was the impact?

Processes were streamlined and managers received training on simplicity values. Over time, simplicity has become part of General Electric's DNA. Thanks to that, decision-making and planning at GE have become significantly faster: it is made clear from the onset who should be involved, and when.

When Jack Welch arrived, GE had 411,000 employees and within five years it had 299,000: 37,000 left when GE businesses were sold and 81,000 left as part of the slimming down of existing businesses. When Jack Welch arrived, GE was earning $26.8bn in revenues and had a market value of $14bn. The year before he left, the company was earning $130bn and had a market value of $410bn. At that time it was the largest and most valuable company in the world.

What can you do at the Enable stage?
Equip people with new simplicity tools and approaches
The what/how problem: even if people know what you want them to do, it does not follow that they will know how to do it.

In order to win in the long run, you will need to give your managers new skills and tools. Very few of them will have been trained on how to identify and remove harmful complexity, so training people on how to simplify something complex will be an essential element of your change program. The nature of this training will again depend on what you learn in the diagnosis and on the simplification strategy you then set.

Your complexity reduction/simplicity training plan could cover:

- how to diagnose complexity in their area of responsibility (country, department, function);
- general tools, techniques and principles of making the complex simpler;
- training teams on Lean tools/techniques;
- reducing everyday complexity (Chapter 8);
- how to improve their own personal complexity behaviors; and
- training and coaching on specific simplicity toolkits and approaches for
  - organization design simplification (Chapter 4)
  - strategy simplification (Chapter 5)
  - process simplification (Chapter 6)
  - product and service simplification (Chapter 7).

What can you do at the Act stage?

Set clear and measurable objectives for complexity reduction

What gets measured gets done. Make sure you have concrete and measurable goals so you can track progress and prove that the financial and human benefits of simplicity are actually being delivered.

Focus on the specific complexity behaviors that are hurting you most

The culture, history and operating style of each organization is unique. It therefore follows that the types of complexity behavior that are holding you back will be different. Some companies tend to over intellectualize, others tend to micro-manage, others have the habit of over-engineering their products and processes.

As part of your diagnosis you should have identified which complexity behaviors are most common in your organization. Once you know what they are you can do a number of things:

- Communicate that certain complexity behaviors are holding you back as a company and that you want to change these habits.
- Self-awareness: Use 360 surveys (where managers rate themselves and get feedback from colleagues) and regular feedback sessions to help individuals to see where their own strengths and weaknesses are.
- Confession and calling out: encourage your leaders to confess to complexity behaviors if they exhibit them, and give their teams permission to highlight (call out) any circumstances where 'the boss' is exhibiting these behaviors. 'If I am over-intellectualizing this then please tell me, I need to know.' Once the leaders start to show self-awareness, others will follow.

Address the key sources of 'everyday work complexity'

The majority of a manager's day is spent on a variety of things that can be grouped together into the following categories:

- Meetings: small groups or one-to-one conversations.
- Communicating: email, and writing and reading reports.
- Decision-making: making key day-to-day decisions about what to do.

Many of these activities are very complex in themselves and/or they create complexity. It therefore follows that you can't address business complexity unless you make the inputs and outputs of these activities as simple as possible. Much of our client work starts with training people on the rules and best practices for managing these everyday work activities as simply as possible. Chapter 8 gives some more detailed thoughts on how to do this.

MAJOR DIY RETAILER: CHANGING INGRAINED HABITS

What was the complexity problem?

The culture in our client's organization was very risk-averse – this was getting in the way of turning things around quickly. Decision-making was hindered, leading to mistrust and a lack of empowerment. Although the company valued entrepreneurship in its people, in practice, any creativity was stifled by laborious sign-off processes and a general resistance to change. This, in turn, lowered morale, especially among the more junior staff.

How did the power of simplicity help?

We worked with the client to understand the root causes of the problem and found that unnecessary complexity was stopping people from getting things done. Together, we identified opportunities to remove this complexity, explicitly giving people permission not to do certain things.

For example, the whole team was spending a significant amount of time analyzing sales performance, even if the results were close to the forecast. By identifying that this activity was not driving value, managers told their teams to stop doing this, and also empowered them to make the decision themselves – contrary to how things were usually done.

Alongside this, we led a behavior change program with the leadership team to help them embrace simplicity as a value within their organization and their teams.

What was the impact?

- Time and cost savings by allowing people to stop doing things that aren't adding value.
- Empowerment and motivation for the whole team.
- Managers' time freed up by reducing the level of micro-management.
- Stronger focus on value drivers of the business.

Get the whole company working on some Simplicity 101 projects

If you have done a good job with your complexity diagnosis (see Chapter 2) you will have identified some small(er) problems that are creating complexity in your company (e.g. the expense claim process, booking travel) that can be tackled by a small group of enabled and empowered people within your organization, free from the 'help' of other functions and/or consultancies!

The next step (in our view) is to get the whole company doing something about these sorts of complexity fast. Putting tangible actions in place quickly creates belief in the idea of simplicity and shows you mean business. More importantly it creates a 'learning by doing effect' so behaviors start to change and new habits start to form. This is often called 'live action learning'.

Simplicity 101: A great way to do this is to identify some easy simplification projects that any team/department can rapidly implement themselves, with very little support or guidance from the top or center of the company.

> *One of our financial service clients created a 'Simplicity 101 Guide Book' that went to all managers with direct reports. The book outlined the purpose of the complexity reduction program, the goals they had set and the Simplicity Beliefs and Principles that the senior team had agreed to live by. The booklet also suggested several ways that people could immediately start to simplify work in their areas of the company. Finally they outlined some 'rules' for dealing with everyday complexity issues like poorly managed meetings, communication, etc.*

The exact nature of Simplicity 101 for your organization will be driven by what you discover in the diagnosis phase (see Chapter 2) and by the simplification strategy that you set. There is no point implementing Simplicity 101 projects unless they help get you to your overall simplification strategy.

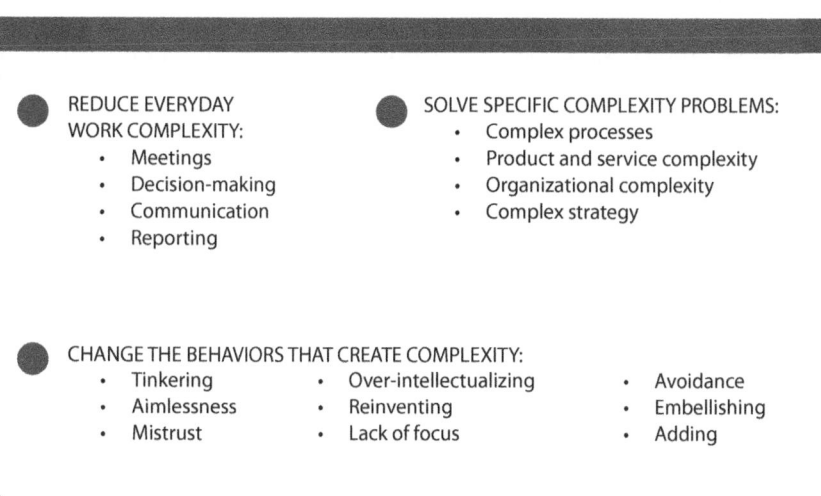

FIGURE 3.4
Three different ways to act against complexity

Start to work on your biggest complexity problems
Your diagnosis will have identified some simple simplification projects but will also have highlighted some big thorny complexity problems that will require a lot of energy to solve.

Examples could be a core business process that runs across different functions and different geographies (e.g. innovation) or the design of your global matrix. These problems will not be solvable by small and motivated groups of people learning about simplicity, doing 101 projects, etc.

Each of these problems will require specific project teams, with clear plans and remits to work together to reduce complexity. Again, the Organization, Strategy, Process and Product/Service chapters each give you clear ideas on how to fix these bigger problems.

What can you do at the Reinforce stage?
Finally, you need make sure that simplicity is reinforced throughout your organization on a day-to-day basis. If it is just a short-term burst of activity, the energy will soon die as other problems and priorities come along. So you will need to continue the drive for simplicity each year. This means you need ongoing plans to continue with the Engage, Enable and Act work.

Create annual complexity reduction plans
Each year ask your team/department/individuals to identify some new complexity problems that need to be solved, e.g. simplify a departmental process, reduce organizational complexity, etc. Then set measurable team, individual and/or departmental objectives for complexity reduction over the next 12 months.

Build simplicity into your core HR processes
Simplicity needs to be one of the values/behaviors that you measure, recruit for and reward. So it is useful to integrate simplicity into the following processes.

- **Feedback and development:** Regularly seek and offer feedback on how successful your people are at living the value of simplicity, and set personal and team development goals.
- **Coach** teams and individuals on the new skills and behaviors they need.
- **Recruitment:** Make simplicity a core part of the selection and promotion process; test for Integrative Complexity (the added complexity that results from a particular new hire).

- **Reward and recognition:** Have a clear program for praising successful simplification projects and rewarding people for success on this dimension.

Build 'complexity impact' into your decision-making process
Before you make major decisions, you will (or should) always consider the financial, regulatory and environmental implications of your decisions. You should also make sure that all business plans consider the complexity impact of the activity/plan you are proposing. There are just two simple questions to ask:

- What impact will this decision, plan or activity have on the overall level of complexity in my organization?
- Is this the simplest way to get to the desired outcome?

Finally keep talking…
- Regularly communicate your progress. How are we doing? What are the next steps? When the leadership stops talking about simplicity, people will assume the battle is won or that it is no longer a priority.
- Share best practice: make sure your best examples are written up as cases that can be shared across the company. This can be done through internal websites or physical resource centers in your offices where people can find simplification tools, case studies, handbooks, etc.

Applying the toolkit to other situations: team or departmental change approaches
A major cross-company program may not be needed or possible. It might be beyond your sphere of control or not a big cross-company issue, but this does not mean you should ignore the problem if you believe your team, department or function is too complex.

We work with many 'enlightened' departmental or function heads who see that complexity is a major problem in their area of the company and want to take action to reduce complexity in their area. They often become trailblazers for a new approach which is quickly copied by other departmental heads or grows to become a company-wide complexity reduction initiative (and they all get promoted and many of them are now millionaires …).

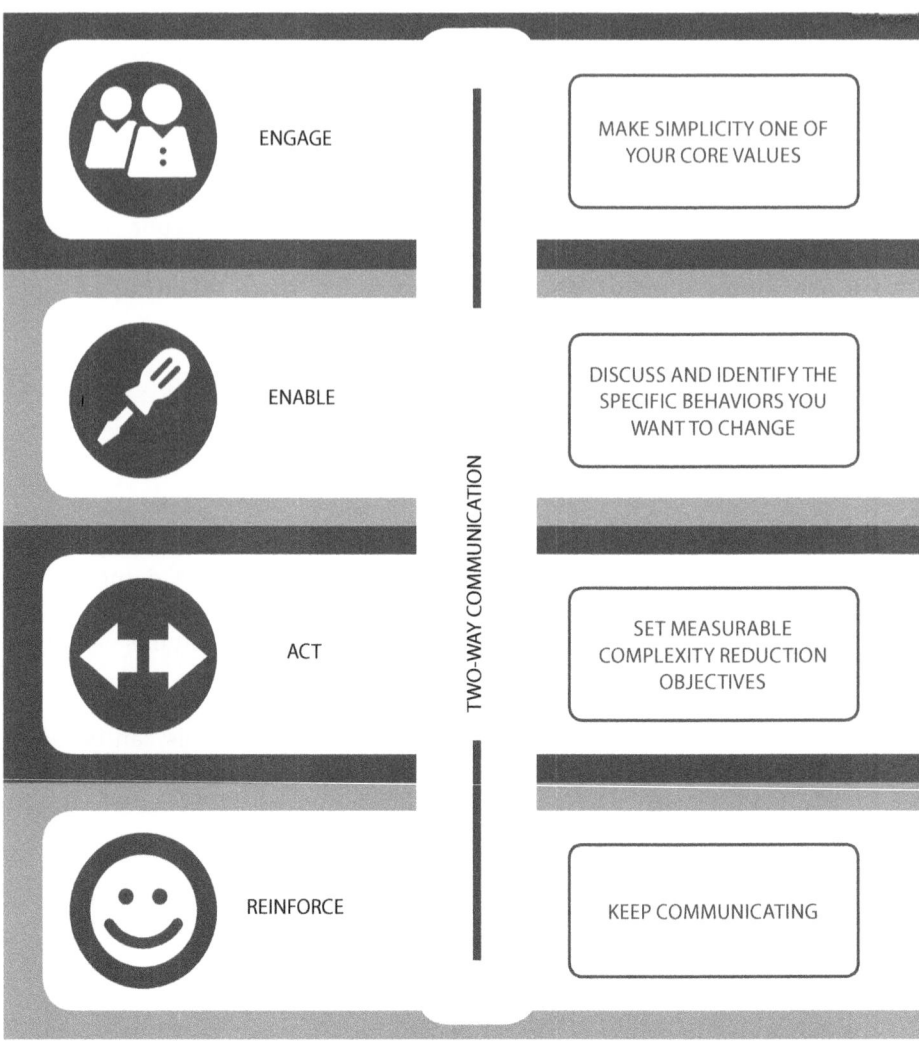

FIGURE 3.5
Overview of toolkit for complexity behavior change

Engage
- Create a team to lead the change project.
- Run a detailed team/departmental complexity diagnosis to identify the behaviors and the specific aspects of this team's work that cause complexity (e.g. complex processes, organization design issues, etc.).
- Develop a clear strategy for reducing complexity in your area/ department.

GET YOUR LEADERS/INFLUENCERS TO START MODELING SIMPLICITY	ENGAGE THE WHOLE COMPANY BY DEMONSTRATING THE BENEFITS OF CHANGE

DEVELOP EVERYDAY SIMPLICITY PRINCIPLES AND RULES	EQUIP YOUR PEOPLE WITH NEW SIMPLICITY TOOLS

START TO PRACTISE SIMPLICITY BEHAVIORS	IMPLEMENT SOME SIMPLICITY 101 PROJECTS	START WORKING ON MAJOR SIMPLIFICATION PROJECTS

DEVELOP ANNUAL COMPLEXITY REDUCTION PLANS	ASSESS THE COMPLEXITY IMPACT OF NEW INITIATIVES/ PLANS	BUILD SIMPLICITY INTO HR PROCESSES

- Communicate the need for change and what your complexity reduction strategy is.

Enable
- Discuss the behaviors you want to change and agree how you can change them together.
- Equip your people with new simplicity tools.

Act
- Set measurable complexity reduction objectives.
- Start to practice the new simplicity behaviors.
- Implement Simplicity 101 and Everyday Simplicity Rules
- Set up separate project teams to tackle the big complexity issues identified in the diagnosis (e.g. problem processes, rationalizing the product/service portfolio).

Reinforce
- Communicate progress and success.
- Recognize and reward key successes.
- Identify future complexity reduction ideas and objectives.

Applying the toolkit to other situations: individual change approaches (for leaders, influencers, managers)

The final situation where you may want to use this toolkit is to change your own behaviors or those of individuals around you. This would be the case where you feel you personally have a tendency to overcomplicate things and that is holding you back. Or someone in your team/company is a complicator and needs some help and support to change.

Engage
- Discuss the benefits of change both for the individual and for the company.
- Use a personal complexity 360 to identify individual strengths and weaknesses.
- Discuss the behaviors you want to change and agree how you can change them together.

Enable
- Create a coaching and development plan.
- Equip the individual with any new skills they need.

Act
- Set measurable objectives for learning and growth.
- Start to practice the new simplicity behaviors.

Reinforce
- Provide regular feedback and coaching.
- Recognize and reward key successes.
- Identify further development opportunities and set objectives.

Bottom line: You can easily reduce complexity through specific projects like redesigning a process or a simplifying a product range. But if you don't change people's complexity behaviors, or give them the new skills they need, the complexity will be back quite soon, *and it will bring its friends ...*

FIVE KEY POINTS ON PEOPLE COMPLEXITY

1. People lie at the heart of all of the forms of complexity we discuss in this book.
2. Different personalities, agendas, skills and needs, plus a wide range of changing relationships and connections between people in business organizations, underlie complexity.
3. General management behavior, internal communications behavior and the content and politics of meetings are three forms of people complexity rated highly in our survey.
4. Changing costly complexity behavior requires a systematic approach: engage, enable, act, reinforce.
5. The behavior of senior management is key. Corporate leaders need to lead the simplicity revolution.

---

6. From people to organizations

As we said at the start: complexity stems from the number and variety of components in a system, the relationships between these components and the pace at which these are changing.

Organizations are complex because they contain a diverse range of people with their own agendas, motivations and preferences with many interactions and interrelationships. Both the people and their relationships are changing all the time. (As a result most organizations are more like a series of DIY mistakes than a neat pyramid.)

In the next chapter we look at the challenge of complexity reduction in organizations.

For more on how to cope with people complexity go to:
http://www.simplicitypartnership.com/

Chapter 4
How to Simplify:
Organizations

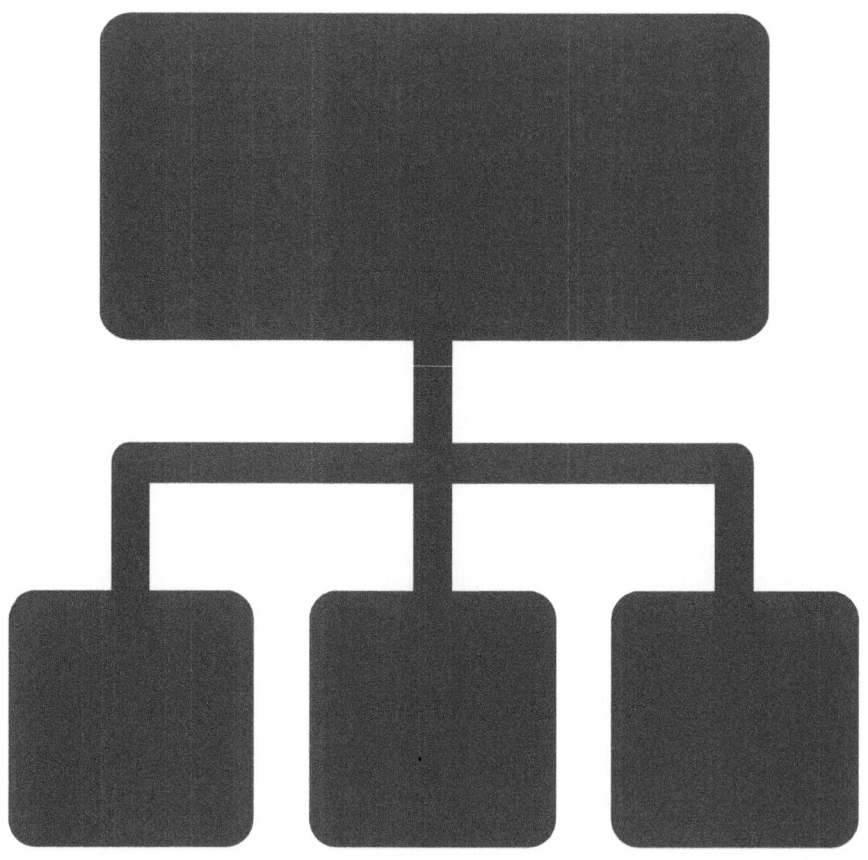

COPING WITH COMPLEXITY: STORIES FROM THE FRONT

A chessboard is a finite system of 64 squares, 32 pieces (six varieties) and strict, simple rules limiting the variety of movements by each piece. However, the total number of possible moves is huge: greater than the number of atoms in the universe and greater than the number of milliseconds the world has been in existence!

But … there are rules and these rules mean that although there are 64 squares on the board, a pawn will only move into one of four squares at most in front of it (and normally only three). Think about the comparisons between a chess board, with these specific rules for movement, and an organization.

If we think that chess pieces are complex, then imagine the complex permutations in a social system where the components (you and me) have free will and complex interrelationships. Control and coordination is necessary, but hugely difficult. Without it there is chaos, but try to add too much structure and too many rules to these free-willed components and you stifle the life out of the organization and the people in it. Simple, clear boundaries and a balance between freedom and control is everything.

The simple truth: In many big companies the organization design has evolved to be too complex to focus on the most important things, to perform key activities efficiently or to make important decisions fast enough.

1. Organizations: complex and simple

The simple truth is that the organization design of many companies, large and small, has evolved to be too complex. This prevents people in these companies from focusing on the most important things, performing key activities efficiently or making important decisions fast enough. Managers working in these kinds of companies know this (and they have let us know – see our research, below) but sorting it all out is one those challenges that usually gets put on the 'too difficult' pile.

Many firms do tackle this through restructuring initiatives. However, these very often focus just on a part of the organization, restricted either to specific functions or divisions, or IT systems or specific processes, rather than the whole thing. Restructuring can also be a response to catalysts like large acquisitions or entry into new markets. They may then involve adding more new divisions, functions, processes and/or activities without consolidating, integrating or removing existing ones. This does not help streamline the rest of the organization and often has the opposite effect of adding complexity across all of these dimensions.

The way that organizations are designed, evolve and are restructured has a massive influence on how – and how well – we work together in organizations. So the organization design dimension of complexity is critical.

What do we mean by organization complexity?

Remember in Chapter 1 where we defined and discussed how *complicated* is different from *complex*? Airplanes are complicated – and have become ever-more complicated (larger, faster, with more features, parts, controls etc ...) – but they are (relatively) predictable. Change an input or tweak a control lever and they respond as we would anticipate. In a similar way some organizations are more stable and predictable than others. They are therefore more complicated than complex. Others are the opposite.

Organizational complexity varies according to a combination of structure (divisional, functional including multinationality), the centralization or decentralization of power and decision-making authority and various attributes of people (particularly the degree of specialization), products/ services, and technologies.

For example, think about why a school would be considered a less complex organization than a hospital. It has one objective – education – and maybe three hierarchical layers from head to janitor, and very limited specialization (administrators, teachers, clerical staff and maybe cleaners). A hospital also has one objective – to improve people's health – but the solutions, or products and services, come in a variety of forms and require more specialists, departments and management layers. Communication and coordination is far more complex in hospitals than schools.

What do we mean by organization design?

Organization design is about the alignment of structures, processes, roles and responsibilities with the strategy of the business. We know, since the early work of Alfred Chandler at Harvard (1962) on the ways that structure and strategy co-evolve, that better organization designs underpin better strategies and better strategies lead to better organization designs. The two can reinforce each other or undermine each other.

> The beauty of Henry Beck's
> 1933 legendary map of the
> London Underground lies in
> what was left out.

The most obvious sign of an organization's design structure is the divisional hierarchy. Firms with many different kinds of products, like Unilever or P&G, often adopt a 'product structure', where the product divisions dominate the organizational hierarchy, with subordinate regional or country departments and functions below them. 'Functional structures' (often adopted by energy and telecoms firms for example) are where the R&D, production and marketing (etc.) departments head up the structure, with product and/or country divisions below them. 'Regional structures' are where the regions (North America, EMEA, Asia etc.) dominate the structure. In most cases, however, these are varieties of the well-known matrix structure, where local departments answer to regional, product division and functional heads.

Getting matrix organizations to work really well is still one of the major challenges facing many senior managers. In theory they help build economies of scale and balance the strategic drivers from regional markets, product groups and functions. In practice the dual (or multiple) lines of command can create confusion in terms of prioritization, goal-setting and coordination.

Despite this, the design of the organization still helps to determine how effectively and efficiently assets, resources, investments and capabilities are coordinated to maintain the delivery of goods and services to current markets. But it also influences how well the firm stays aligned with the changing needs of these markets, and to new competitors, new technologies and other threats and opportunities in the competitive environment. 'Agility' and responsiveness of firms and therefore their survival depends on an ever-evolving organization design. Similarly inertia – the inability to adapt and respond – stems from static designs and out-of-date legacy processes, systems and behaviors.

We will come back to some of these issues later. First, let's try and outline some more components of organization design. Figure 4.1 shows one way of breaking this down, with clear links to our other dimensions of complexity: processes, people, strategy, and products and services.

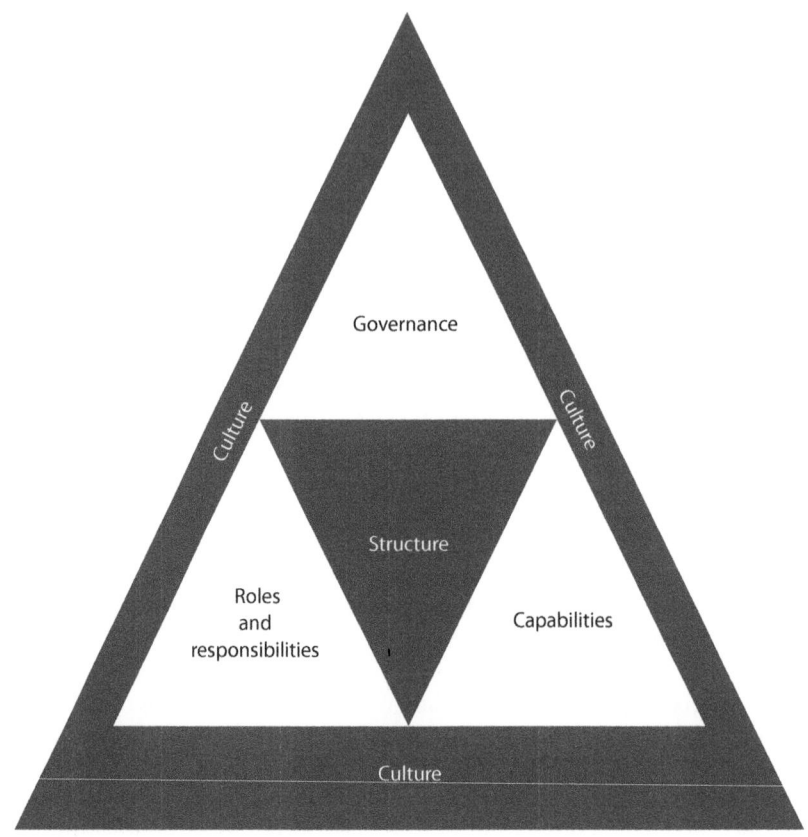

FIGURE 4.1
The organization design pyramid

- Governance: who can make what decisions and the documented policies and procedures that guide decision-making.
- Structure: the layers, divisions and sub-units of the organization, how the work is divided, allocated, coordinated and supervised.
- Capabilities: the specialist knowledge and skills that are needed and the routines and practices that develop and apply these.
- Roles and responsibilities: who does what to get the work done.
- Culture: the way we do things, communication and behaviors.

The work by Chandler, mentioned above, has been developed further by other management thinkers, including J.R. Galbraith (the systemic approach and the 'star model'), Henry Mintzberg and Peter Drucker. Drucker's in-depth analysis of General Motors, for example, led to a profusion of case studies on 'best practice' organizations. One thing they all agreed on is that these components of organizations are all interrelated and interacting. So any attempt to change or improve organization design needs to tackle these dimensions together.

A simpler version of how we can define good organization design cuts across all of these dimensions. Good organization design is about getting the *right people* doing the *right things*, in the *right way*.

- The right people: people with the knowledge, skills and behaviors you need to win.
- Doing the right things: aligned and focused only on activities, strategies and projects that add value.
- In the right way: working in the most effective and efficient way possible.

PHILIPS: ALIGNING STRUCTURE WITH STRATEGY

What was the complexity problem?

Philips wanted to create a market-driven, people-centric company with a strategy and a structure that fully reflected the needs of its customer base. But it also had a leading R&D and design center in Eindhoven (and eight other innovation centers around the world), with some of the best technical and creative talent in the consumer electronics industry. It knew – from 120 years in the business – that *connecting technological opportunities with customer desires was the key to being a leading innovator in the industry.*

Successful implementation required a realignment of the organization.

How did the power of simplicity help?

Philips simplified its business structure by creating three core sectors with strong single-headed management: Philips Healthcare, Philips Lighting, and Philips Consumer Lifestyle. The latter, for instance, encompasses divisions previously known as Consumer Electronics (CE) and Domestic Appliances and Personal Care (DAP).

This was the first step to consolidate the structure and in turn the product portfolio. This enabled clearer operational links between its 124 production sites, the 100 countries in which it had marketing, sales and distribution facilities, and its nine R&D centers. A simpler matrix structure was developed to coordinate and connect the firm's 122,000 employees globally to deliver value at the point of contact with the customer, through flexible cross-functional teams (an initiative badged as 'team up to excel').

What was the impact?

The business structure is now more focused on the end consumer. Philips's managers have a much deeper insight into customer needs and connect these back more directly to R&D and design activities and investments. As a result, the firm is better able to accurately develop and market innovative products with higher levels of profitability. Flexible cross-functional team structures within the matrix also give it more 'structural agility' in the face of changing consumer needs and evolving markets.

Complexity in modern organization structures

The design of the modern corporation has evolved a long way from its simpler predecessor.

The proliferation of product and service variety, following the growing segmentation of markets; the addition of various new information and communication technologies (ICT); the increased specialization of expertise and knowledge (which adds to the complexity of coordinating across specialists); the geographic spread of inputs and outputs, driven by globalization and driving firms to be multinational – all of these trends have added to the complexity of the modern corporation.

Managers now have to cope with more variety and more change. If we reflect on our definition of complexity (see Chapter 1) this means different kinds of components (people, tasks and organizational forms) and different kinds of relationships between these components. It also means coping with change in both. They have to deal with many different kinds of consumers, cultures, institutions and regulatory change. They also have to deal with many different kinds of organizational forms including alliances, joint ventures, acquisitions, outsourcing partnerships and a range of intra-firm and inter-firm contracts. Dynamic capabilities, agility and continual innovation – with more rapidly evolving processes, products and services – to cope with turbulent competitive environments are the buzzwords of the day.

As a result of all of this modern corporations (1) are structured differently and in a more complex way; and (2) change their structures and designs much more frequently, with knock-on effects on people's roles and responsibilities, decision-making structures and strategic clarity.

Another reason for the increased complexity of the modern corporation is the general shift from manufacturing to knowledge-based services. We reminded you earlier about the airplane being *complicated* rather than *complex*, and part of the reason is that you get less uncertainty and more predictability when you take people out of the system. There are relatively few people involved in flying a plane; most of it is done by the technology and machinery.

To some extent there is a direct correlation between the number of people involved in any activity and the complexity of that activity! Manufacturing process lines are computer-controlled and dominated by sophisticated equipment rather than operators. They are more complicated than complex, which enables very precise analysis of input–output relationships to reduce input costs and scrap yields and increase reliability and productivity. This is why they are such good candidates for 'lean' improvement procedures and business process re-engineering (BPR) practices (see more on this in Chapter 6 on process complexity).

Most modern organizations are dominated by people. Their specialist expertise provides the input, and specialist services or knowledge-based content (software programs, media, financial services, etc.) is the output. Input–output relationships and consequently organizational designs are much more complex. Change one element and the knock-on effects and influence over productivity and performance are much less predictable. Organization design therefore has to be that much better to cope.

Organization design and the value chain

As we said above, organization design is about who does what where. This includes the way a firm organizes its division of labor, its functions and its business units in relation to each other. But it is also related to what the firm does and what it leaves to the market.

If Apple designed, made and marketed the iPhone entirely in-house it would be a much more complex – and less profitable – firm than it is now. In fact it focuses on the parts of the iPhone value chain that add most value. It does the R&D and product design at one end of the value chain and the marketing, brand development and after-sales services at the other end, leaving the rest to other firms around the world. In the case of the iPhone 4, this means letting firms like ST Microelectronics, Murata, Infineon and Foxconn develop and make the components and assemble them into the final product. For an iPhone 4 costing $560 these partner firms make the product and get $178. Apple, with its techie wizards, design gurus and marketing talent, gets $360. It has made a strategic choice about what it will focus on and what it will leave to the market. It is doing the right thing.

This focus allows the firm to maintain a simple structure, aligned with clear outputs. It has no need for a semiconductor design department or production plants, or an assembly operation. The Apple organization is dominated by creative and innovative people AND they know what they are doing. Their strategic targets are clear and simple.

Moreover, this simplifies the range of functions, divisions and back office operations the firm needs to cope with, and allows it to limit its geographic spread (it does not have to manage component operations in places like China). So, in terms of where and how it positions itself within the value chain, it is doing the right thing, in the right way.

2. How do you know when your organization is TOO complex?

Over time, organization designs have evolved to become much more complex. In fact we have yet to meet a company that has evolved towards a simpler way of organizing people and decision-making. So in today's modern organization design there are many, many more people, with a wider variety of skills and functions. These people are managing wider and more complex product/service portfolios across international boundaries. Most big companies are now organized in an international matrix, decision-making is more consensus driven, and individual roles and responsibilities are less clear, with many people having a similar role. In addition, it is less clear who ultimately makes a decision and how decisions are made.

No wonder that many companies now complain that their organization design is too complex, and making even simple decisions is too slow and uncertain.

Organizational complexity: the symptoms

- **Busy but ineffective people:** People appear to be permanently busy and stressed, but the company is not progressing in the right direction. It is difficult to get even simple things done, e.g. travel authority, small expenditure sign-off.
- **Inter-department conflict:** A lack of alignment and overlapping responsibilities means that departments are working on the same things or against each other.
- **Lots of KPIs and measures:** Everything is measured and reported as managers try to understand and control what is happening at the levels below them.
- **Intensive performance management:** Arising from persistent inter-departmental conflict and lack of coordination.
- **Late or no decisions:** Too many people involved in key decisions, too much or irrelevant information and people reluctant to take a risk.
- **Poor morale and engagement:** People and departments are pulling in different directions, which frustrates people.
- **Lots of decision committees:** No clear accountability so committees are set up to make decisions.
- **Drawn-out sign-off process:** Overlaps in roles and decision authority mean lots of people have to agree things.
- **Doing the same things in different ways:** Departments work independently to achieve the same objectives.

What are the causes of organizational complexity?

Understanding the causes of organizational complexity can help with both prevention and cure. There are a number of different reasons why your organization may have become too complex; Table 4.1 lists the most common ones.

AREA	ISSUE
Governance	• Unclear or laborious decisions and sign-off processes • No accountability, split accountability or unclear accountability • Performance metrics and rewards not aligned with strategy and objectives • Conflict resolution – no clear process for resolving strategic disagreements
Structure	• Structure not aligned with strategy • Formal structure and informal structure not aligned • Too many organizational layers • Too many reporting (people-to-people) touchpoints (e.g. spans of control too wide or too many matrix interfaces) • Too many organizational unit connections (e.g. too many functions, geographical units, product or process teams) • Back office functions not aligned with needs of frontline functions • Too many external connections or relationships (e.g. suppliers, customers, etc.)
Capabilities	• Lacking skills to deliver work required • Lacking knowledge/information to deliver work required • Training and development misaligned with required capabilities • Talent not identified and nurtured the right way
Roles and responsibilities	• Lack of clarity in the relationship between organizational units (which unit owns a process – the function? the project team?) • Role diversity – number of specialist roles within a company • Multiple hats – managers and directors asked to wear too many 'hats' • Lack of role clarity and understanding of how roles create value (unclear vertical and horizontal relationships, role duplication and overlap)
Culture	• Too many rules, controls and intervention: a lack of trust • Too little intervention, guidance and boundaries: lack of strategic clarity • Over-centralization and defensive, territorial management • Too much devolvement and a lack of coordination and shared sense of purpose

TABLE 4.1
Causes of organization complexity

3. What does our research show?

Our survey of 600 executives in 300 European firms of over 5000 employees (see Chapter 1) showed us which kinds of organizational complexity created the biggest headaches for them.

Table 4.2 lists various sources of complexity showing how managers ranked these. High-impact sources include: 'levels of management and/

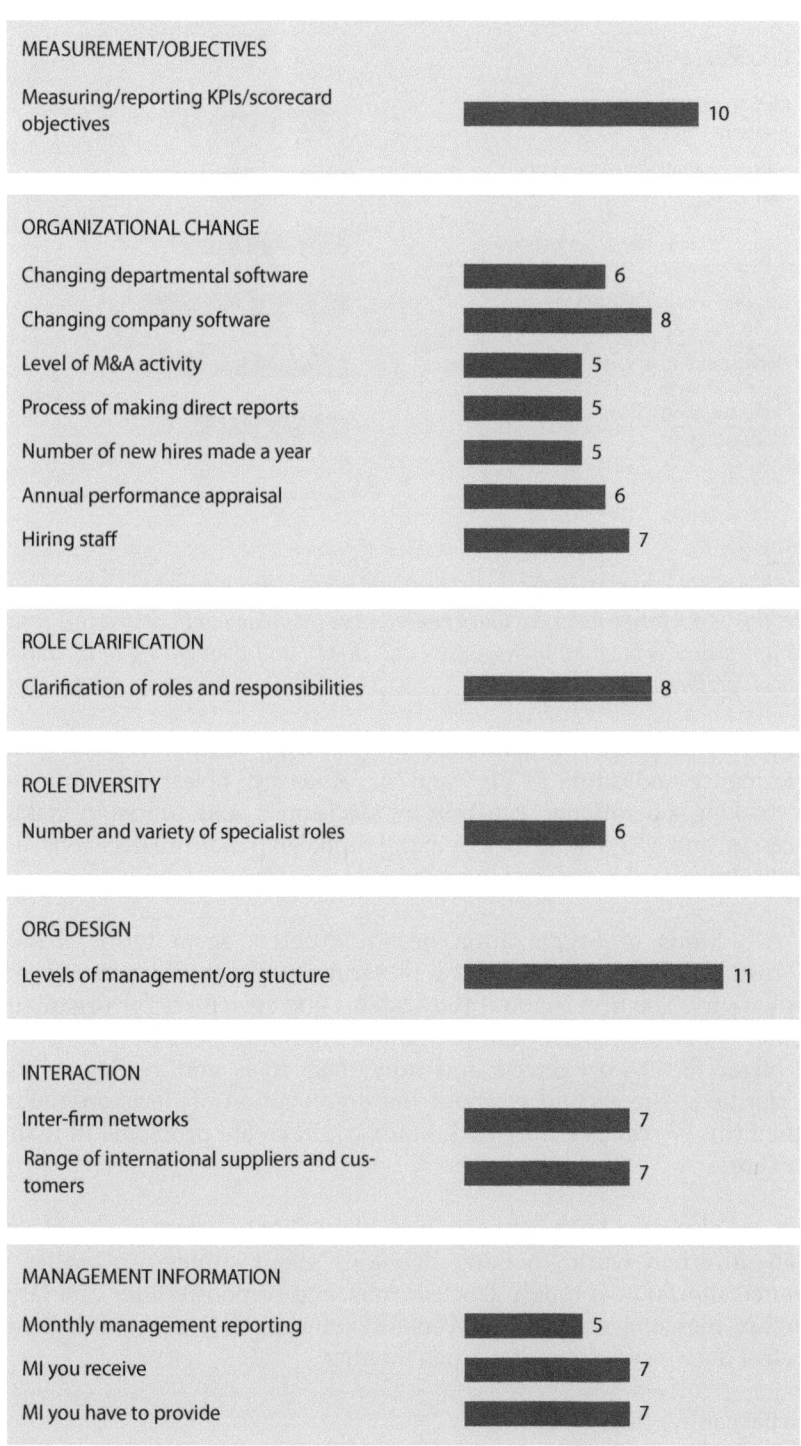

MEASUREMENT/OBJECTIVES

Measuring/reporting KPIs/scorecard objectives — 10

ORGANIZATIONAL CHANGE

Changing departmental software — 6

Changing company software — 8

Level of M&A activity — 5

Process of making direct reports — 5

Number of new hires made a year — 5

Annual performance appraisal — 6

Hiring staff — 7

ROLE CLARIFICATION

Clarification of roles and responsibilities — 8

ROLE DIVERSITY

Number and variety of specialist roles — 6

ORG DESIGN

Levels of management/org stucture — 11

INTERACTION

Inter-firm networks — 7

Range of international suppliers and customers — 7

MANAGEMENT INFORMATION

Monthly management reporting — 5

MI you receive — 7

MI you have to provide — 7

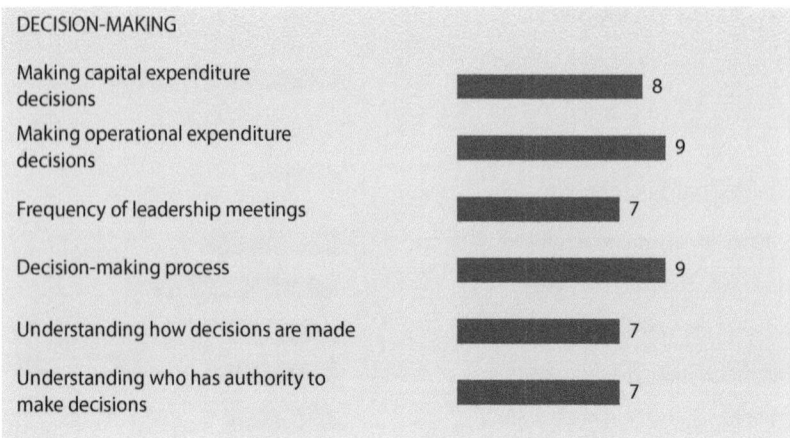

TABLE 4.2
The impact of organizational sources of complexity on the business
Note: this is a relative measure that combines the frequency with which this source
of complexity was cited by managers in our survey and their rating of the impact
it has on performance.

or the organizational structure' and 'measuring and/or reporting key performance indicators (KPIs) and/or scorecard objectives', followed by: 'making operational expenditure decisions'; and 'decision-making processes' and as a whole, then 'making capital expenditure decisions' and 'clarification of roles and responsibilities'.

So, two kinds of organization design problem seem to be driving the costlier kinds of complexity, in terms of constraining managers' productivity. The first is about the systems and structures for organizing people – how their performance is monitored and measured, how they are hierarchically organized and how their roles and responsibilities are clarified. The second is about the organization of decision-making in the firm. We can see how both kinds could create problems in matrix structures.

There are also clear links between these highlighted sources of complexity. In an uncertain world, making decisions about strategic priorities or resource allocation is tough. Unclear roles and responsibilities and large, complex hierarchies (lots of layers of management) make quick and effective decision-making that much tougher.

So what can we do about it?

4. How can you simplify your organization design?

In the rest of this chapter we address two questions.

- How can I take my current organization design and make it simpler? In this case your strategy has not changed significantly, but your complexity diagnosis is showing that your organization has become too complex, so you cannot execute your strategy effectively. It is time to remove the complexity caused by those successive incremental changes to your organization.
- How do I create a simpler organization design? In this situation your organization needs a fundamental overhaul, either because your strategy is radically different, or because the current design is so broken that it is time to go back to the drawing board.

Simplifying your current organization design
The start point for simpler organization design: Right people, right things, right way

If you do not need to fundamentally change your organization design, but you just want to make things simpler for people, so they can execute your strategy more effectively, then there are many things that can be done to simplify your current model. In this section we focus on the key things that will help you to make your current organization design simpler.

Right things: your strategy guides you on the right things

Good organization design always starts with your simple strategy: the sole purpose of organization design is to organize your people so they can deliver the strategy that you have set. It follows logically that a review of your strategy will always need to happen before you start to discuss organizational design options. There may be many different organizational design options, but they should all be informed by your simple strategy.

A great deal of complexity in organization design comes from a mismatch with strategy. If a business is striving to become a global leader in innovation then a very different organization design is required from a business that wants to grow through being great at customer service. The innovation business will benefit from a flat and networked structure that fosters collaboration and the generation of ideas. Similarly, it will want to recruit people who are technically gifted and thought leaders. The business that is focused on customer service will want to standardize things to ensure the quality of customer experience and will likely need to push accountability down the organization and empower its people to help their customers.

So you should not start any organizational design work unless you are 100 per cent clear on your strategy. You need to be sure the strategy is right and sure that everyone understands it.

Complex strategy = complex organization design. If your strategy is too complex, then obviously your organization design will be too complex as well. You also need to question whether your strategy is too complex (see Chapter 5) or whether people's understanding of your strategy is too vague.

Stop playing with that organization! Your strategy should not be changing too often, so major changes in your organization design should be rare. However, in many of our projects we notice that our clients have been through a constant evolution of organization designs. As we have already observed, most things evolve to become more complex, not simpler, so this 'organizational tinkering' will inevitably result in organizational designs becoming too complex. Restructuring is now so common that it is estimated that most large companies are constantly restructuring to some degree. This means that organizations are in a constant state of flux, and the benefits associated with restructuring are rarely realized before the next restructure. This inevitably creates complexity as jobs, processes, structures and all other elements of organizational design are constantly changing and more and more materials, policies, guidance etc., are created in an effort to clarify things.

Decisions on the design of your organization should never be based on the following factors:

- Minor changes in strategy: small changes in strategy are not a good reason to change your organization design.
- How you were historically organized: what worked in the past may not be right now. If your strategy has changed significantly then your organization design may need to change.
- How your competitors are organized: their strategy will be different from yours, so you cannot copy their design.
- Individual employees: you should avoid creating roles/structures around individuals and their personal situation, goals or needs.

If your diagnosis shows your organization design is too complex (for whatever reason) then it might be time to strip back the organizational design to what really matters and remove the white noise that distracts people from value-adding activities.

Right things: your strategy also tells you what to measure
Your organization should be designed to simply focus on delivering your strategy or your ten simple success keys (see Chapter 5).

Measure fewer things, measure the right things: Once you've set your simple, clear strategy, you can track how you're doing. But beware: the old adage goes 'what gets measured gets done'. And it's true.

Measures are an important part of work coordination, as they offer people targets and goals to strive for, which is a proven motivator. However, measures can have a dramatic effect on the complexity of your organization, because if you measure too many things, or you set the wrong measures, then without doubt you will cause more even more organizational complexity.

Too many measures: As we know, complexity occurs when new elements are added, the interconnections between them grow and pressure is increased. There is a propensity in the management of large organizations to introduce measures in an effort to understand what is going on in their business. Although this can indeed help managers keep an eye on things, too many measures can distract people from the real value-adding work. The more different things you ask your managers to measure the more complex their work will become, and these complexities will stop them working on other more productive things. Every time you ask for a new measure, someone somewhere has to come up with a way of getting that measure. They then have to report it back. You then have to discuss it and decide what to do about it. In other words, energy gets directed into measuring things, not doing things. But the problem does not stop there.

If you set too many measures for your managers, eventually the measures will start to conflict and contradict each other. So the measure will create confusion. Are we trying to increase market share or grow our profits? If your people are being measured on and rewarded for the wrong things, your strategy will not be executed.

Measuring activity not outcome: The other danger here is measuring activity rather than outcome. Your measures should not focus on activities (how long a customer support call lasts) but on outcomes (how happy the customer was with the answers they got).

> *Here's an example from a project we worked on. A new Customer Service Director wanted to ensure his call centers (which deal with sales and product support enquiries) were always well staffed to answer phones.*

To do this, he needed to understand average call lengths, so he asked the team leaders to measure the call lengths over a period of four weeks. The average call length was found to be around six minutes. Very soon, team leaders in the call center started to wonder why some people were taking longer than this 'average', because taking longer than six minutes on a call added costs and made it harder to plan resources. So they set a target for all calls to be six minutes and linked that to departmental bonuses. Within weeks of this happening they noticed that the other metric they measured, call center satisfaction, had dramatically gone down. Not all enquiries could be completed in six minutes, so staff were finishing calls as soon as possible after the six-minute time span had expired, even if the client query was not resolved! Customers then had to call back, inevitably talk to a different person and start all over again.

You can see how what started as a rather innocuous measure has quickly become a target that not only takes resource away from the business of customer service but actually begins to undermine customer service and increase resource demands. Measures and targets are such an important influence on what your people are doing that they cannot afford to be anything other than clear, simple and aligned to drive strategy execution.

Some practical advice on setting simpler measures:

- Make sure all measures are directly linked to your strategy and departmental value drivers. If the strategy of a global bank is to be number one for customer service, then the people in the call centers and branches must be measured on the satisfaction of their customers and not just sales or productivity.
- Make sure that for the overall company you have no more than five key measures to focus on.
- Make sure each and every departmental and managerial measure is linked to the company measures.
- Make sure that all measures are outcome-based (e.g. number of successful product launches) not activity-based (number of innovation ideas generated each month).
- Make sure there are no contradictions between measures (e.g. market share and profit) and that no measures have unintended consequences (short call-center times and customer dissatisfaction).

Right way: optimize layers and spans of control
Layers add complexity: The layers of your organization describe how many layers there are, from CEO down to your frontline staff at the lowest

layer. Layers exist to divide up decision authority within your company. Accountability and decision authority tend to increase as people move up the organizational hierarchy. Each layer of your organization adds both people costs and complexity costs to your business, so an organizational layer should only exist where a discrete level of decision accountability is required. Studies have shown that the maximum number of layers from CEO down to the shop floor or customer should be no more than eight, and best practice is closer to six.

If you have more than eight layers in your organization, this factor alone is almost certainly driving complexity and we would recommend a de-layering exercise. In organizations with more than eight layers we usually find very high levels of duplication, with too many people involved in each project/decision. Individual roles and responsibilities are therefore unclear, which makes processes and decision-making more complex than they should be.

> 26% of our sample have more than
> 10 management levels in their
> organization (19% more than 16).

Spans of control may also add to complexity: Span of control refers to the number of people that report to a single manager. A span of control exists to break up and coordinate the work that needs to be done. If spans are too large, it becomes difficult for a manager to understand and coordinate the work of his or her people. If you remember, we said that organization design was really about getting the right people doing the right things in the right ways. If you have too many people to look after, you will quickly lose sight of who's doing what and how well they are doing it.

Again, studies have shown that the maximum span of control a manger can control is between six and twelve, depending on the skill level of the work being performed. Extending spans beyond twelve means bad complexity tends to grow again. This is logical because there is a limit to a manager's ability to handle the number of decisions, issues and activities within their sphere of control. In response, managers will tend to create more KPIs, processes and reporting demands to help them manage the sheer volume of activities, issues and communications. Hence as the span of control becomes too wide, complexity grows.

As a general rule, the more skilled and specialized the work, the smaller the span of control should be. Relatively skilled departments (e.g. engineers, scientists, account managers) should aim for spans of around six to nine, while less highly skilled or task based departments seem to be able to cope with spans of nine to twelve, and sometimes as many as fifteen. Beyond this number, the manager will struggle to understand the work being done in the team and will struggle to effectively coordinate her/his people, which may in turn add to complexity

In smaller organizations, as you get down to lower levels of management, it might be very difficult to achieve a span of control as wide as six. For example, a small organization might only need four regulatory managers, one overall regulatory department head and three regulatory managers each looking after different product areas. In this example the regulatory manager would have a span of control of three. To increase this manager's span of control we would need to add another functional cluster to her/his responsibilities, but there may not be another functional cluster which logically fits with regulatory management. In this case the span of control cannot be increased to six. We would encourage the aspiration of trying to get to spans within the six-to-twelve range, but in many organizations there will be a few exceptions. But the exceptions should be few!

Cluster like activities and skills together: To reduce complexity it is also important for teams and departments to be logically clustered together in groups where the skills, experience and outputs are similar. They should also be managed by people with a good understanding of the work. Organizational complexity will increase if you have very different skills or roles under a manager. For example, having 'buildings and facilities' managed by HR seems like a reasonable place to put it on an organization chart, but what is an HR manager likely to know about buildings and facilities management? Would it be better to have a wider span and have a separate Buildings and Facilities Manager as well? These are the kinds of debates that need to be had to ensure that your organization design is complex enough to deliver your strategy, but not more complex that. We call this 'requisite complexity' (after William Ross Ashby – a cybernetics expert; cybernetics being the 'science of coordination, control and communication').

Spans and layers are interrelated: The more layers you have in the organization and the wider the spans of control, the more complex your organization will become. Activities will be duplicated, more people than necessary will be involved in activities and staff will be unclear about where accountability rests. All of these things will cause complexity.

Unfortunately, however, it is not always a question of simply reducing both spans and layers. If you are keeping the overall number of people in your organization constant, then by reducing the number of layers to lessen duplication, you will now have wider spans of control. This may drive up complexity since there are now more people for each manager to coordinate. If you are reducing headcount there may be an opportunity to reduce both the number of layers and the average span of control, but there will still be a balancing act to perform. Ultimately it comes down to what is right for your organization to execute its strategy. To remove complexity in organizational structure successfully, you must trade off its number of layers against its spans of control.

The ready reckoner in Figure 4.3 is helpful as it shows you for the size of your current organization what number of layers and average span of control you should currently have. So if you have 50,000 people in your company then your current layers/average spans should fall somewhere in the shaded area. If the design of your 50,000 person organization does not fall in the shaded area, then you should take time to understand why your organization has either more layers or wider spans that it might need. There

LAYERS*	6	7	8	9	10	11	12
8	2,015,539	6,725,601	19,173,961	48,427,561	111,111,111	235,794,769	469,070,941
7	335,923	960,800	2,396,745	5,380,840	11,111,111	21,435,888	39,089,245
6	55,987	137,257	299,593	597,871	1,111,111	19,48,717	3,257,437
5	9331	19,608	37,449	66,430	111,111	177,156	271,453
4	1555	2801	4681	7381	11,111	16,105	22,621
3	259	400	585	820	1111	1464	1885
2	43	57	73	91	111	133	157
1	7	8	9	10	11	12	13

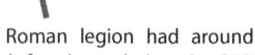

A Roman legion had around 5000–6000 people, with four layers below the CEO and average span of control of around eight people.

FIGURE 4.3
Layers and spans ready reckoner: organization headcounts for different combinations of spans of control and layers of organization
*Represents layers below CEO.
An organization of 50,000 people should aim for either five layers (below the CEO) with an average span of control of eight–nine people; or six layers with an average span of control of six people.

might be good reasons, but you should understand them. Understanding this will give you clues on how you might be able to reduce organizational complexity.

At full strength a Roman legion was made up of between 5030 and 6000 soldiers. Through hard battle experience this highly efficient fighting machine had worked out the optimal organization structure for them to triumph in battle. The overall legion commander (CEO) had four layers of 'management and staff' below him. The bottom layer of a Roman legion consisted of the front-line, fighting legionaries. Within the legion the widest span of control was ten people; the narrowest span of control was six. The average span of control was just over eight.

How to check decision authority to reduce layers: Reviewing decision authority can help determine whether your structure has too many layers.

Here's the simplest way to review decision authority:

- First list the current layers in your organization and write out the current responsibilities and decision accountability assigned to each layer (see Figure 4.4).
- Now identify how each layer uniquely adds value and helps with the implementation of your strategy.
- Next try to identify if any layers maybe superfluous to requirements by asking two questions:
  - Does each layer have distinct and increasing decision authority?
  - Can you identify any overlap in responsibilities or decision-making authority between the layers?
- Try to work out the minimum number of layers that you could operate with. Ask yourself:
  - What levels of decision-making authority are necessary to effectively perform your key activities/strategies/processes?
  - What discrete role does each layer play in making sure your strategy is brilliantly executed?
  - Does each layer add significant value or prevent significant risk?

One warning: Fewer layers can lead to efficiencies and can empower staff to be more innovative. However, the process can be taken too far. A certain minimum number of levels is likely to be needed to ensure appropriate management and control to avoid senior managers being too busy managing operations to scan the environment and shape the future.

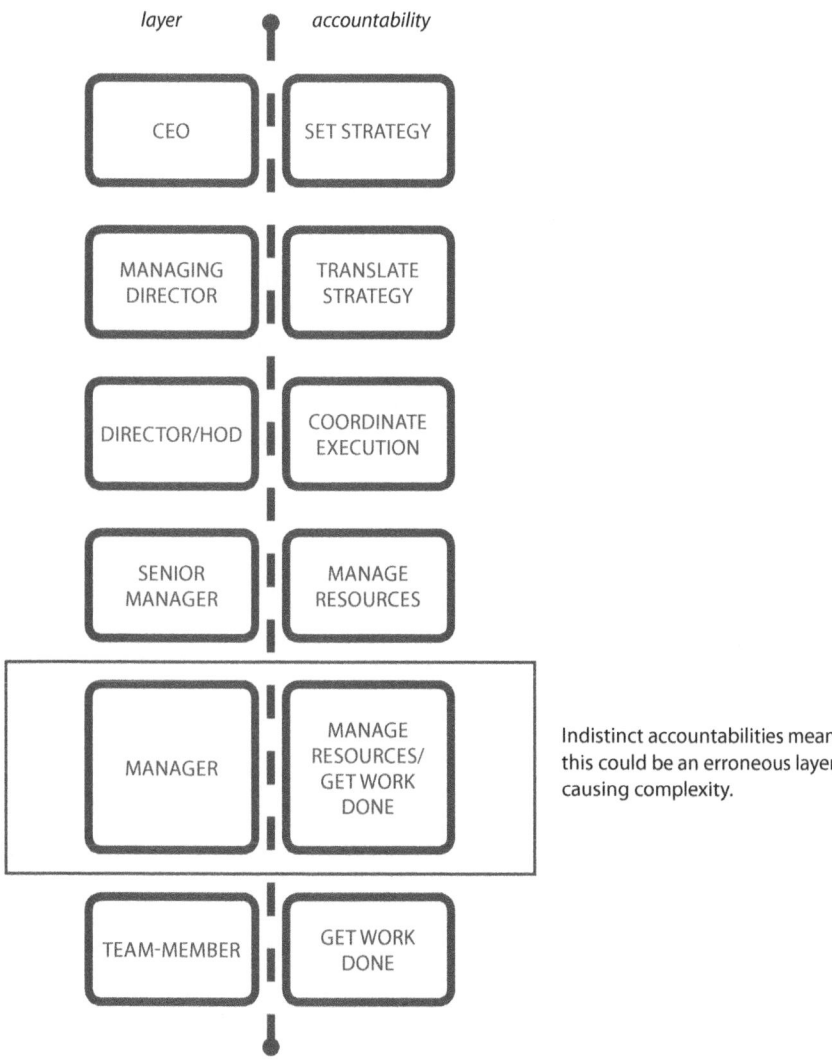

FIGURE 4.4
Layers and accountability

How to optimize spans of control: Work should be broken down into logical 'clusters' of activity where specific focus, skills or experience is required. Your aim is to end up with between six and twelve people reporting to each manager.

Fewer than six: you probably have more managers than you need, which will increase costs and add complexity.

Beyond twelve: your managers will be unable to effectively manage their direct reports and will create unnecessary complexity in a vain attempt to control their people and work.

- Identify whether the nature of the work the cluster does is high-skill, medium-skill or low-skill. If it is high-skill then we would tend to aim for a span of control around six; if the skill level is low then up to twelve, or even fifteen, may be manageable.
- Identify the important activities that need to be performed and how these activities can most logically be clustered together.
- How many people and what skills do you need to effectively deliver these most important activities and maintain your core processes? What is the most logical way to cluster/group activities together to deliver these critical projects/activities/processes?

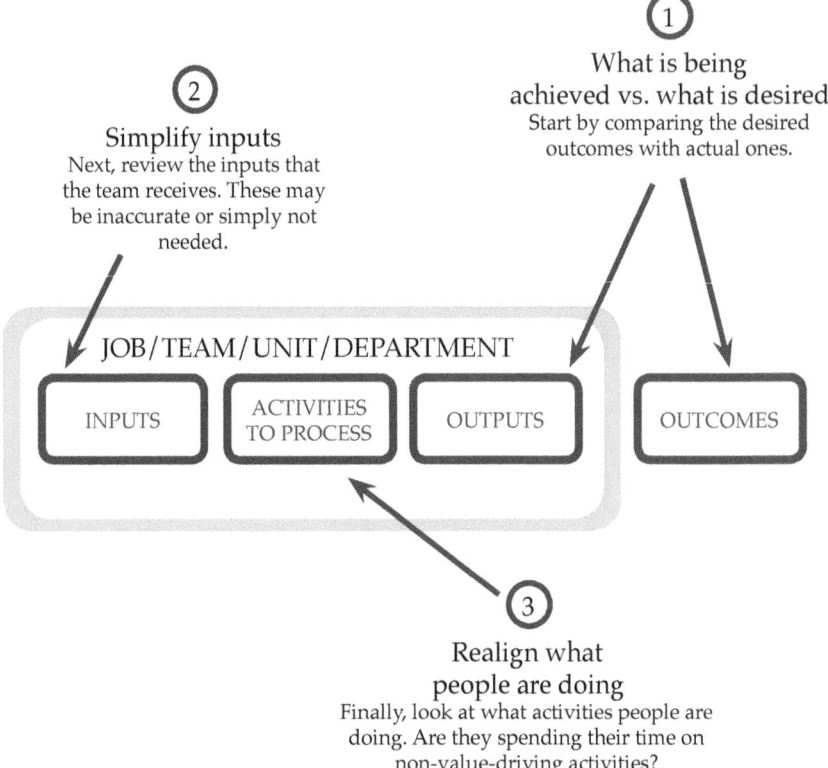

FIGURE 4.5
Inputs, activities, outputs and outcomes

- Describe the overall role of each cluster in simple terms. If work and tasks do not naturally fit together then it is likely that complexity will arise once this working unit is put under time pressure.
- Make sure you are clear on how each cluster adds value for the company; if this is not clear ask why that is, and don't be afraid to be brave and just stop doing some things.

Another important consideration in making your spans of control work is the interaction between roles, teams and departments (Figure 4.5). Research has shown that, under pressure, the most effective and efficient teams are those that understand each other's roles. This is why psychologists working with elite teams spend a lot of time helping the various elements of the team to understand what the others do in order to improve inter-group working. It is also one of the advantages of job rotation (often practiced in Japanese firms, for example), although there are also disadvantages (such as the trade-off of having weaker specialists). Shared understanding means that each element of the team or department knows what other elements need from them to succeed and can produce the right things in the right way at the right time.

If you find that the performance of your teams and departments begins to falter under pressure, that they are not coordinated or spend too much time checking and clarifying rather than just getting on with the work, then chances are that it is because they do not understand each other's work well enough.

Right way: simplify decision-making

From our work with big organizations it is very clear that decision-making can be a major source of complexity. Large numbers of people from different parts of the business are involved in many decisions. Often it is unclear how major decisions will be made, what information will be needed and who will ultimately decide on the right course of action. The result is that it is often difficult to get simple things done quickly, let alone make the major strategic decisions you need to deliver decisive action on important issues.

The symptoms of complexity in decision-making: There are many symptoms that might indicate to you that your decision-making is too complex. These include:

- **Late or no decisions:** Too many people involved, too much or irrelevant information and people who are reluctant to take a risk.

- **Decision committees:** Accountability is unclear or decisions are considered too risky, so committees are set up to spread the burden and attempt to make a better decision.
- **Revisiting:** The decision was made some time ago and now new people are involved and want to check things.
- **Sunk cost:** The decision may have been wrong but a lot has been invested so we plough on.
- **Loudest wins:** This is what is known as 'group think' and happens when powerful individuals dominate a group.
- **We know the way already:** But there is a strict process that must be adhered too so we go at the prescribed pace.

Some of the underlying causes of complexity in decision-making: These symptoms are often the tip of the proverbial iceberg. There are often intangible issues, hidden from view, that make decision-making processes more convoluted and time-consuming than necessary.

Some of the more common issues that we come across are:

- **Mistrust:** Large organizations are not always comfortable trusting decisions to a single person or a small group of people. So we often find many companies have large numbers of decision committees or a culture of making decisions in large groups. This is not to say that making a decision as a group is bad. Indeed, studies show that diverse groups can often make better-quality decisions and are the best way to escape from group think or move away from locked-in beliefs of specific cliques or elites. However, almost invariably the speed of the decision is slowed.
- **Accountability is unclear:** The mere scale of operations in global companies means that there is often someone doing a similar job, or there will be area/department that will be impacted by your decisions so they need to be involved in some way. Add in the interconnections and dependencies of today's matrix organizations and the pool of accountability gets pretty murky. Not having a single person where the buck stops for certain decisions drives complexity, as people with vested interests or even tenuous interests become involved in decision-making.
- **Information overload:** The information age means that real-time data is out of date the moment it is read. This creates an extremely dynamic decision environment where resources, data and often the goals for making decisions are in almost perpetual motion. Add to this the fact that some information comes from systems or sources that people do not trust, and we have another driver of complexity in decision-making.

- **People like to create:** As we know from the people chapter (Chapter 3) of this book, people are predisposed to create and 'improve' things. When this disposition is brought to bear on decision-making it can lead to many of the symptoms we outlined above. People seem to enjoy the brainstorming, problem-solving part of decision-making – that part up-front when all options and courses of action are considered. It is often only the problem holder who seems anxious for one course of action to be identified and executed. How many times have you been in a decision-making committee where at least one person is still throwing in ideas long after the decision has been made?

CONAGRA FOODS: SHEDDING SURPLUS LAYERS

What was the complexity problem?

In 2005, marketing and sales were at the heart of the ConAgra business but CEO Gary Rodkin found that the structure didn't give him the oversight and transparency he needed in these core areas. Also, the business suffered from a lack of accountability in other processes and functions due to an overly devolved structure.

How did the power of simplicity help?

ConAgra realigned the operating structure from three channels to two, with the previous ConAgra Food Service being merged with ConAgra Food Ingredients to form ConAgra Foods Commercial.

They reshuffled and centralized some corporate and shared services units to better support the business, as well as to drive accountability, simplification and collaboration.

All supply chain organizations were then consolidated under a single Executive Vice President of Manufacturing and Supply Chain, with responsibility for manufacturing, warehousing, logistics, purchasing, and customer service.

What was the impact?

- Aligning managers directly with key priorities resulted in better execution and effectiveness.
- Reducing the number of business units gave the CEO better oversight of sales and marketing to maximize impact with both customers and consumers.
- Centralizing corporate areas like HR and R&D freed up the business units to focus on execution and improving performance.
- Consolidating the supply chain organization allowed ConAgra to reduce handoffs (links in the chain) and drive productivity, thereby improving efficiency across the entire supply chain.

Five steps to simplify decision-making in large organizations

1. Be clear on WHAT you are deciding.
2. Consider the accuracy versus time trade-off.
3. Optimize WHO is involved.
4. Be clear on HOW you will decide.
5. Make the decision and stick to it!

1. Be clear on WHAT you are deciding: Decision-making is complex if you are not clear on what you are deciding. In some meetings it is often unclear IF you are deciding something or just talking about it. So always make sure everyone is clear on exactly what the decision is, e.g. to decide if we hire this candidate, to decide if we make this investment, to decide if we will launch this new product.

At this point you should also make sure that you eliminate any decisions that simply don't need to be discussed and made at all. These questions can help you weed out pointless decisions:

- Does the decision fit with your strategy?
- Do you have the resources and/or capability to carry out a decision?
- Will value be added by making a decision?

2. Consider the accuracy versus time trade-off: Next consider if you need a fast decision or a very accurate decision. This will help you determine who should be involved in making the decision and how the decision should be made, i.e. the process that you will go through to make the decision. Typically large organizations tend to be better at making accurate decisions than they are at making timely decisions, and making a very accurate decision often means adding in more people, more information, more steps and sign-off points which leads to more complexity and reduced pace. So rather than being roughly right in good time, many companies end up being precisely right, far too late!

Figure 4.6 illustrates the trade-off to be made between speed and accuracy. For each decision you should consciously decide on the level of precision that is needed before embarking on the decision-making process. There are times when a good decision fast will be better than a perfect solution too late. You may miss the boat on a market opportunity like Nokia did when it failed to make a decision to move into the smartphone market in time. Knowing where your decision sits on the matrix in Figure 4.6 will help you in choosing how to decide.

3. Optimize WHO is involved: Another sure-fire way to add complexity is to have too many people involved in the decision, to have the wrong people involved or to be unclear on the roles that each person will play. Choosing to go it alone with a decision may be the right choice in some situations, but could result in rejection of the decision in other departments, or you might miss a key perspective. You might go it alone and come up with the best decision possible, then be brought back or even reprimanded for acting unilaterally when perhaps consensus-building and acceptance of the decision was as important as the decision itself. Conversely, the decision-

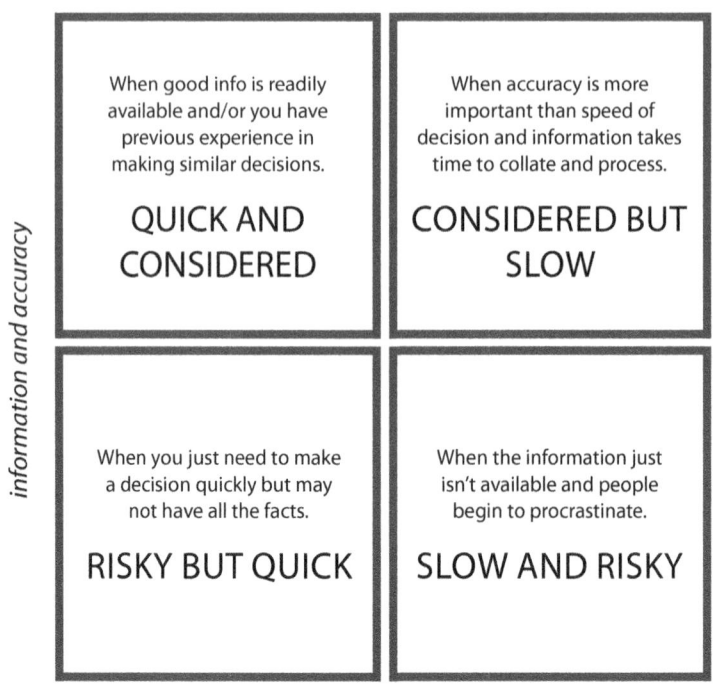

information and accuracy

When good info is readily available and/or you have previous experience in making similar decisions.

QUICK AND CONSIDERED

When accuracy is more important than speed of decision and information takes time to collate and process.

CONSIDERED BUT SLOW

When you just need to make a decision quickly but may not have all the facts.

RISKY BUT QUICK

When the information just isn't available and people begin to procrastinate.

SLOW AND RISKY

time and lack of risk

FIGURE 4.6
Information and accuracy versus time and lack of risk

maker who is tasked with making a decision by their boss and brings a vast number of people into the process may be in equal trouble. So, deciding who to involve is a critical step in the decision process.

- **The right number of people, no more, no less:** You should minimize the number of people involved in the decision, but not at the expense of decision quality. Only involve someone in the decision if:
  - they have unique skills and experience that will be critical to making a good decision;
  - the decision has major implications on their part of your organization; and
  - if their acceptance/buy-in to the decision will be essential for successful implementation of the decision.
- **Don't involve several people from each function/department.** Encourage them to send one empowered contributor, making it clear that it is their responsibility to consult with their team members before the decision and report back after the decision.

- **Clarify decision accountability:** You can immediately improve your organization's decision-making pace by making one person, and one person only, accountable for the final decision. They can then consult the right people to make a good decision rather than tasking the group to come up with a decision. The best way to do this is to have RACIs (see below) for all the most common and important decisions.
- **Put decision authority back at the right level:** In times of austerity, there is a propensity to pull accountability for things like external spend or even internal improvements up to leadership to give a sense of control. This can indeed rein in costs but, if not done properly, risks disempowering people throughout the organization. It is these people who are closer to customers and markets and therefore better placed to spot opportunities. Spending some time assigning them the right level of decision authority and training people to make good and timely decisions will mean that you no longer have to revise policies and put in stringent cost controls should the market take a downturn. Similarly, your organization will be more responsive to its customers as people are empowered to make things happen.

4. Be clear on HOW you will decide: In decision-making, confusion also reigns when it is unclear what the decision-making process will be. When will we meet? How will we all input our thinking? Will a discussion paper be circulated and discussed before the meeting? Will we use consensus? Will we use voting? Make sure that the decision-making process is crystal clear before you start and, if appropriate, adopt a rational decision-making model.

- **Map out the decision process:** Map out exactly how the decision will be made but make sure you minimize the number of steps/stages and remove duplication of steps or sign-offs.
- **Identify critical information needs:** Decision-making will be complicated by the lack of information or conversely by an overload of irrelevant information. So at the start of the decision process make sure you understand all the information that each person/function will need in order to decide. Minimize the amount of information used by focusing only on 'critical information needs' and removing all else. Different types of decision will need different types of information, so think carefully about the right level and type of information for the decision you are planning.

> 18% of our sample receive six or
> more management reports a month
> (9% receive more than 16).

- **Have clear 'decision lock' points:** Having clear 'decision lock' points is helpful as well. A 'decision lock' tells people when the final decision will be made and fixed. This encourages people to make sure they input into the decision at the right time, as they will know that the decision cannot be revisited after that.
- **Standardize common decision types:** If this type of decision is very common (e.g. go/no go decision on a new product launch) then it is helpful to standardize the information needs and the decision process. This way, managers quickly get to know the process for getting approval/ sign-off. Reckitt Benckiser, for example, use a particular research methodology to decide, and everyone knows that new product ideas will have to pass this test before they can be given the green light. If their ideas do not pass this test then there's no point asking for launch approval.
- **Use the right decision style for the situation/culture of your company:** There are three broad styles of decision:
  - **Autocratic:** The classic command and control decision. The leader points the way and the troops make it happen. No questions asked.
  - **Consultative:** Before making a decision, you would speak to people and gather some data. A single person still makes the decision but others are involved in providing information.
  - **Collaborative:** This is where a decision is reached by a group rather than an individual.

Matching the decision style to the situation is important and will play a big role in determining the success of your decision-making. Therefore, it is worth taking some time to understand the variables such as time, accuracy, level of commitment, etc., and selecting a style of decision-making that is appropriate. For example, making an autocratic decision about the performance management of your team may not be a good idea if the team is unionized!

In general, a consultative or collaborative style is most appropriate when:

- you need information from others to solve a problem;
- the problem is not well defined;
- you need people's buy-in to your course of action;
- time is less important than accuracy.

An autocratic style is most efficient when:

- you have clear accountability for the decision;
- the team will accept your decision;
- there is little time available.

5. Make the decision and stick to it! Making good decisions simply is difficult, but worth it. However, if your organization constantly revisits and changes decisions, this will create additional complexity as the whole organization changes direction. In addition, managers will not commit fully to making good decisions if they believe the decisions will not stick, or if they know they can easily be unpicked at a later date. Make sure you have clear decision locks and that decisions are only revisited in very exceptional circumstances.

Even simpler: using the reduce/clarify/standardize framework you can quickly identify many ways to simplify your organization design.

Reduce
- The number of decisions that you start working on
- The number of people involved in decision-making
- The number of steps in the decision-making process
- The level at which decisions are made

Clarify
- How and when key decisions will be made
- Who will be involved in making key decisions

Standardize
- Standardize decision-making processes and sign-off procedures for recurring decision types
- Remove duplication so that, wherever possible, only one person has the final say in a decision

Right way: simplify the matrix
Many major companies now operate with matrix organization structures. These have become essential structures for running successful multi-functional and multi-region companies.

However, the matrix organization is an inherently complicated structure. In fact, the matrix organization is probably the most complicated form of organization you can create. As we discussed in Chapter 1, the complexity of a system increases whenever you increase the number of components, the variety of components, the interconnections between components and/or the pace of change. With this concept in mind it is clear that matrix organizations increase the number, variety and interconnections of components involved in your organization design. So the matrix is by its very concept a form of complication.

Add human behavior to complexity of connection and the complexity increases further. Humans are essentially tribal creatures. A trip to any football game will quickly remind you of this. We tend to be very loyal to our tribe and will defend our tribe and/or attack other tribes. We are also naturally hierarchical, looking to a higher authority for direction.

- **Divided loyalty:** A matrix organization immediately creates a divided loyalty, with two or more tribes to be loyal to and two or more hierarchies to operate within.
- **Loss of control over our destiny:** Matrix organizations also shift control from one tribe, to two or more tribes. So we no longer have the same level of control over decisions or actions.
- **Ambiguity:** People also prefer or find it easier to work in situations where there is clarity and certainty. But matrix organizations tend to create ambiguity about how things get done: which tribe is in charge? Which hierarchy is the one to work up? Many people find this ambiguity frustrating, and this reduces human engagement and sometimes brings the worst out in people.

But the matrix design has many benefits, particularly because it links strategic drivers from the business or product divisions (including economies of scale, product platforms and branding or new product development priorities across all markets, often from other multinational customers) directly with country market drivers (including local customer preferences, regulations, supplier opportunities, etc.). So it is here to stay for good reasons. If you believe that everything should be made as simple as possible, but no simpler than that, then the key question is: how can you make the matrix organization as simple as possible?

Minimize the number of matrix connections: In our view, the complexity that is caused by multiple or unclear connections is probably the most challenging form of complexity to deal with, particularly when the connections are not easy for you to see or control. This tends to be a major part of the problem in poorly designed and/or poorly managed matrix designs. Your organization becomes like a tangled knot of kite string where the interconnections, meeting points and rules are very unclear, confusing and inefficient. We see many organizations where senior managers have two or three matrix roles, so they are being asked to be a part of too many matrices. Best practice dictates that a manager should have one solid line of reporting to a functional/departmental head and a maximum of one matrix report to another area.

Do not let the matrix go too deep: Similarly the matrix should not go too deep into the layers of your organization. In our view a matrix should not be operating below the third layer in your organization. The senior managers in your organization will have the skills and experience to operate effectively in the matrix; more junior ones will not have the leadership and people skills needed. Senior managers can also navigate their way to the top of the organization to get clarity and rulings on matrix disputes. This is harder if you are lower down the organization, so the inherent ambiguity of the matrix will cause more tension and inertia lower down the company.

Minimize the number of decisions which are made in the matrix: The next point is to use the matrix sparingly, by being clear on the decisions that are matrix decisions and those that are purely departmental/hierarchical decisions. Certain key decisions and activities need to be done within the matrix in order for the company to be successful. But not all major decisions/ activities need to be matrix decisions; most can still be departmental or functional. The key here is to list all the major decisions that need multi-departmental/functional input in order to create value and deliver your strategy. The acid test is again simple. Will we create more value (or reduce risk) by making this decision across the matrix, or will more value be created by making this a functional decision/action? As another rule of thumb, if more than 20 per cent of your daily decisions require matrix alignment you are likely to have significant difficulties making decisions and driving your strategy forward.

Most people are unsure when to employ or not employ the matrix, so make sure you clearly communicate which decisions they are expected to make using the matrix and which ones are not matrix decisions. When new situations arise, quickly agree if this new situation requires matrix input or not. If you have many new decisions/situations arising that could be matrix points, then create some guiding principles to help people decide for themselves.

Crystal clear roles and responsibilities: Now you are clear on which specific decisions are made within the matrix, you will then need to be clear on the roles and responsibilities of the people involved in each of those matrix issues/decisions.

For each matrix decision there should be a clear and simple RACI (see below). Even within the matrix there should still be a single point of accountability. It needs to be clear who this person is, and if they are not directly involved in matrix decisions then you must clarify the escalation process for taking issues that need resolving to the person who is accountable. People can deal with conflict, but only if they know how it will be resolved.

As far as possible you should standardize the way matrix decision processes work across the whole company and all its divisions. This will mean that as people move around the organization, the way the matrix works will always be consistent, which will allow people to quickly learn how to work in the matrix. It is very hard to do anything where the rules are inconsistent or change very rapidly.

Align goals and measures: Misaligned goals, measures and rewards are also a major cause of complexity in matrix management. This is a very obvious point, we know, but still it is frequently forgotten. If managers within the matrix have different or contradictory objectives (e.g. where one matrix manager is incentivized on volume, and his matrix counterpart is incentivized on profit margins) then it will be difficult to make good matrix decisions. The result will be conflict, tension and inertia. So make sure you have joint scorecards and shared objectives throughout the matrix and that these goals and measures are clearly linked to your strategy/value drivers. As we outlined above, you should also minimize the number of measures/ KPIs you use and always ensure that every measure relates directly to your strategy or key driver of value creation.

We always recommend that these goals should be carefully constructed and tested to avoid unintended consequences.

Develop and reward good matrix behaviors: If you want to invest in some good training, then invest in training people on how to work effectively in a matrix organization. Managers often lack skills or understanding of how to operate within a matrix, which means that even when you have designed the simplest matrix possible it can still fall down simply because of people's behaviors.
Define the behaviors that are essential for good matrix operation and encourage and reward them throughout the organization. Examples of good matrix behaviors are:

- **Whole-company perspective:** Encourage loyalty to the whole organization above loyalty to one's own departmental/functional tribe. Encourage managers to look at every decision from all perspectives, not just their functional perspective.
- **Active listening:** Teach people how to practice active listening so they can understand all perspectives fully before making decisions.
- **Getting it right, not being right:** Encourage people to focus on what is right for the company, not on winning the argument or proving that their function knows best.
- **Better together thinking:** Help people to understand that two heads are always better than one, and that in modern business it is impossible for one person to make progress without input, help and alignment from others. Also help them to understand that even a good decision

made in one function will not be well implemented unless the right people are involved and committed to that decision.

- **Timely, open communication:** Encourage people to openly communicate across the matrix and to be transparent in their communication.

GLOBAL FOOD COMPANY: SIMPLIFYING THE MATRIX

What was the complexity problem?

Decision-making at this global food company was both slow and risk averse. This was because each senior manager needed to consult and align with several teams and people before being able to action relatively minor day-to-day decisions. It was also unclear who would have the final say in the event of a disagreement.

How did the power of simplicity help?

The management redefined what was considered 'day-to-day' in decision-making, so that more power was devolved further down the organization. The RACI for all day-to-day decisions was simplified radically to reduce the number of people involved in any given decision to a maximum of three.

This dramatically reduced the number of connections each person had within the matrix, so that for most day-to-day decisions, they'd only need to align with one other person, in addition to their line manager.

Teams were coached on how to make great decisions with speed and simplicity.

Important matrix decisions are now managed through a series of executive committees that meet face-to-face every month to make the major decisions requiring more involvement and alignment with other geographies or functions. For each committee, there is one person with 'final call' rights to make a decision whenever consensus can't be reached.

What was the impact?

- All day-to-day matrix decisions can now be made by two to three people maximum.
- Decision-making processes and rights are simple and clear to everyone.
- The speed and quality of decision-making have improved.
- Senior managers now have more time to focus on longer-term strategic initiatives.

Right people: clarify roles and reduce role duplication

For your organization design to be effective, it is essential that people know exactly what their roles are, how things are meant to be done and who they are meant to work with most closely. Duplication of activity / responsibility also needs to be removed.

Simplify and clarify job descriptions: Overlapping, misdirected or overly complex job descriptions are another common driver of organizational complexity. If the job description is unclear then people will not know how to focus their time; in addition, they will unwittingly drift into working on other people's jobs, which will cause frustration and confusion. We are regularly given job descriptions for middle managers with a long list of tasks that sounds more suitable for the CEO than for a functional expert or middle manager.

How to simplify job descriptions
- Start the job description by describing (simply!) how the role contributes to delivery of your strategy and creates long-term value for the organization, i.e. why does this role exist at all?
- Identify the five key activities, processes or projects that the role is specifically there to focus on. There should be no more than five major items in this section.
- Identify the two or three key outcome measures (see above) that this role is responsible for.
- List the key skills and behaviors that will be essential for success.
- Make sure interdependencies with other people/functions are identified and spelled out. Make it clear HOW you want these people/functions to collaborate effectively.
- Ensure that there is no duplication of responsibility between this role and other roles, either within the department/function or between other departments/functions.
- Where people must work together toward a common goal, ensure that they understand each other's job descriptions and how their roles fit together.

Seek out and remove or clarify duplication: Duplication of activities/responsibility is very common in big companies. The sheer size of many organizations means that it is very hard to avoid this, as people cannot possibly know what everyone else does and is working on. However, duplication of role/activity is wasteful in cost terms and demotivating to your people. In fact very few things are more frustrating at work than thinking that you are responsible for something and then finding that another part of the organization is working on the same thing or is being asked to create something similar. Duplication also means that you will develop several different ways of doing the same thing, which again is inefficient and confusing, and creates conflict as people argue over which way is best. You should aim to ensure that there is no duplication by designing roles properly. Where duplication or overlap occurs, people should be encouraged to point it out so that the managers/leaders can get together and remove overlapping tasks and responsibilities.

Get radical with your RACI: Most companies now have RACIs – or something similar. RACIs describe who is **Responsible**, **Accountable**, **Consulted** and **Involved** in each major decision, project or activity. These are essential to ensuring that people are clear on how key decisions are made. However, there are three key problems with RACIs that need to be designed out:

- **Key activities/decisions only:** In many companies creating, discussing and agreeing RACIs has become a full-time occupation for managers. You should only create RACI tables for the major or essential activities that involve cross-team/department working. A simple functional decision or action should not need a RACI: it is clear who is responsible and who is accountable (the departmental/team head).
- **Minimize the number of people:** The next problem with RACIs is that usually there are still too many people in each category, i.e. more than one person in the accountable box and many in the responsible box! We advocate an approach called radical RACI, where there is a maximum of two people responsible for delivery of the project/activity/process and just one person who is ultimately accountable.
- **Communicate how we do things around here:** RACIs are rarely communicated well. So often people are unclear about how things are meant to be done. As a result they will either do things in the wrong way, or get frustrated because they do not know how to move things forward. RACIs should be clearly communicated so that people understand how things are done and what their part is in the decision/ process/activity.

Right people: clarify and build capability

At the start of the chapter, we made the point that simple organization design is all about getting the right people doing the right things, in the right way.

The 'right people' means making sure you have people with the experience, skills and behaviors you will need to win. If your people do not have the knowledge and skills to do their jobs effectively then they will focus on the wrong things. Or they will be doing the right things, but in the wrong way. This will cause complexity.

As part of your organization design you need to:

- identify the activities required to execute strategy throughout the organization;

- define the key skills, experience and behaviors that people will need to have, so they can to perform these activities brilliantly and move your company forward; and
- identify any key skills gaps – conduct a skills assessment survey with validation from managers and experts as appropriate, to identify if you have any major skills gaps.

This is likely to leave you with three categories of people:

- The Stars – your most capable people who can coach others
- The Potentials – those who have a few skills gaps in their capability, but who can be developed
- The Strugglers – those who do not have the required capabilities/skills to meet the demands of the roles

There will obviously be a difference in what happens next for these three groups. The Stars can be quickly put to use delivering work and coaching the Potentials to become stars. This leaves the Strugglers and it is not an option for either the business or the individual to ignore these people as both parties will suffer. In large organizations, the prognosis for these people is not as bad as it sounds as they can often be redeployed into more appropriate roles.

Then, finally, define, design and deliver pragmatic and cost-effective development interventions to close any gaps.

5. Zero basing: a simple approach to creating a new organization design

When is it time to go back to the drawing board and create a new organization design from scratch?

> Two American tourists were travelling through Ireland trying to find a small village where some distant relatives had once lived. They were very lost and the map was useless, so they stopped and asked a local man for directions. He listened attentively as they explained their problem and then thought for a while before saying … 'Well, I wouldn't start from here.'

Many business leaders would not start with their current organization design if given the choice. It may be apparent that simplifying your current organization design is not going to be enough to implement your strategy. This will usually be because your strategy has changed radically, or because the current design has evolved away from the original design and is now so broken that it is time to go back to the drawing board.

In some cases we would recommend creating a zero based organization solution, in essence designing your organization from scratch. Imagine you were starting your business today with your existing product/ service portfolio and your existing geographical spread. How would you organize your company/function if you were starting over, afresh? The reason for doing this is because starting with your current design will lead to another round of incremental tweaking and revisions. This incremental approach to organization design is what got you to this overly complex, cumbersome design in the first place. If you take the same approach as last time, the outcome will be the same and the result will be an even more complex organization, not a less complex one! Even if you cannot or do not want to implement the zero based option you could have a try at creating it. This might give you and your management team the creative tension or provocation needed to inspire new ideas on how you could be organized, or encourage you to take more radical steps.

If you feel a zero based approach is needed, then we would recommend following these steps to create this new simple organization design.

Step 1: Make sure everyone understands your strategy

The first step is always to make sure that everyone involved in the organization design project has a very clear picture of your strategy, as this will drive your organization design. If they do not understand your strategy in detail they will design the wrong organization. So take time to align the design team around the strategy. A good question to ask at this point is: how will our organization design need to change so we can implement our strategy?

Step 2: Understand how people are currently using their time

Next you should understand how people are currently using their time. Remember that our research shows that a significant proportion of management time is directed to non-value-adding activities and processes. This will be true in your organization. So you need to understand which activities, projects and processes are currently occupying people's time. This can be done using work diaries, workshop sessions or work observation as described in the diagnosis chapter. This goes back to the core questions we have raised before. Are we currently doing the right things? Are we doing the right things in the right way?

This might appear to be a rather retrospective exercise when you are designing a future organization, but before you start to change your organization it is important to understand how it currently works and understanding how people actually spend their time.

Step 3: Identify what people should be doing with their time

To implement my strategy, what activities do I want my people to spend time on? What specialist skills/know-how do I need to meet my key customers' needs and execute my strategy brilliantly? What new ways of working/behaviors will we need?

This is the most important step. Your strategy will define what drives value in your organization and what you will need to do in order to win in your market. The next step is to identify the work activities, processes and projects that your organization should be doing in order to implement your strategy.

When we do this we use the detailed inputs from the ten Simple Success Keys exercise (see Chapter 5), as this describes all of the important activities, projects, strategies and processes that your new organization needs to focus on.

The output from this 'what should we be doing' exercise can usually be summarized as answers to the following simple questions:

- What are all the key activities/projects/processes that the organization will need to focus on so it can deliver its strategy?
- What specialist skills and capabilities do we need to have to implement our strategy? Do we need new skills/capabilities or to transform our skills and capabilities in any way?
- What ways of working or behaviors will it be essential for us to exhibit? To deliver our strategy do we need any major changes in our ways of working, culture or behavior?

Actually doing versus should be doing: When you compare what people are actually doing with their time with this new list of activities, you will notice that currently a lot of time is directed to activities that do not contribute enough to achievement of your strategy. Asking why this is the case can quickly identify that you do not currently have the right structure or the right people in place to deliver your strategy.

Another useful exercise is to conduct a Stop/Start/Continue exercise on all the major activities that your people are currently spending their time on and ask the question:

- In order to achieve our strategy what activities/behaviors do we need to STOP doing altogether?
- In order to achieve our strategy what activities/behaviors do we need to START doing very well?
- In order to achieve our strategy what activities/behaviors do we need to CONTINUE being excellent at?

Step 4: Cluster activities into logical groupings

What is the most logical way to cluster these skills and activities together into distinct functions/departments? How will each of these functions/departments uniquely contribute towards value creation for your company?

Once you understand all the key activities and projects, the next work will be to see how they naturally and logically group together. The idea is to put things that naturally belong together into the same part of the organization. There are clear economies of know-how and/or scale if activities that require similar skills are grouped together. It is easier to create the right management structure if people are managing activities that they know well.

- **Skills clusters:** Put things that require similar skills together, e.g. all activities that relate to creating great new products/services, all things that relate to making and delivering products to customers.
- **Location clusters:** Put things that need to be physically located together in one place, e.g. all activities related to success in a strategic geography.
- **Outcome clusters:** Put things that link together towards a common outcome together, e.g. reporting on the financial health of the company.

The point here is that work is simpler when similar things are in one place, but more complex if someone is being asked to perform a series of diverse and unconnected activities which they do not have the skills and experience for. The risk of duplication is also much greater when similar skills/activities are spread out across the company.

It is important that you challenge the status quo here. It's easy to conclude that the key clusters are the same as currently, i.e. sales, marketing, R&D, finance, production, key regions. However, this is a great time to challenge this. For example:

- If innovation is an important key to achieving your strategy, you may want to create an innovation cluster made up of marketing, market research and R&D people, all reporting to one boss. This may be more efficient than having three separate bosses pulling R&D, marketing and market research people in different directions.

- If you want to improve your customer satisfaction ratings, you might move customer services from under sales and have them report direct to the CEO.
- If new technologies are the key to future growth, you might want the head of future technologies on the main board.

Step 5: Who will need to collaborate and how?

The next step is to map out the key collaborations that will be essential for you to deliver your strategy. You will need to identify any clusters/departments that need to work together effectively and seamlessly in order to win.

Almost certainly you will need people from different regions and or functions to work closely together across your organization in order to deliver your strategy. For example, marketing will need to work closely with R&D. If you are trying to develop new products for one specific region then R&D will need to work closely with the local managers in that region. So defining who will collaborate and how is a critical stage. The simplest way to identify the collaboration model is to map out all the essential connections between clusters, using a network map like the one in Figure 4.7.

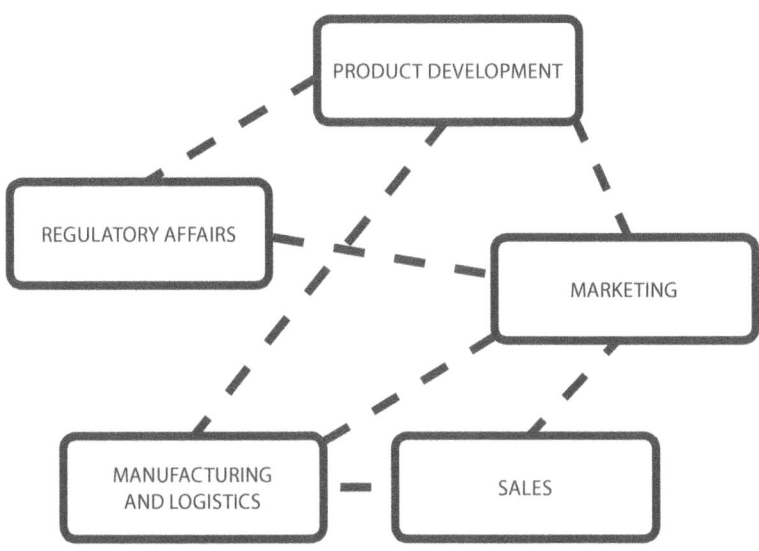

FIGURE 4.7
Network map

In some cases the collaboration model will need to be permanent, in which case you will create a matrix design to facilitate the collaboration. However, make sure that you really do need a matrix for your collaboration model to work. In some cases the collaboration only needs to exist for the duration of a key project. After the project has ended the need for collaboration might reduce.

Step 6: Now create your new organization design

With the output of the previous steps in your hand, you will now have enough information and understanding to map out the first two layers of your organization. You should start with some clear design principles drawn from your value drivers, i.e. if innovation is central, then design part of the structure around this principle, grouping specialists to create new products.

Set targets for layers and spans of control: To define the overall shape of your organization, you should try and set a target for how many layers you want and some guidelines on minimum and maximum spans of control. You can use the ready reckoner in Figure 4.3.

Start at the top: Write down the key 'clusters' (departments/functions/ activities) you will need at the top of your organization in order to deliver your strategy brilliantly. These clusters are the first layer of your organization. Logically the clusters that are most important to achievement of your strategy should report to the CEO. Things that are secondary or supporting functions do not need to report to the CEO regularly. Any clusters that are important, but not central to delivering your strategy, should appear in the second layer of the organization. Remember, the CEO's span of control should be between six and twelve people.

There may be several options, so try and capture them all. To decide between different options, simply answer the question: which option gives me the highest chance of delivering my strategy and why?

Design the matrix/collaboration model: At this point you need to identify the best matrix/collaboration model to make sure things that need to work together are able to do so well. This will be clear from the exercise above, but now you need to decide how you will build these connections into the day-to-day operation of your organization.

Then go to the second layer: Once the top layer is clear, you need to identify the clusters of roles/functions that each top-layer cluster will need in order for that function to create value and deliver on your strategy.

So you should now go through the same process for the next layer, identifying key clusters that will report to each of the departments/functions that are in the first layer of your organization. The top two layers are primarily the responsibility of the CEO and his direct reports, so they should work together on this second layer of the organization.

Keep it lean: In order to ensure the organization is as lean as possible, you should challenge your managers to design their organization to be as efficient as possible in total headcount and cost. People always want more resources than they need. If they currently run a similar department/function, ask them how they would design their function/department if they only had half the number of people available to them. What if you only had one-quarter of them? The aim here is to design the organization with fewer people than you think you need.

Set clear design rules/guidelines: If you are leaving the task of detailed design to the managers who will run each team, then make sure you set very clear guidelines for them on how you want them to design. This will include guidelines on which activities/strategies are most important for them to deliver well, how you want them to collaborate and with whom, and rules on spans of control. Again, these need to be closely connected to the above design principles underpinned by your value drivers.

Then carry on down the layers: You will then move down each layer, one by one, answering the same basic questions for the next level:

- Do we understand our strategy?
- What is this part of the organization currently doing with its time?
- What should it be doing with its time to create value and contribute directly to the achievement of the company strategy?
- How will people need to collaborate within this part of the organization?
- What key skills and capabilities do we need? How do these skills logically cluster together?
- What key roles/functions will we need to have in our part of the organization in order to deliver our strategy?
- What measures and KPIs do we need to keep track of progress?

Step 7: Implement your new organization design
- Develop a clear communication plan to explain your strategy, why the organization design is changing and how you want people to operate.
- Define your values, ways of working and behaviors for successful implementation of your strategy.

- Write clear job descriptions that show how the individual/team creates value and contributes towards the central strategy (see above). Make sure people understand their roles and how other parts of the organization contribute to the success of the business as well.
- Develop RACIs for the most important decisions that will be taken (see above).
- Move the right people into the new organization. A transparent and fair process of capability assessment and role allocation is a common method that can be used here. You are looking for people with the right capabilities to succeed in the new organization so you will likely find yourself with three groups of people coming out of the assessment:
  - Stars: These are the most capable people and they can be utilized to coach the next group.
  - Developers: These people have shown that they have the basics to succeed in the new organization but will need to grow into the roles.
  - Won't make it: These people don't have the capability required to make the new organization a success. You will need to manage their transition to other roles or out of the organization very sensitively.

FIVE KEY POINTS ON ORGANIZATION COMPLEXITY

1. Organization design is about the alignment of structures, processes, roles and responsibilities with the strategy of the business.
2. Complex organizations are confusing for those that work in them, inflexible for those that try to manage them and unpredictable for those that try to improve them.
3. Our research shows that 'levels of management', 'measuring and reporting key performance indicators (KPIs)', 'decision-making processes' and 'clarification of roles and responsibilities' are high-impact sources of organizational complexity.
4. Good organization design is about getting the right people doing the right things, in the right way.
5. Simplifying business organizations requires: a focus on the simple success keys; optimizing layers and spans of control; simplifying decision-making processes (reduce, clarify, standardize) and managing the matrix; clarifying roles and responsibilities; and possibly zero basing.

---

6. From the organization to the strategy

If you have made it this far you have got through our longest chapter! There is lots of stuff here, some which will be more relevant than the rest for you and your management challenges. We know from our research – and from talking to senior executives wrestling with these issues – that the design and operation of the organization is critical to its overall success. Managers in giant firms like Vodafone, Unilever and HSBC are trying to cope with hugely complex organizations, spanning many diverse country markets, cultures and institutional environments. Some have over 300,000 employees (Walmart has over 2 million!) divided into multiple divisions, departments and management layers.

The complexity can be overwhelming. A game of chess does not even get close!

As we said at the start – getting the structure right helps you get the strategy right. Simpler structures and simpler strategies reinforce each other for better performance.

And strategy is what we look at in the next chapter.

For more on how to cope with organization complexity go to: http://www.simplicitypartnership.com/

Chapter 5
How to Simplify: Strategy

COPING WITH COMPLEXITY: STORIES FROM THE FRONT

Can you tell what it is yet? (Show me your strategy)

A common exercise to kick off a strategy workshop with senior managers is to ask participants to do a 'Show It' exercise. The idea is to demonstrate how a complex idea can more easily be explained using pictures and images, rather than words.

To make this exercise work we need a subject/topic that everyone knows well. Since we are dealing with the top leaders the topic is obvious – create a picture, diagram or images to explain your company strategy to your people.

What we discover (every time we do this exercise) is not that people are poor at using pictures to tell a story; we know that, which is why we do the exercise. The surprise is that the majority of these very senior execs do not fully understand their own company strategy well enough to simply draw it.

This demonstrates one (or both) of two important common problems with corporate strategies: (1) they are not clear and focused, even for those at the top; and (2) they are not easy to communicate simply, distinctly and quickly.

1. Strategy causes complexity

One of the most surprising findings in our research is that strategic complexity drivers are seen by managers as the second biggest source of all harmful complexity in business (after the external sources).

These survey findings do not just reflect the fact that the world is a complex place and guiding a large firm through this complexity is difficult to do. Managers' responses said more than this: they said the *strategy itself* can be a major source of complexity. This is ironic, given that the role of strategy

> Precisely 50% of the managers in our complexity survey are juggling five or more strategic initiatives at any one time. 12% are trying to cope with 16 or more!

is to provide clear and consistent guidance on what a company needs to do in order to win. Large numbers of people are supposed to be inspired and directed by the strategy you have developed, but our study suggests that in many big companies they are not. They are confused by it (and part of the problem is that 'it' is usually 'them' – lots of strategic initiatives, not one clear strategy).

On top of this, managers tell us that the way that strategies are developed and implemented, and the decision-making processes and practices themselves, are a major source of costly complexity.

Obviously strategic decision-making is not easy. It involves understanding external threats and opportunities that are relevant to the performance, or even survival, of the firm and developing plans to respond to them (see 'What is strategy?' below). Clearly the Board, the CEO and the senior management of a firm have a responsibility for strategy. But strategic decision-making takes place at all levels of the business. Everyone in a firm makes decisions about how and where to allocate their time and resources. This adds to the complexity of the business.

What is strategy?

Strategy is concerned with the direction and scope of an organization over the long term.

Its aim is to achieve advantage for the organization through its configuration of resources and capabilities within a competitive environment.

To be successful it must continually meet the changing needs of markets and the expectations of stakeholders.

Viable strategies need to answer the following questions:

- What are the aims, values and expectations of those who have power in and around the business (stakeholders)?
- Where is the business trying to get to in the long term (direction)?
- Which products and services should a business make and which should it buy (boundaries)?
- Where and how do these products and services add value?
- Which markets should a business compete in and what kinds of activities are involved in such markets (markets, scope)?
- How can the business perform better than the competition in those markets (advantage)?
- What resources (assets, finance) and capabilities (expertise, knowledge, relationships) are required in order to be able to compete?

- What external factors affect the businesses' ability to compete (environment)?

So let's clarify what we mean – and what we want to focus on here. This chapter of our book is not going to tell you what your strategy should be. That is your job. We are going to tell how strategy is a major source of complexity that can damage your performance. Then we are going describe some of the ways in which you can help simplify and clarify strategy in your business.

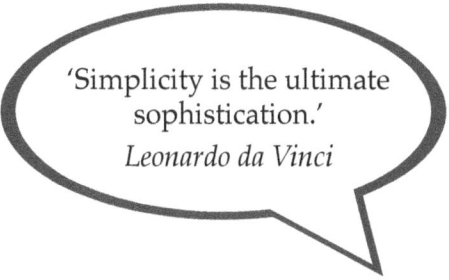

'Simplicity is the ultimate sophistication.'
Leonardo da Vinci

What are the causes of strategic complexity?
Our research (see below) reveals four major problems with strategy in modern businesses that give rise to excessive complexity:

1. Too many changes in strategy (shifting goalposts)
2. Too many strategies (initiative overload)
3. Unclear strategy (confused priorities)
4. An overly complex strategic planning process

All four are linked, and firms normally suffer from more than one and often all four together.

There can be many contributing factors, including:

- No clarity on what customers value in your target markets
- Lack of a clear vision of what you want to achieve
- Too many objectives or having the wrong objectives
- Lack of ownership and commitment by leadership team
- Strategy not communicated to/understood clearly by those who must implement it
- Lack of integration and alignment among functions, business units or geographies
- Personal goals and incentives not linked to strategy and goals

As you can see, these – and many more examples – link our four main complexity problems and the questions in the 'What is strategy?'section above.

Multiple strategic initiatives and frequent changes in strategy are both major complicating factors in firms. These can result in managers being unclear about what the strategy is or how to prioritize across many different initiatives. This means that they work hard doing the wrong things, don't deliver on time and find it difficult to communicate the strategy to others. Equally, if there are too many strategic projects, your managers will disperse their efforts too thinly and will not deliver the most important projects as quickly as they would if things were more focused.

SENIOR MANAGEMENT STRETCH
Time of leaders tied up in planning, debate over priorities, etc.

STAFF AIMLESSNESS
Failure to set clear direction or attempting too many strategic initiatives means staff are unable to effectively prioritize work.

POOR DELIVERY
Too many priorities or lack of strong communication mean manager spreads resources too thinly or allocates them to the wrong areas.

ANALYSIS-PARALYSIS
Everything is measured and reported on, as people don't know what the most important drivers of success are.

POOR MORALE AND ENGAGEMENT
People and departments are pulling in different directions, which frustrates.

SLAVES TO PROCESS
In the absence of clear priorities or direction, staff will revert to standard processes, stifling pace and innovation.

FUNCTION/UNIT DRIFT
Unclear or overly complex strategy means different parts of large businesses are often marching to different drums.

CUSTOMER CONFUSION
Customers and suppliers unclear about what you stand for and what differentiates you from competitors.

CHANGE STAGNATION
Staff become immune to changes in strategy, even when these are merited by market forces.

FIGURE 5.1
What are the symptoms of overly complex strategy?

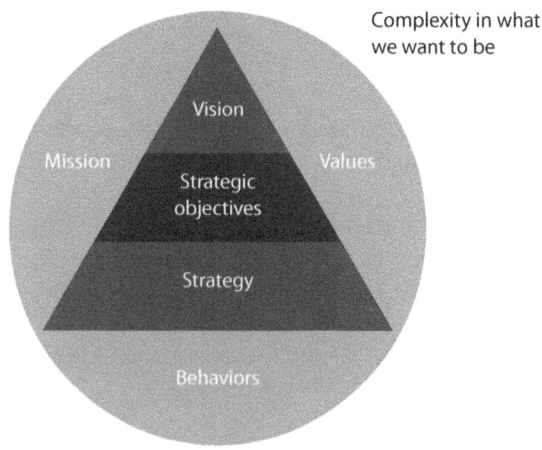

Complexity in what
we want to be

Complexity in our
objectives, or what we
must achieve to get there

Complexity in core strategy, or how we will
achieve objectives, which can also cause:
• Complexity in how we translate strategy into
  operational plans and budgets
• Complexity in how we measure and report on
  progress against the strategy

FIGURE 5.2
Where will strategic complexity hide?

Part of the problem is the strategic planning process itself. This was seen in our survey (see below) as being too long and complicated in many companies. This process often ties up many hours of senior management time each year, but can often fail to provide the strategic focus and clarity needed.

Our research suggests that all of these strategic complexity problems are common in modern business and that they all have a major impact on success. Finding true strategic simplicity should be a key objective of any leader who wants to eradicate and prevent harmful complexity. When you tell people what your strategy is, do they understand it immediately or does it require a lot of explanation or justification? If the latter, then either it's not a good strategy or it's not being communicated simply.

2. What does our research show?

In our introduction (Chapter 1), we gave an overview of the findings of our survey of 600 executives in 300 European firms of over 5000 employees. Here we are going to look at some of the findings that relate to strategy. This source of harmful complexity came second, after 'external' sources, but ahead of all the other internal complexity sources (people, processes, organization design, products and services).

What did experienced managers tell us were the sources of complexity that had the highest impact on their personal productivity?

As Table 5.1 shows, 'changes in company core strategy', 'the core business strategy itself' and 'the annual budgeting process' are the highest ranked sources. In fact these all lie in the top ten of our overall survey, when we exclude 'external' complexity sources. The survey includes over 100 complexity sources across the five internal complexity dimensions: people, processes, products and services, organization design and strategy.

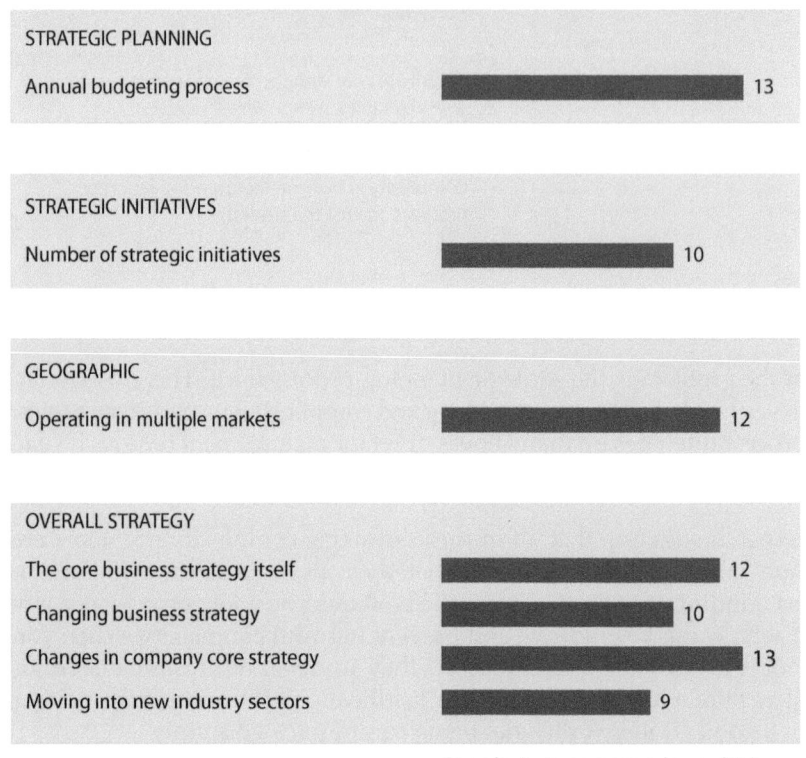

STRATEGIC PLANNING

Annual budgeting process   13

STRATEGIC INITIATIVES

Number of strategic initiatives   10

GEOGRAPHIC

Operating in multiple markets   12

OVERALL STRATEGY

The core business strategy itself   12

Changing business strategy   10

Changes in company core strategy   13

Moving into new industry sectors   9

Complexity impact score: low to high

TABLE 5.1
The impact of strategy-related sources of complexity on the business
Note: this is a relative measure that combines the frequency with which this source of complexity was cited by managers in our survey and their rating of the impact it has on performance.

Also damaging, according to respondents, are 'the number of strategic initiatives', which comes under the category of internal strategic management and clarifying priorities. 'Operating in multiple markets' (international strategy), 'launching new products/services' (innovation strategy) and 'moving into new industry sectors' (competitor and market strategy) on the other hand lie at the interface between the firm and its competitive environment. Decision-making across these three complexity areas is about aligning the organization in response to external threats and opportunities.

So, we can connect our survey responses – what experienced managers tell us are major sources of high-impact complexity – to the original four causes of strategy complexity listed at the start of this chapter: (1) too many changes in strategy (shifting goalposts); (2) too many strategies (initiative overload); (3) unclear strategy (confused priorities); and (4) an overly complex strategic planning process.

These sources of costly complexity keep good managers awake at night.

Now the key question is what can you do about it?

> 75% of firms in our survey have four or more stages in their capital expenditure sign-off process. For 11% there are over 10 stages – and for 7% of firms over 15 stages!

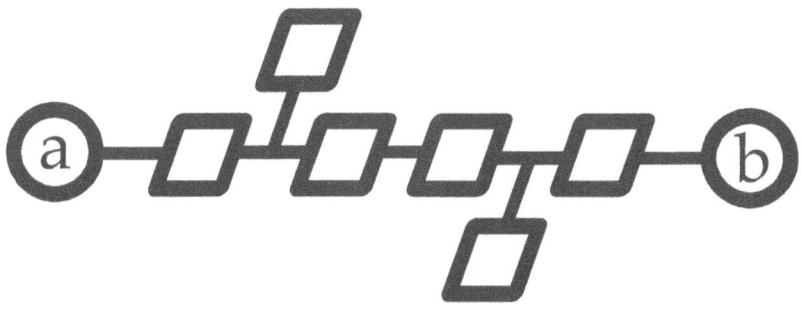

IBM: TURNING A SINKING SHIP AROUND

What was the complexity problem?

In 1993, IBM posted a loss of $8bn: at the time, the largest shortfall recorded in the history of corporate America. Its enterprise was sprawled across countless industries and business areas – IBM was literally spreading itself too thinly.

How did the power of simplicity help?

These financial woes led the board to oust their CEO – after all, a fish rots from the head. An outsider with fresh perspective, Louis V. Gerstner, Jr., was trusted with the task of nursing the ailing company back to health.

Gerstner decided to focus on high-margin opportunities (namely, IBM's global services businesses). This meant mercilessly pruning back anything with a lower margin, such as DRAM, IBM Network, printers and hard drives. Furthermore, Gerstner broke IBM's longstanding no-layoff policy, letting go 85,000 employees in three years and thereby cutting $7bn in costs.

Under Gerstner's guidance, the remaining businesses were brought closer together, allowing IBMers to coordinate their activities more easily. This also let them to devise a strategy to support their core products and services. Due to that, more staff are now able to be outward-focused.

IBM's acquisition of the consultancy division of PricewaterhouseCoopers in 2002 is proof of a maintained focus and reinforces their position as the biggest provider of IT services.

What was the impact?

The new focused and simplified strategy helped IBM to return to profitability. Bringing shared services in-house has allowed the firm to lower costs by about 25 per cent over the past five years. It also ensures that nine out of ten employees now focus on value-adding activities.

---

3. Simply add value: do the right things the right way

As we said in Chapter 1, the role of work is to create value. Each day when we go to work we should focus only on activities that truly create value for our organization.

We should ask ourselves two key questions:

- The right things: Are we doing the right things? That is, are we spending our time and the firm's resources on activities that create value?
- In the right way: Are we doing these things in the right way? That is, are we being efficient with the methods, processes and organizations we have designed to get these right things done?

Anything that does not create value, or creates it in a convoluted or inefficient way (adding more costs than value), needs to be stopped.

This is a good 'acid test' of strategy. If you or others do not know what the 'right things are' then this is a sure sign that your organization is suffering from one or more of the four major strategy-related complexity problems described above.

Strategy acts as a simple guide to show people what needs to be done for your organization to add value. So if your strategy is wrong, unclear or poorly communicated, you will have a team of busy fools, actively and energetically filling up their days, doing the wrongs things in the wrong way.

Strategy drives product portfolio, organization and process design decisions

Strategic complexity can have a cascade effect, giving rise to complexity problems elsewhere in the business. If your strategy is too complex then inevitably your organization will be too complex, your processes will become too complex and you will probably have too many markets, customers, products and services to look after.

If we consider the strategic planning process, the cascading effect happens in two directions, affecting what we can call 'strategy-input' processes and 'strategy-output' processes. On the input side we have the budget planning and reporting machinery of the firm. In large firms this involves a massive exercise in information and data generation and transmission, much of it going upwards for senior management monitoring, control and decision-making. On the output side we have monthly, quarterly, annual and long-term targets, goals, projects, expectations, missions and visions. As implied, this machinery does much more than providing an input into strategic decision-making, but when asked, managers are often unsure what large parts of it are for.

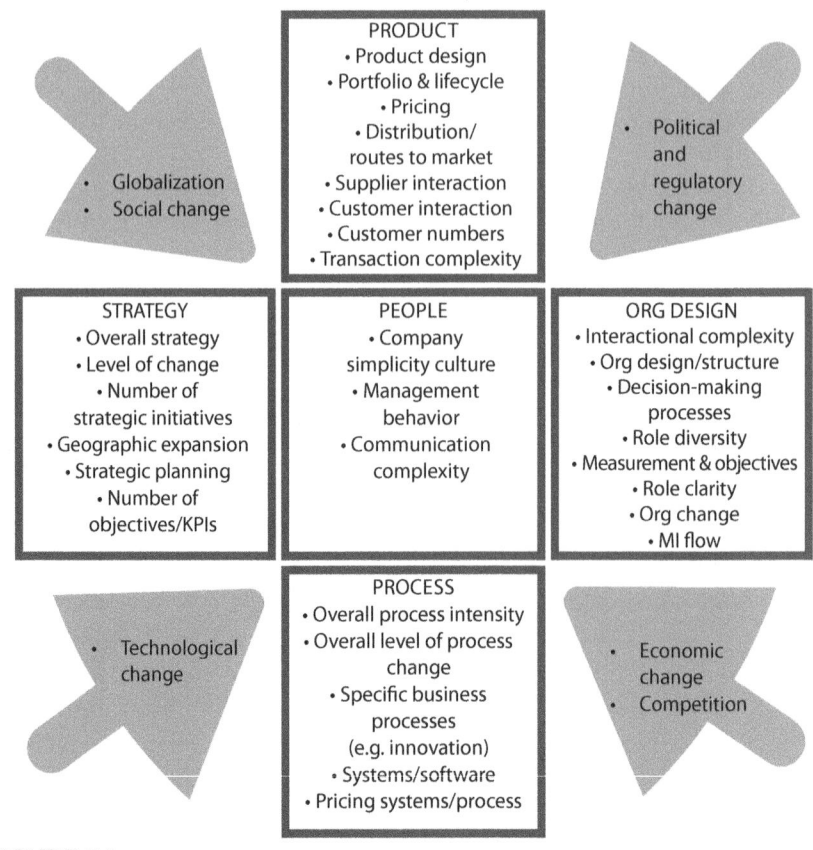

FIGURE 5.3
The complexity cross

When we originally created the complexity cross we put strategy in the middle box, as it was clear to us that a messed up strategy would mess up everything else as well. We ended up putting people in the middle, as obviously it is the people who create the strategies that confuse everything else!

> 'Golf is deceptively simple
> and endlessly complicated.'
> *Attributed to Arnold Palmer*

But the point still remains, if your strategy is wrong, constantly changing or poorly communicated, people will spend their time on the wrong things, but they will also create the wrong organization design, the wrong types of products and the wrong processes, develop the wrong skills and behave in the wrong way. So if these aspects of your company are too complicated, the chances are it all started with a complex, poorly communicated or changing strategy.

Strategy as simple rules

Managers are faced with hundreds of opportunities every week. Strategy is about picking the right one or two to invest time and money (theirs and often other people's) into. This applies at the highest level, when CEOs are considering the trade-offs between acquiring competitors, entering new markets or investing in R&D joint ventures with major partners. But it also applies further down the business, when managers are choosing one IT system over another, selecting new recruits, allocating budgets to projects or spending time supporting one customer over another. The very business of business is tied up with strategic trade-offs.

We argue that you should not respond to a complicated world with elaborate strategies; you need to develop a small number of simple rules (see below for how to do this). This contrasts with traditional schools of thought in strategy which advocate market positioning and/or resource leveraging as the foundations of good strategy. We would argue these may be a stable foundation for strategy in stable markets and a predictable world. Turbulence and complexity outside require simple rules inside.

Here are three examples ...

T-shirt makers have a major strategic dilemma over which designs of shirts to manufacture. Pick a good design that everyone wants and you gain huge economies of scale in production, distribution and marketing; if you don't, you will lose money. This is one version of the common strategic problem of standardization versus customization. Doing lots of different things costs more. It adds coordination costs and complexity costs. Spreadshirt (www.spreadshirt. co.uk) cut through this complexity using 'crowdsourcing' – an open-innovation approach. Rather than 'internalizing' the problem – trying to second-guess customer demand with an in-house market research team – Spreadshirt run a design competition ('laFraise' – now Europe's largest). Each week designers from all over the world put forward their latest creations and the Spreadshirt community (inside and outside the firm) votes for the best. Winners get prizes as well as their designs printed and sold globally. The firm, just 300 people with revenues of $19m, is effectively a design 'broker' and marketing operation and outsources manufacturing, distribution and much of the rest.

At the other end of the spectrum, 3M is a multinational firm with over 75,000 employees producing over 55,000 products. It is undoubtedly big and complex yet, despite a recessionary environment, sales have increased by 11 per cent and margins increased by 23 per cent. How? Well, we know that it's famous for product innovation (and for the story of the yellow sticky-notes). 3M's simple strategic rule is to require divisions to continually generate 30 per cent of their revenues from new products introduced in the past five years. This has created a range of processes and behaviors clearly targeting this single measure. These innovation-generating routines have prepared the company particularly well for emerging markets, where it is enjoying success ahead of more sluggish rivals.

Insurance companies trying to be customer-led are confused about what customers value. Is it price, quality and reliability, reputation and trustworthiness? A well-known online insurance firm cut through this complexity to focus on *speed* as its key differentiator in the market place. This turned out to be great for simple branding ('we will turnaround an insurance quote in two days, maximum!') but even more effective for clarifying its internal strategy, streamlining delivery processes and focusing everyone's efforts inside the firm. Customers knew what they were about – but so did employees.

Some examples of simple rules …

Some of the simplest and most effective rules are all around us, on the roads and highways we use every day. Without a line down the center of the road and a simple understanding among all drivers to keep to one side of this line, chaos would ensue. Stop signs, roundabouts (one of the most effective simplifying devices ever invented!), pedestrian crossings and so on: relatively few simple rules give order to potentially costly complexity.

Here are some for businesses.

Borderline rules: Where, in terms of our products, services, markets, customers, do we compete? And where do we not compete? These rules specify which kinds of opportunities managers should focus on and which are outside the scope of the business. They also help with the 'make versus buy' questions: what should we be doing and what should we leave to the market (i.e. other firms).

Priority rules: How do we judge which opportunities are more important than others in terms of investing our time and resources into exploring, developing or completing particular initiatives? These rules help us rank our opportunities and place limits and target measures (like ROI – return on investment, or NPV – net present value, to assess investments) to distinguish between good and bad ones.

Stop rules: How do we know when to stop doing things that are costing us more than they are benefitting us, our customers or our stakeholders? These rules, again often using performance measures (like minimum profitability), help us to close down operations and stop activities that are costing us more than they are worth.

These kinds of questions are at the heart of some of the analytical frameworks that management and business consultants use, from the growth-share matrix ('Boston Box') to net-present-value (NPV) accounting. Our view is that thinking in terms of simplifying rules is equally, if not more, useful.

Rules also tend to be the product of common sense and experience rather than clever thinking. But they can also become a source of damaging complexity in their own right. If they are too broad or vague, they do not clarify the business strategy. If they become out of date, they provide the wrong guidance and/or can be based around the wrong measures. If they multiply, they can overwhelm managers or constrict their initiative with controls and bureaucracy. Some scholars have even suggested that having more than ten rules becomes problematic.

INTERCONTINENTAL HOTELS: REFOCUSING ON CORE STRENGTHS

What was the complexity problem?

Intercontinental Hotels had made a strategic choice to focus on running hotels as a service provider, rather than owning the real estate and running the hotels as it used to. But its operational strategy was still one of a hotel owner, leading to overly complicated delivery, sourcing processes and decisions.

How did the power of simplicity help?

They listed all their core processes and activities in each function across the organization so they could see everything that each function was trying to do. Processes were then classified by the nature of the activity (transactional, knowledge-based, etc.), how well they needed to perform the activity and how important it was to the delivery of Intercontinental's strategic objective of being the best hotel services provider. Many of the processes the company was running turned out to be legacy activities that related to its days as an owner and operator of hotels, but were not relevant to its new strategy.

This allowed the company to eliminate, centralize or outsource many activities which were non-core, leaving its people free to focus on the most value-adding activities/processes. The operational strategy was re-shaped and simplified around the remaining core activities.

What was the impact?
- Increased staff focus on what most drives value in the organization.
- Cost savings from eliminating non-core activities or delivering them differently.

4. How to reduce strategic complexity

How can you make strategy simpler in big companies?

Thanks to business gurus and consultancies the simple concept of strategy has become a complex process, the output of which is often impenetrably difficult for people lower down the organization to understand or act upon. So one way to fight this is to think of and develop strategy in more human and intuitive ways. Strategy is simply about guiding large numbers of people to do the things you need them to do, without having to explain in excruciating detail what it is that you want each individual to do.

Here are some simple ways to make the creation and output of strategy much simpler ...

Simplify your annual strategy, planning and budgeting process
The Global Simplicity Index identified that the process of developing/
reviewing strategy and setting annual plans (often both go together) was
in itself very complex and time-consuming. Some of the respondents in our
study reported that they spend 16 weeks of the year (yes, about one-third
of their year!) preparing the strategy and plans for next year. This certainly
reflects our own observations where the very process of creating strategies
and plans becomes a major internally focused industry. Is this really how
we want our leaders and managers to spend their time?

In fact, as outlined in Chapter 1, we find strong evidence that managers
in weaker-performing firms spend far too much time battling internal
complexity and too little time focused on real strategic threats and
opportunities from their external competitive environment. Elaborate
planning processes, lengthy budget cycles and loads of irrelevant emails
distract their attention from the real strategy drivers – such as changes in
customer needs, technological opportunities or new competitors.

> Budget planning takes four or more
> weeks of the year for 61% of firms
> we surveyed; over 10 weeks for 15%
> and a staggering 16 weeks or
> longer for 10%!

If the process is encouraging the right thought processes and mind-sets
for successful strategy then it is not wrong. The problem is that creating
complex processes makes the brain lazy, because managers will focus on
compliance with the process, believing that the answer will automatically
pop out at the end if they follow the steps or complete the templates that
have been laid down. This is never true in knowledge-based processes,
so in effect over-processing some things creates low-quality outcomes. In
other words, brains solve problems, not processes. Your strategy should
encourage a very strong focus on external factors, not internal activities
and bureaucracy.

Examples of external factors that your strategy and planning process
should emphasize are:

- anticipating customer needs and trends in more detail;
- identifying growth markets/segments;
- understanding, anticipating and neutralizing competitor moves;

- identifying emerging technologies; and
- working out how to use your competencies/skills to win in the market.

So we urge all CEOs and CFOs to revisit the processes they use for strategy, planning and budgeting to make sure they are short and simple and that they encourage the right kind of strategic thinking in your business.

Strategy as answers to simple questions

As described above, we think organizations need to clarify their strategies and simplify their strategic decision-making processes by developing some simple rules. Another way of looking at this is to think of strategy as no more than answers to some very simple questions. This can make strategy creation and communication much simpler.

The following questions are linked to our earlier definition of strategy.

Mission: What's our purpose? What are we trying to achieve?

Situation analysis: Where are we now in terms of performance, strengths, major issues and major opportunities (often captured as a SWOT – strengths, weaknesses, opportunities and threats – matrix)?

Vision: Where do we want to be?

Values and behaviors: What strongly held values/beliefs do we have? What are the winning behaviors we will need to exhibit?

Where are we going to compete? Which segments, markets, products, customers, geographies provide us with the greatest opportunity to achieve our ambitions? And ... which of these are the 'must win' battles that we will focus our efforts on most aggressively?

The choice of where you fight will, in turn, be informed by a variety of questions:

- Core competencies: What are we great at? What are we poor at? What could we be great at? Also called differentiators (or your 'unique selling proposition'), these might be assets or capabilities that competitors find difficult to steal, imitate, develop quickly or buy from somewhere.
- Market attractiveness: Which markets/segments/customers are most attractive to compete for today? How will this change in the future?

WHERE SHOULD WE PLAY?
Which markets, customers and products and services
will we focus on to achieve our goals?

HOW WILL WE WIN?
How will we win in our chosen focus areas?

FIGURE 5.4
Where to play and how to win?

How will we win? Now that we have decided on which battles to fight, we then need to identify what we will need to do in order to win in each of these markets.

- How do we best use our core competencies/strengths to win each battle? Do we need to address any weaknesses to win each battle?
- Barriers to success: what's stopping us winning in our chosen areas?
- Who will be our key competitors in these chosen battle fields? What are their strengths and weaknesses? How do we beat them?
- What are the key success factors for winning in each of these chosen battle fields? How can we ensure we are organized, skilled and resourced to outperform competitors and customer expectations on each of these key success factors?

Simple strategy tools

Using some simple strategy tools/frameworks can help you answer these simple strategy questions quite quickly. These are familiar or even 'classic' strategy tools. Some people might feel a bit ashamed to use these as they are simple, but in our view they are not simplistic. They are still around after all these years because they work!

Situation analysis tools

- **PEST:** a classic framework and often used alongside SWOT (below) for analyzing potential country markets as investment propositions. This can be a simple list of the current and likely future political, economic, social and technological characteristics of a particular country market, used to compare it with other markets. This helps managers to judge relative costs, risks and market rewards and select investment locations. (Add Legal and Environment to get 'PESTLE' if you prefer.)

- **SWOT:** the classic and still the best way to summarize your current situation and where you could/should go next. This can be a simple list of your strengths and weaknesses vis-à-vis competitors, coupled with an assessment of strategic opportunities and threats associated with changes in the competitive environment, from new technologies to regulatory changes that allow easier access to key markets. More sophisticated SWOTs can employ data and in-depth analysis to understand current and potential future assets and capabilities compared to competitors and in relation to different investment opportunities.

Visioning tool

This tool asks you to imagine what success would look like and feel like to you and to your colleagues, your customers and other stakeholders (Figure 5.5). The results of this brainstorming are used to create a compelling vision of success for your company.

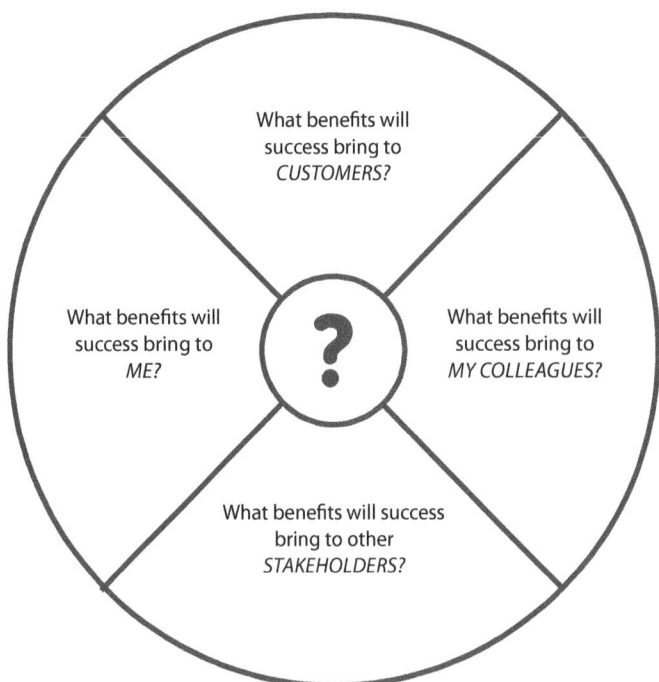

FIGURE 5.5
Visioning success

'Where are we going to compete' tools
- **Attractiveness/Strength Tool:** This looks at the attractiveness of different markets/segments/customers and your company's strengths in each of these markets/segments/customers. You can then use the grid to decide which strategies and priorities to adopt. The most famous version – the original – is the BCG Grid (or the 'Boston Box'; see Figure 5.6), also known as the growth-share matrix, but this model has evolved to consider more factors than just market share and market attractiveness and to think about the current situation and future potential.
- **Relative Product/Brand Differentiation Tool:** This looks at how strongly differentiated your products are and how attractive the market is. Investing more in highly differentiated products that compete in attractive markets is one of the most profitable strategies you can employ.

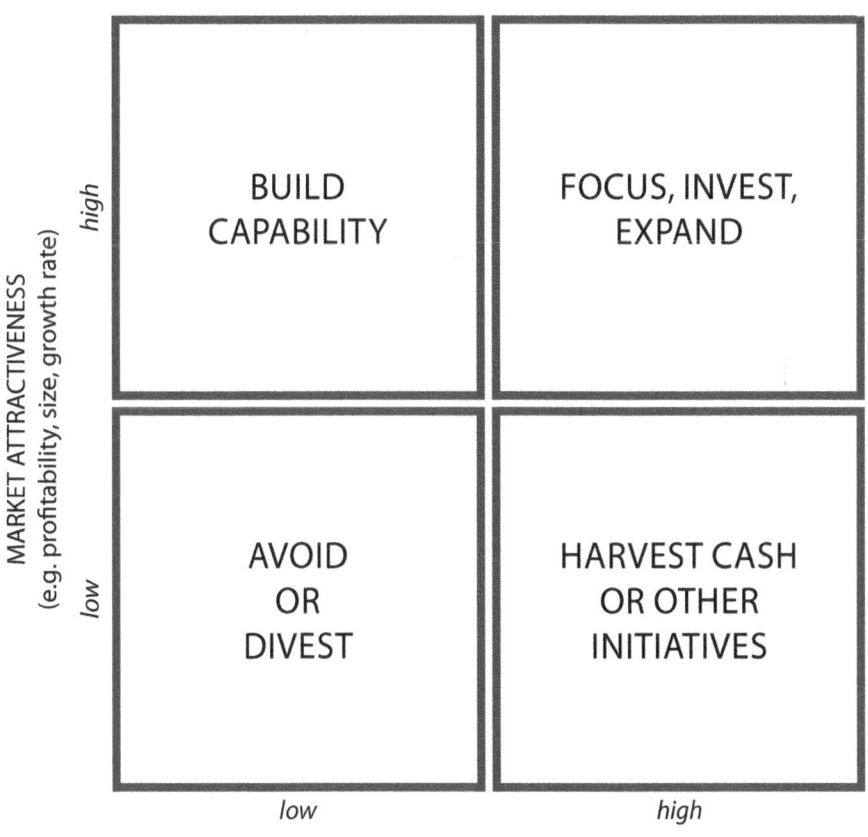

FIGURE 5.6
The BCG grid

- **Customer segmentation:** Rather than looking at your customers as one homogeneous mass, segmentation divides customers up into sub-groups with distinctly different needs/characteristics from other sub-groups. There are many different ways to do this. The point is you should never think of your customers as one group. This allows you to think about the trade-offs between standardization and customization, as mentioned earlier in this chapter. It also provides a useful extension of product portfolio analysis.
- **Innovation Portfolio Tool:** This tool (Figure 5.7) explores the relative benefits/risks of focusing on current products/services versus developing innovative new products/services. New markets are often more risky and are hard to develop new products in (because you know them less well); yet they offer big growth opportunities, as sales cannibalization is low. These opportunities, need to be balanced against the opportunity for getting more out of your existing products and markets. Having all your innovation in high risk categories is dangerous, so you should have a spread of innovation opportunities across this grid (Figure 5.7).

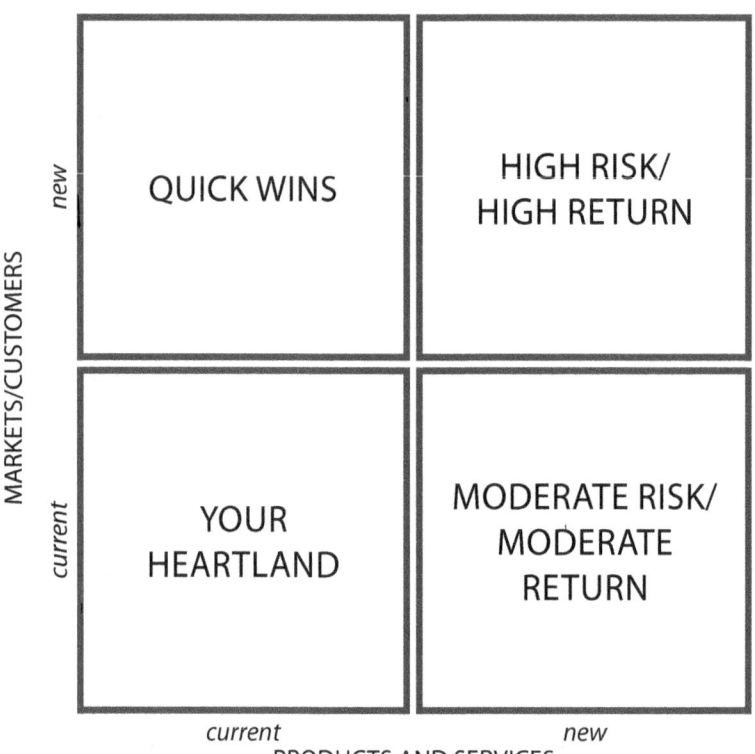

FIGURE 5.7
Innovation portfolio tool

GLOBAL TECHNOLOGY COMPANY: R&D STRATEGY OVERHAUL

What was the complexity problem?
The overall R&D strategy of this global technology giant lacked clarity and focus and, as result, there were over 60 global innovation projects, many of which were off-strategy, duplicative or inter-dependent.

How did the power of simplicity help?
The company created a new set of harsher selection criteria tailored to kill projects that couldn't prove a high market potential and chance of success.

Historically money had been shared thinly across lots of projects, so as not to leave any unfunded. This time, 'reverse budgeting' was used, where each project team calculated the resources needed to maximize the chance of success. Project funding was then allocated to ensure success on the highest potential project first, then the next project was given all the funding it needed and so on until no more budget was left. Only seven projects got full funding; the remaining 53 were shelved for later or killed off.

Projects were de-linked, and then fully resourced so that no project team was dependent on a team in another function or location for the success of their projects.

All of the core innovation processes were streamlined, so that projects could move much faster through each stage of senior management approval, with fewer steps and fewer people involved in the major decisions.

The whole company was then reorganized around key roles to make sure these seven projects made it to market and were successful when they got there.

Over 20 of the 53 waitlisted projects were outsourced to partner companies. Of these, nine have since come to market as joint ventures.

What was the impact?
- All seven projects made it to market, ahead of (or in line with) plan.
- Over the past five years, revenue growth has increased by an average of 14 per cent each year and profit by an average of 17 per cent.

- **Stop/Start/Continue Tool:** Used less often and yet quite powerful, this asks the questions 'in order to be successful, what do we need to stop doing? What do we need to start doing? What do we need to continue doing well?' (Figure 5.8).

STOP/START/CONTINUE

What do we need to **STOP** doing?	• Investment in industrial components business in mature markets • Discounting to buy volume in emerging markets
What do we need to **START** doing?	• Building marketing and sales capability in Asia • Embedding simplicity as a core way of working
What do we need to **CONTINUE** doing?	• Investing in new, sustainable and eco-friendly technologies

FIGURE 5.8
Stop/Start/Continue Tool

WE NEED TO MOVE FROM > TO

FROM focusing on low-margin high-volume models	**TO** focusing on innovation on premium segments
FROM doing everything ourselves; suspicion of partnership as a model	**TO** using external technology suppliers to reduce cost/risk and speed up development of new technology
FROM large number of small innovation projects	**TO** align and focus the whole company on three major innovations every year

FIGURE 5.9
From/To Tool

Values and behaviors tool
- **From/To Tool:** This tool helps you to think about your people, values, behaviors and culture and asks where you are now and where you need to be in the future, e.g. we need to move from being internally focused to being externally focused, or we need to move from being risk averse to being risk aware (Figure 5.9).

'How will we win' check list
This check list gives some of the many questions which might help you to identify different ways to win in the markets/segments you have decided to compete in.

How do I simply win? Some ideas on how you can win in your chosen markets: Here are some different ways that you can potentially win the battle for growth in your market:

- Identify sectors of the market that are growing fast, understand why they are growing and make sure your product/service is able to best exploit this growth area.
- Identify the unique brand or business strengths that you have relative to your competitors. Relentlessly exploit your strengths.
- Identify key weaknesses of your competitors that you can address/ improve on with your product/service. Mercilessly exploit their weaknesses.
- Identify a segment of the market with unmet needs that you can address better or more quickly than the competition.
- Identify ways you can improve your product or service to outflank your competitors, raising the stakes and making them less relevant, or making them appear lower in quality.
- Introduce new technology that makes your product/brand seem superior to those of your competitors.
- Invest more heavily in marketing and sales, innovation, quality etc.
- Improve the price value equation.
- Identify new consumer trends, habits or behaviors that you can take advantage of.
- Change customer behaviors to embrace your product/brand.
- Identify an insight that your competitors have not identified. This could be an insight about the category, your brand, customers or your competitors.
- Reposition your product to be more relevant to your customers than the competition.
- Identify new ways to differentiate your product/service. Being different does not mean you are better than the competition, but standing out more in your market will always give you a competitive advantage.
- In some cases your focus itself can become a strategic advantage; in other words, by focusing on a different sort of person or geography you can differentiate yourself.

Our experience working with firms across many kinds of industry also shows that it is often the conversation that happens around these frameworks that adds most value. Individual managers are already coping with more information than they can deal with, trying to keep up with rapidly changing competitive environments as well as internal organizational turmoil. When groups of managers with different areas of experience and knowledge, from different departments and often from different cultural backgrounds come together to make strategic decisions, complexity is multiplied!

The above tools help groups of managers build a simple consensus about strategic strengths and weaknesses and the best way forward from a complex range of options and possibilities. They each provide simple rules for thinking, discussing and deciding.

5. Strategy as a list of simple success keys

Strategy is really about working out what is most important … and then tirelessly focusing on a few very important things. Less important things can be ignored or deferred to a later date.

Another simple way of looking at strategy is to see it as a prioritized To Do list for your business. A friend and colleague of ours is a high powered working mother with two young kids and a husband with a senior role that means he travels a lot. The whole family was moving to Asia, and the complexity of doing her current job to her very high standards, moving house, finding new schools, dealing with the bureaucracy etc. was very challenging. 'How on earth do you manage that?' I asked. 'Well,' she said, 'really it's just a list, isn't it? I work out what really needs to be done, prioritize, and then I work through the list.'

So an alternative way to create and/or communicate your strategy is to develop a list of the most important 'Simple Success Keys' for your business or department (Figure 5.10). It is easier to communicate a list of ten projects than a more cerebral or esoteric strategy statement. If people can see the ten key things that the company needs to do well in order to win, they will quickly start to work out how they can contribute.

Once you know what the Ten Simple Success Keys are for your business, it should be easy to organize yourself to deliver them.

Here's how it's done …
Work through each of these questions to identify Success Keys under each heading – add more or remove the ones you think are less relevant for your business:

- **Key markets/segments:** Which current markets or market segments are most important? Which new markets or segments will you need to enter in order to be successful?

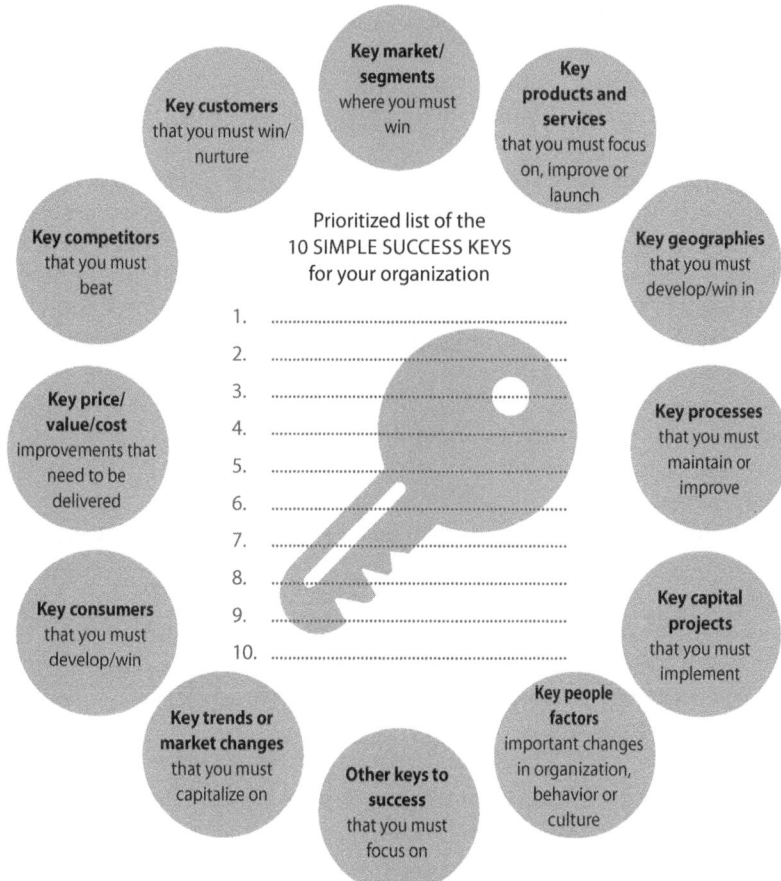

FIGURE 5.10
Identify your ten simple success keys

- **Key customers:** Which current customers do you most need to look after? Which new customers would you like to acquire?
- **Key products/services:** Which current products/services offer greatest prospect for profit and/or growth? Which products/services need to be improved? Which new product/service innovations do you need to focus on?
- **Key trends/market changes:** Are there any major changes in the dynamics of your market that you must exploit or defend your company against?
- **Key competitors:** Which existing competitors do you need to most need to win against? Which new competitors will enter the market and how will you compete and win against them?
- **Key price/value/cost improvements:** In which areas do you most need to defend the value/price of your product versus your competitors?

What are the major cost saving opportunities? How can you improve value for your customers?

- **Key consumers:** Which consumer behaviors do you need to encourage/change? Which new consumers do you need to acquire and develop?
- **Key geographies:** Which countries/regions offer the greatest prospects for profit and/or growth? Which geographies need to be strengthen or exited? Which new geographies do you need to enter?
- **Key processes:** Which business processes are most important for the health/smooth running of your business? Which processes need improvement or simplifying? Do you need some new processes to ensure your future success?
- **Key capital projects:** Which capital projects need to be implemented/managed well? Which new capital projects could have a big impact on your future success?
- **Key people factors:** Which areas of your organization design most need to be nurtured or improved? Do you need to redesign your organization to deliver your strategy? Which key individuals do you need to look after/manage? What key skills do you need to develop/improve? Which key management behaviors do you need to encourage/improve?
- **Other keys to success:** Which other projects, initiatives or strategies will be essential to your success in the future?

Now you have a long list, you will need to prioritize the list so you end up with Ten Simple Success Keys for your company.

The Ranking Tool is the simplest way to do this. First agree on the five (maximum) criteria that you will use to decide on the importance of each Success Key you have listed. For example:

- Importance to health of current business
- Future growth/profit potential
- Likelihood of delivering the project on budget/on time

If necessary or helpful, collect data, inputs or measures for each of the selection criteria for each of the projects. Then rank each project as either high (3 points), medium (2 points) or low (1 point).

Or use a simple Pareto Analysis to identify which 20 per cent from the full list of Success Keys will help you to achieve 80 per cent of your objectives/goals.

6. How can you communicate strategy better in big organizations?

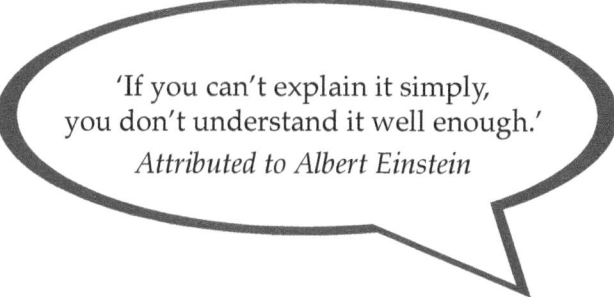

'If you can't explain it simply,
you don't understand it well enough.'
Attributed to Albert Einstein

A good strategy is useless if it is not well understood by the whole organization, because the whole point of strategy is that it provides direction for thousands of people, acting as a guiding light or filter to direct people to the type of decisions/actions you want them to take on a day-to-day basis. It follows that if people don't understand your strategy then they will run fast in the wrong direction (or just sit and do nothing).

Our research shows that in many companies the majority of people do not actually understand their company strategy well enough, and this is supported by other evidence. Effectory are one of the biggest companies specializing in employee surveys. Their summarized results from over 300,000 employee surveys showed that less than 50 per cent of employees believed their leaders were effectively communicating or promoting the company strategy and values of the company. As a result, 54 per cent of employees did not understand the basics of the strategy they are supposed to be following. In some companies less than 20 per cent of employees understood the company strategy.

To us this seems like insanity: we spend millions of dollars in management time and consultancy fees to create a great strategy, then we spend virtually no time and money communicating it well. We do deserve to fail if we continue to assume that the work is done when the strategy is written. This is the beginning of the journey for the majority of your people. They cannot add value if they don't understand your strategy.

We learned a great phrase from a copy-writer in a workshop once: 'To explain is to fail.' This truly applies to communication of your company strategy to your whole workforce. You will not be there in every meeting or forum to explain what you want people to do. So the communication of your strategy has to be universally understood by your whole organization.

Once people do understand your strategy, millions of kilowatts of human energy will immediately be invested into making your strategy work, as clever people will soon work out how to do something once they know what you want them to do.

For us, one clear leadership imperative is to invest more time and energy into making sure your strategy is well understood and that the implications for each department and individual are carefully spelled out. In fact, as a leader, once you have a simple strategy at least 30–40 per cent of your daily activities should focus around the ongoing communication and reinforcement of the strategy you want your people to execute.

> 'The first step is to do the simple stuff and then move into the more complex areas once you've built the trust.'
>
> *Attributed to Tony Cocker,*
> *Chief Executive, EON UK plc*

How to ensure your strategy is easier to understand

- Use simple words and concepts to describe your strategy. Making your strategy sound clever or complex is self-defeating. You might feel smart, but your people will be confused. Examples of impenetrably complex strategies we have seen:
    - 'Reinvent the role that biscuits play in the day of a modern consumer's snack life.'
    - 'To engage local people in a dialogue about a new paradigm of care in the community for 2020.'
    - 'To deliver a systematic and sustained program of efficiency and measures for improved effectiveness, translated into sustainable local delivery to ensure the delivery of more stretching centrally derived targets.' (With thanks to 'Pseuds Corner', *Private Eye.*)
- Summarize your strategy on one single page (see Figures 5.11 and 5.12).
- Turn your strategy into an image/diagram.
- Turn your strategy into a set of simple rules or a simple To Do list for your company.

- Make your simple strategy into a screen saver for every computer.
- Road test your strategy with a small sample of your employees before you launch it (testing for 'do you understand it?', not do you agree with it or think it's right!)

A software company:

VISION, MISSION AND STRATEGY

MISSION
Allow people to enjoy their home technology, free from hassle or fear of attack.

VISION
To transform the market for home PC maintenance and protection.

VALUES
Speed, collaboration, pioneering, simplicity.

STRATEGY

- **our objectives**
  $500bn profit by 2020.

- **our scope**
  Global home user PC maintenance and protection software.

- **our competitive advantage**
  INNOVATION: continual development of the best PC protection and maintenance software, in terms of overall performance and customer ease of use.
  SERVICE: the quickest and simplest company to do business with.
  VALUE: lowest overall license fees over 5-year life.

FIGURE 5.11
A strategy summarized on one page

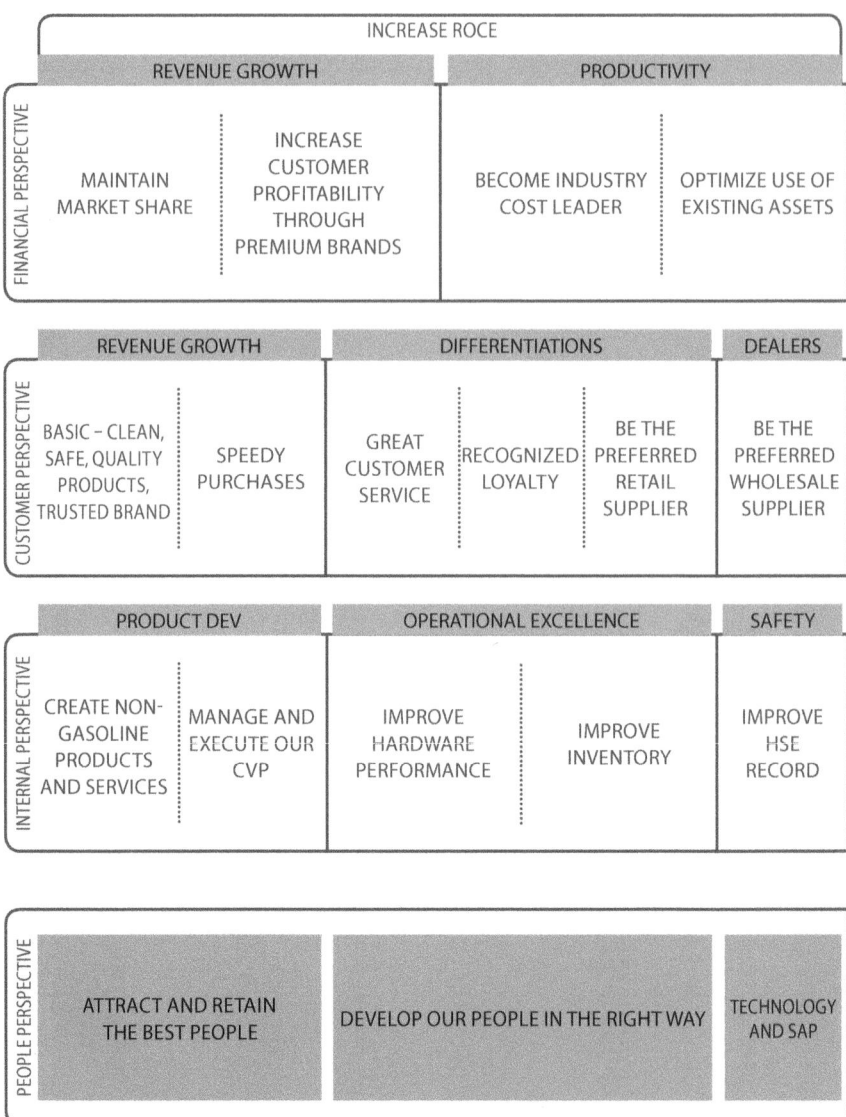

FIGURE 5.12
A strategy summarized on one page

- Discuss the strategy with each individual/team and define how their day-to-day role creates value and how it contributes to achievement of the company's strategy.
- Provide concrete examples of the sort of things you will do and will not do as part of the strategy.

- Turn it into a story of what your company will be like in the future.
- Turn it into a short, inspiring video and play it all the time.
- Use the stop/start/continue tool to make the strategy more tangible and clear.
- Constantly provide real life examples of where your strategy is being successful.

Strategy of the month! Changing your strategy too often

One of the major findings from our studies is that some people are confused by what they see as constantly changing strategy and/or a continuous flow of new strategic initiatives, all of which are the top priority.

Perception is reality. In fact your strategy may not be changing at all; it might be that your people don't understand your strategy, so it might just be that the arrival of new initiatives or projects might make it appear that the strategy has changed. So when news is communicated it is therefore critical that you make sure you overtly state whether this news is a change of strategy.

For example, if a new product is launched by your competitor you may say 'This major competitor product launch does not change our core strategy, but it does mean that we now need to re-focus on product X rather than product Y so that we can successfully execute our strategy.' Or 'our strategy continues to be focused on the successful launch of product X, but clearly we need to refine the product formulation to account for this competitor.'

In fact all senior exec communications (emails, team updates, town hall meetings, etc.) are great opportunities to remind people of what your strategy is and that it has not changed.

Remember: if you don't have a simple strategy, or you don't communicate it well, good people will still come to work and fill up their days, but most of the day they will be running fast in the wrong direction. If you change strategy, or they think you have, they will turn to face in another direction. But that direction may also be wrong. At the very worst you may have clever, capable people running around in circles.

FIVE KEY POINTS ON STRATEGY COMPLEXITY
1. Strategy comes top of our five categories of internal complexity sources (ahead of people, processes, organization, products and services) in our management survey.
2. Strategic decision-making is complex and in many companies the processes for discussing, deciding and communicating strategy are part of the problem, not the solution.
3. There are four major problems with strategy in modern businesses that give rise to excessive complexity: too many changes in strategy (shifting goalposts); too many strategies (initiative overload); unclear strategy (confused priorities); and an overly complex strategic planning process.
4. Ask yourself: are you doing the right things in the right way?
5. You should not respond to a complicated world with elaborate strategies; you need to develop a small number of simple rules, such as borderline rules, priority rules and stop rules.

7. From strategy to processes

So, you should now have some clear ideas on how to draw up a simple strategy for your firm and communicate it effectively throughout the organization.

One of the big findings of our research is that strategy-related processes – procedures and practices for developing strategy – are a major part of the complexity problem. Doing the right thing strategically is inevitably connected to doing things in the right way. Organizational effectiveness is linked to organizational efficiency. We move now from the former to the latter to look in Chapter 6 at how process complexity reduces firm performance and how it can be tackled.

For more on how to cope with strategic complexity go to: http://www.simplicitypartnership.com/

Chapter 6
How to Simplify: Processes

COPING WITH COMPLEXITY: STORIES FROM THE FRONT

A friend of mine – a doctor – once had a meeting at a government health agency office in London. Given the London traffic he went on his bike and was asked to sign the 'bicycle register' at reception. While waiting for his meeting to start he became curious about the practice, given that car owners who parked outside did not need to sign this register. Why is this necessary, he asked the receptionist? She did not know, but when he asked what they did with the registers she took him to a back room where several shelves were stacked with completed registers dating back many, many years. A little more research revealed that the 'bike registration' process was initiated during the Second World War as part of an incentive system to save fuel costs! Nobody had ever questioned the need to continue the practice and it was part of the standard training for all receptionists.

This is an example of a legacy process: a habitual routine that everyone follows and no one questions. Most examples of redundant processes are less obvious than this one, but as in this case it is often outsiders, rather than those in the organization, who question whether such processes are adding any value.

Over the last two or three decades, business process reengineering (BPR – or 'lean') has become a major focus for many businesses and industries. Often it has added significant value by perfecting and controlling how work gets done. This has in turn allowed process design to contribute significantly to the creation of competitive advantage, improvement in quality and consistency, and reduction in cost.

However, as we observed in the people chapter, clever humans have a natural tendency to over-engineer things; the result of this is that in many cases process creation (there is a process for everything) and refinement (constant tinkering with the process) has now gone too far. As a result, our research identifies major issues with process complexity in big companies.

- **Too many:** In many big companies there are now too many processes; there may be formal processes for everything big and small, even if it is not really necessary to have a detailed process for everything.
- **Too much duplication:** In different countries/departments, there are different processes for doing the same or similar things, but economies of learning and best-practice sharing are hampered by lack of standardization or by 'territorial' reinvention.
- **Too complex for the task in hand:** In addition, our research showed that in many cases processes have become more complex than they

need to be for the purpose in hand. In some case this has resulted from continual fine tuning and adding on to existing processes, but in others it is simply that we have created a sledgehammer to crack a nut.

1. Processes: complex and simple

A business process is 'a set of related tasks performed to achieve a defined business outcome'. Processes represent the daily routines of the firm.

Processes are a valuable and necessary part of all major organizations, because they provide a number of important benefits. They:

- allow lower-skilled people to achieve a higher-skilled outcomes
- improve conformity, which allows you to
  - reduce or eliminate risk
  - maintain a certain level of quality
- drive efficiency by identifying the best way to consistently achieve a desired outcome within defined cost and quality parameters.

They can evolve into efficient habits that help you achieve routine tasks quickly ... or into useless traditions, maintained for the wrong reasons and getting in the way of more important stuff.

PROCESS LEVEL	NOVELTY: INPUT/OUTPUT PREDICTABILITY	WHAT?	FOR EXAMPLE?
STRATEGIC	Novel, unpredictable processes	Think through, consult, assess, compare, look at options, scenarios, risks, etc.	New product development, M&A, new market entry initiatives
TACTICAL	Predictable, cyclical decision-making processes	Think, consult, assess, and then do it	Budget-planning, resource allocation, recruitment and training
BASIC	Routine and mundane processes	Just do it! Repeat work	Repeat orders, standard expenditures, everyday communications

FIGURE 6.1
Different kinds of business processes

There is a link between the management hierarchy and the types of processes outlined in Figure 6.1, with senior management doing more of the strategic stuff and those lower down the hierarchy doing more of the 'doing' stuff. However, a very large number of managers today do all three.

Although processes can be described as 'hierarchical' or flow-oriented, role-oriented, goal-oriented or time-oriented (like the processes Gantt charts capture), most are 'transformational' in some form or other. That means they transform a set of inputs into outputs. A sequence of activities adds value at each stage. There may be sub-processes, branching options and decision gates, as well as cross-departmental or inter-firm inputs that need to be communicated and coordinated.

Too many complex processes?

There are two drivers of process complexity in the modern world that seem to be creating headaches for everyone – in and outside the workplace. One is the rise of health, safety and security procedures that have been designed as a response to very unusual events. The second is the rise of the 'professional administrator', a person whose life is dedicated to developing more and more control, checking, monitoring and reporting systems for the rest of us.

Shocking events, from tsunami to oil rig disasters, 9/11 to banking crises, trigger a flow of regulations, procedures and processes. Understandably no one wants these things to happen again, but adding more and more complex processes is rarely the solution. Controversial we know, but does anyone really think the huge increase in complex security processes at every airport will stop another terrorist attack? Once we ramp up the number of procedures, it is difficult to dismantle the new organization structure. Inertia sets in and the new processes are embedded.

At the other end of the scale, process creep – driven by 'process creeps' – can create a stranglehold on management. The increasing sophistication of administrators that are several steps removed from adding value to customers and focused on adding, developing, revising or extending the internal processes until our bells and whistles have bells and whistles on them is a powerful force. These people can certainly organize, clarify and streamline – but they can also over-elaborate, overwhelm and paralyze.

These two drivers add to the already strong momentum behind the growth of complex processes in the modern firm.

JOHNSON & JOHNSON: R&D PROCESS SIMPLIFICATION

What was the complexity problem?
In the early 2000s, R&D processes at Johnson & Johnson (J&J) were extremely siloed – each R&D site across the globe was largely independent, with their own processes for developing products.

At the same time, the pharmaceutical industry was becoming more globalized, with products discovered, manufactured and distributed in different parts of the world, increasing cooperation between regulators, and so on. Process silos were making it harder to combine resources to compete effectively, as well as to meet increasingly heavy compliance and reporting burdens.

How did the power of simplicity help?
The Global Head of Quality Assurance at J&J instituted a global integration and simplification initiative. It began by targeting the highest-impact R&D processes: auditing clinical trials, preparing for regulatory inspections and close-out audit exceptions.

The simplification process also sought to engage the entire R&D organization. New initiatives were commissioned every four months, so that after two years, the entire R&D process had been simplified and almost every staff member had participated in at least one initiative, which made acceptance of new processes much easier.

What was the impact?
The productivity of the R&D function increased by 50 per cent from 2002 to 2004. The standardized R&D function became more agile, meaning it was able to easily incorporate J&J's biotech arm when the decision was made to merge it into the wider pharma business.

---

2. What does our research show?

Over-complex and redundant processes cost you money, energy and enthusiasm. Relative to our other five sources of complexity (external, strategy, people, products and services, and organization design), business processes turn out to be a relatively low-impact source of complexity in our management survey. No process-related complexity comes in our top 30 high-impact sources of complexity. This suggests that firms have gone some way already down the track of re-engineering, slimming down and removing the frustration of complex processes.

However, the 600 managers in our survey of European firms placed 'major project processes', 'production processes' and 'core business processes' at the top of their ranking of process-related sources of costly complexity. This fits with the other areas of complexity highlighted in our studies. As discussed in the first chapter, the growing uncertainties of strategic decision-making and continuous restructuring initiatives are examples of sources of complexity that cut across the six categories, linking external sources of complexity with internal strategy, processes, organization design, products and services, and people.

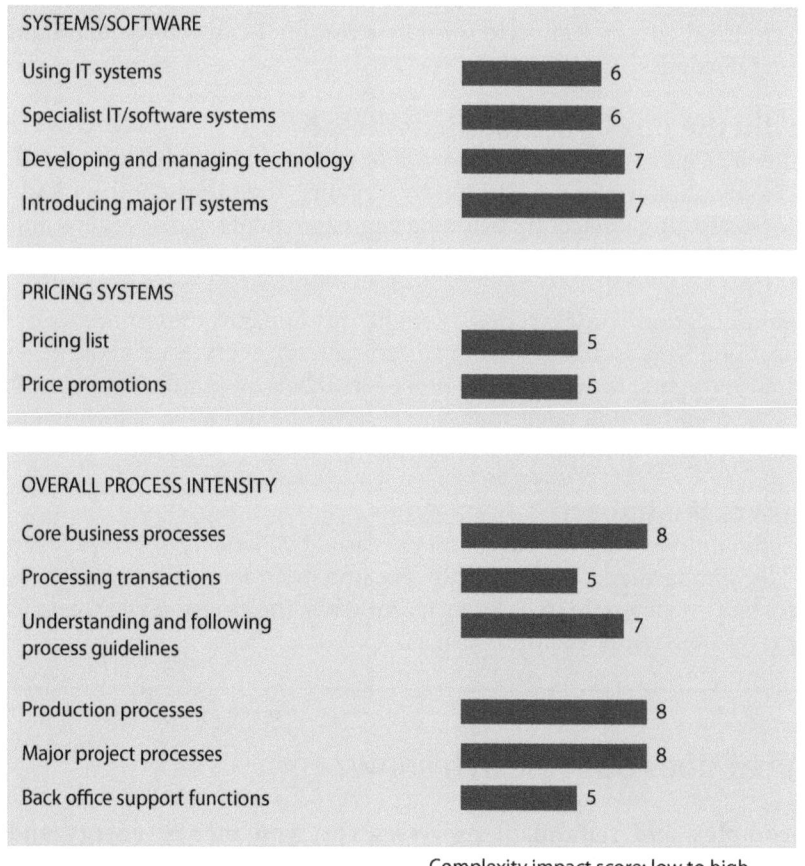

Complexity impact score: low to high

TABLE 6.1
The impact of process-related sources of complexity on the business
Note: This is a relative measure that combines the frequency with which this source of complexity was cited by managers in our survey and their rating of the impact it has on performance.

When we looked at the kinds of complexity affecting poor-performing firms, as compared to top-performing firms, it was a surprise to find that process-related complexity was ranked much higher for the poor performers. In fact 'monthly management reporting', 'annual performance appraisal' and 'customer support' processes came in the top ten of our overall list of over 100 sources of complexity. This matches the result we found for 'people' sources of complexity (see Chapter 3).

As we emphasized in the first chapter, poor-performing firms are 'introverts' in terms of their focus on internal sources of costly complexity. Respondents in these firms are overwhelmed by people and process-related complexity. And because of this, they are losing sight of the significant range of opportunities and threats in the external competitive environment.

3. Can BPR or Lean help you simplify your processes?

All your key processes need to be regularly reviewed and removed or revised to improve overall business efficiency. The competitive advantages you can gain from being 'lean' have been shown over and over again in the manufacturing sector. Japanese automotive and consumer electronics firms demonstrated many of these in their rise to the top in the 1970s and 1980s. In the 1990s BPR (business process re-engineering) became a popular way of trying to extend the Lean approach to other areas of the business (a survey by Deloitte and Touche found that just over 80 per cent of firms had some form of BPR initiative underway). Six Sigma-style audit and control procedures have helped managers maintain the process review and revision cycle.

Knowledge-based processes versus machine-based processes

At this point it is important to make a clear distinction between 'machine-based' and 'knowledge-based' processes, as the way of simplifying these two types of process are very different.

Machine-based processes: In these processes humans interact mainly with machines. Obvious examples are factory production lines, IT-driven processes like logistics systems and transaction closing systems in banks. In these processes human interact with machines. These processes are easy to define and map, and outcomes are often binary: they are either right or wrong, and either in or out of specification. In addition, the connections between steps are very formal and visible. This means that the input and outputs are relatively predictable and measurable. Quality is easy to define, measure and control.

Knowledge-based processes: Knowledge-based processes are very different. In these types of process people interact mainly with other people. There are lots of different ways to achieve the same outcomes. Information may be shared or stored using IT systems, but human- to-human interaction is the essence of the work. A good-quality outcome is subjective to assess, not as simple as saying that this outcome is in or out of specification; i.e. the outcomes are NOT binary. Examples would be the HR, marketing and sales processes in big companies.

Outcomes are far less predictable in these 'knowledge-based' processes, because each 'situation' is very different and can only be solved by human-to-human interaction. Successful outcomes depend on human skills, experience and judgment. These skills cannot be turned into simple process steps. Until machines develop the capability to adapt, think, negotiate and compromise for themselves, this type of process cannot be managed or controlled like a machine or IT system can.

In these types of systems 'brains solve problems, not processes'. A loose process can be specified to create a framework or approach that ensure that you gather the right information, involve the right people, ask the right questions, and comply with regulations ... but the process cannot in itself ensure the outcome you are looking for.

Over-engineering can be very dangerous in these knowledge-based processes. This is because the mere existence of a detailed step-by-step approach may give a false sense of security, making the brain lazy: 'if I follow the process the outcome is certain'. This creates the impression that the process will 'automatically' solve the problem, guarantee quality or prevent risk. In addition, people soon become too focused on complying with the process and lose sight of the overall outcome that the process was originally designed to create.

When Lean is weak

BPR and Lean, because they have been primarily developed for machine-based processes, provide weak solutions outside of the machine-based manufacturing environment. One of the major problems is that they tend to treat people-based processes the same as manufacturing processes. For example, they often attempt to apply the kinds of precise input–output measures we would use for controlling flows of materials and components to knowledge-related processes. This does not work very well.

Manufacturing systems are largely made up of predictable stages in product fabrication based around capable machinery. The more people are involved doing non-routine work, the less predictable the outputs are – in terms of quality, reliability, and so on. Step away from plant lines dominated by automated equipment to deal with production systems dominated by people, with less tangible outputs and a range of non-physical inputs – like specialist knowledge, creative energy, enthusiasm and office politics – and we can quickly see input–output predictability slipping away.

As a process, 'input' knowledge is tacit and context-specific, i.e. knowledge means different things to different people in different contexts – so its value varies depending on who learns it when, where and in relation to what other knowledge. So the ways in which knowledge-based services (such as consulting or financial services, real estate, education, social services, media or entertainment) add value for customers is much more complex. Re-engineering these production systems needs to go beyond a Lean approach.

More people = less predictability: Studies in the 1980s showed how Japanese firms were managing plant-level processes better than their Western rivals in the automotive and consumer electronics industries. Comparative data showed how output quality and productivity levels were much higher, for two reasons. First, they were the first to introduce advanced technology to the production line, including computer-controlled systems for regulating throughput. Fewer employees on the plant floor led to more standardized processes and increased predictability of output quality along with reduced costs. Second, management practices like quality circles, *kanban* and total quality management (TQM) helped to focus the efforts of the remaining plant-floor staff on continual process improvement (*kaizen* activities), using simple rules (such as plan-do-check-act – PDCA – cycles).

Still excellent at manufacturing, the Japanese have failed to bring about the same productivity revolution in service industries. People are at the heart of the processes that add value. Computer-controlled systems and lean standardization approaches cannot help much.

So in our experience, Lean works very well in 'machine-based' processes. However, it has some major limitations when it comes to simplifying knowledge-based processes:

Problems with Lean
- Lean does not work well in unpredictable processes, where the inputs and outcomes are unpredictable and hard to control (e.g. the process of creating a great new advertisement).

- Complex, technical and expensive: The Lean approach is very complex and technical, requiring high levels of skill and experience. This means that in most businesses very few people have the in-house skills to do Lean projects themselves. This means many companies will end up buying in expensive consultancy support to conduct Lean projects.
- Lean can create additional complexity. Lean was originally designed to identify and remove waste in factory and logistics processes. It was never designed to simplify processes. Paradoxically, this highly analytical tool can create more complexity, as removing waste will require the creation of new sub-routines, so the waste is gone, but the process is now more complex!
- User resistance: Finally, the people involved in knowledge-based processes are often very resistant to Lean as an approach. They reject the idea of being treated like a machine. Lean feels disempowering, because the highly technical and complex nature of the Lean process means they cannot do the work themselves, so the work is either 'done for them' or 'done to them', which reduces engagement and commitment by the people who will ultimately run the process when the experts have gone. An approach to simplification that they can do themselves will be more successful for obvious reasons.

So while Lean can be a very effective tool in machine-based processes, it is not the best approach to all the process redesign projects you might be faced with. So choose your tools wisely!

XEROX: TRANSFORMING THE PROCUREMENT SYSTEM

What was the complexity problem?

At Xerox, Non-Production Procurement (NPP) is the term used to refer to all purchases of supplies, other than those used in the actual production of photocopiers. So, all office supplies, from desks and personal computers to pencils and stationery, come under this NPP category.

In the mid-1990s, Xerox was spending $4.3bn per year on NPP. The ordering process was fragmented and over-complex; there were way too many suppliers filling small orders. Within Xerox, the procurement function had been split between too many departments. Complex cross-departmental coordination and communications resulted in delays and an undependable ordering system. Xerox realized that the redesign of this process represented a major opportunity to save money.

How did the power of simplicity help?

Xerox created a process flow chart depicting all of the activities and departments involved in the NPP process. The initial diagram was formidably large and complex, identifying hundreds of activities, bridging departments, systems and specialists. Many of the process steps and sub-process activities were found to be non-value-adding, and were eliminated.

Xerox also decided to identify the larger purchasing opportunities that could be consolidated into exclusive deals with preferred suppliers at a global level. The firm then negotiated better deals with the largest suppliers that could support Xerox throughout the world. By replacing numerous small contracts with a few large ones, the management was able to eliminate a range of redundant processes and reassign procurement personnel as well as simplifying its complex range of contracts.

The team also took the opportunity to completely automate access between Xerox managers and the suppliers, so that all paperwork would be eliminated. The economies of scale in the larger contracts made this viable. Each manager can now access the supply system and complete orders online. Departmental limits and constraints are all handled by the computer system without any need for intervention by accounting personnel.

Other radical changes to the NPP process were also implemented as the system was restructured. For example, credit cards were issued to all managers. With fixed limits on them, managers were encouraged to pay by card whenever they needed to acquire something quickly. By shifting decision-making and responsibility for these occasional rush purchases to departmental managers, a large portion of the NPP bureaucracy was eliminated.

What was the impact?

The new process has saved a significant amount of the procurement administration budget. Hundreds of activities have been reduced to dozens. The inter-firm negotiation, contracting and coordination are now far simpler as a wide range of supplier links have been consolidated into a few large deals. A convoluted system of paper forms has been scrapped and the entire process is now handled online by a new NPP software system. Coordination and management of the resulting procurement process is simpler and the supply chain is more reliable.

4. How to reduce process complexity in your organization

'Making the simple complicated is commonplace; making the complicated simple, awesomely simple, that's creativity.'

Atrributed to Charles Mingus

What are the major symptoms of overly complex processes?

The major symptoms of overly complex processes in your organization are:

- Your managers spend significant amounts of time changing/adapting your processes because they are not working well at present.
- Managers spend significant amounts of time discussing how your internal processes work, to the exclusion of focusing on external factors and the quality of outcomes.
- When things go wrong people blame the process or claim that it's not their fault because they followed the process.
- People describe your organization as being bureaucratic.
- Process 'work arounds' are common and/or compliance with the official processes is very poor.
- People are frustrated by the need to follow a process for more or less everything.

- Your people complain that there is too little time for creativity, for interaction with other employees or for problem solving.

What are the major causes of process complexity?

AREA	ISSUE
Evolution	• The process has evolved with the development of the business • Pace has meant that evolution has been ad hoc and there has not been the opportunity to do a full redesign • Each time there is an error, the process is added to (usually without taking anything away), and without considering whether the cost of change is greater than the cost of error • Like layers of paint on a door, the appearance of the process may be very different now from the wood you started with
Step change	• Inputs to the process have changed significantly (perhaps as systems and focus changes) • The historical process is still operated, perhaps with steps that no longer add any value • The process was never intended to deal with the variety or volume of occurrences that are now being addressed by it • The output from the process is not dovetailing with downstream processes, so workarounds and fixes are applied, perhaps by different functions
Lack of definition	• The process has grown up with the business and has never been written down or defined • The person operating the process has considerable scope to complete the process as they see fit • New joiners take over the process and deal with it in their own way
System workarounds	• Many processes are created to compensate for systems that don't integrate or don't do exactly what you want them to do • Temporary workarounds become the norm – rather than fixing the root systems issue
Over-engineering	• Most processes are over-engineered • Error-correction has meant that the majority of normal occurrences are now processed in a way designed to catch all eventualities – perhaps making the majority of transactions inefficient

TABLE 6.2
The major causes of process complexity

Key steps for reducing process complexity in your organization

In order to reduce the negative impact of process complexity, you will need to do the following three things in this order:

1. Eliminate any redundant or unnecessary processes.
2. Standardize any processes that are similar/duplicated.
3. Streamline all the remaining processes.

'It is far more difficult to be simple than to be complicated; far more difficult to sacrifice skill and easy execution in the proper place, than to expand both indiscriminately.'

John Ruskin

Start by creating a master list of all the major processes in your organization/department

This is in effect a 'stock take' of the process intensity in your organization. Just looking at the list will immediately give you a sense of how process-intense your company has become. If you have identified your Simple Success Keys (see Chapter 5) then you will have already identified which processes are essential to the success of your company, so this can be a good starting point. If you don't already have a list of the key processes, you will need to draw one up and then answer the following questions for each of your existing processes.

- What is the process designed to do? Does it currently work well or poorly?
- How does this process create value for your organization or help with the delivery of your strategy? Examples would be:
  - Reduces risk
  - Improves quality of outcomes
  - Speeds up key activities
  - Creates competitive advantage
  - Essential for servicing our clients effectively
- How necessary is it to have a formally laid down, detailed process for doing this? Instead of having a detailed formal process, can we create a simple set of best practice rules and guidelines?
- Duplication: In other departments/functions or countries do you have several different processes that deliver similar outcomes/products?
- How predictable are the inputs/outputs? Can this process be reliably automated?

- Do you have to do this in-house, or could you outsource it and gain any major benefits?

Now use the results of your analysis and apply the three rules above

1. Eliminate any redundant or unnecessary processes: The bicycle register at the start of the chapter is a great example. Your company is likely to have a lot of redundant processes that can be stopped without creating risk or harming customer satisfaction. Any process where there is no clear connection between a value driver/your strategy and the process should be stopped as quickly as possible. Similarly if there are benefits from outsourcing the process this option should be evaluated quickly.

2. Standardize any processes that are similar/duplicated: Due to a succession of major acquisitions, one of our clients has four different enterprise resource planning (ERP) processes across their organization, which is currently causing chaos. Where there are several different processes for doing the same thing, you should standardize to the simplest one, or design a new simple process (see below) that combines the best of them all. Doing the same activity or achieving the same outcome from two different processes is clearly illogical and value-destructive. Economies of learning and scale will be lost. Each time people change countries or departments they will have to learn a new way to do the same thing. Best practice will be difficult to share. Tension will grow between departments who see the other department doing their work or doing things in the wrong way. Where processes are overlapping you should standardize to one cross-company way of doing things. This will immediately release energy, time and cost from your company. Take care to work out the best process to standardize to. Don't standardize to something which is too complex or over-engineered. If the process is too complex, use the approach below to simplify the process.

> 38% of our survey respondents have six or more specialist IT systems that they use to do their job (13% have more than 16).

3. Streamline all the remaining processes: This last part of the journey focuses on taking existing process and slimming them it down as much as possible. By now your list of processes will be reduced to the most mission-critical processes that your organization needs to perform effectively. Every other process will have been eliminated or standardized. So the final step is to complete process simplification reviews on all the remaining processes. This involves identifying how you can reduce the number of stages, the number of people involved and the documentation, forms, meetings and other bureaucracy involved in running the process.

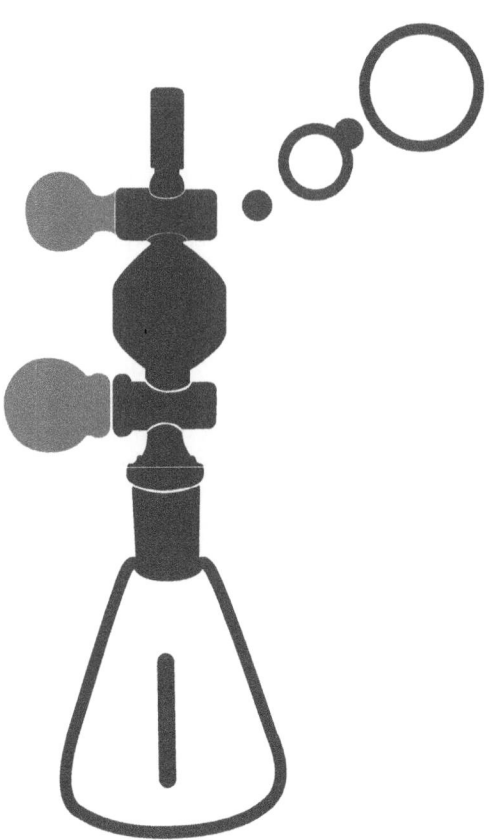

TOP FIVE PHARMACEUTICAL GIANT: GLOBAL MARKETING
PROCESS REVAMP

What was the complexity problem?

The global marketing process in this pharma conglomerate had gradually evolved to become too complex. The process of developing a new global brand strategy now had over 30 separate stages, with each brand project costing several million dollars in management time, consultancy fees and market research.

Too many people were involved in each project, many of whom lacked the skills or experience needed to develop a strong global brand strategy. In addition, most decisions (big and small) were referred upwards in the hierarchy to managers who were not closely involved in the project. In many cases, this resulted in diluted or over-complicated outcomes at each stage.

Not surprisingly, the final product of these projects was often a disappointment. Project-managing this convoluted process and alignment of a massive number of people left little time and energy to focus on the quality of the outcome.

How did the power of simplicity help?

They started by breaking the marketing process down into its constituent steps and mapping it on the wall in their project center. For each step in the process, they identified exactly what was done, who was involved, how the work was completed and how much each stage was costing them in management time and fees.

The value and outcomes of each stage were then reviewed in detail, with examples of best practice outcomes highlighted for each stage/step. This process allowed them to identify several stages that were over-engineered or unnecessary for a successful outcome.

In addition, they noticed that several activities were duplicated by separate teams, or at different stages of the project. The outputs of each stage were therefore standardized, so that there was no need to rewrite them at a later stage.

Finally, they reduced the number of people and functions involved in each project and empowered the remaining ones to make the major decisions, with less reference up the hierarchy.

What was the impact?

- The number of major stages in the global marketing process was reduced from over 30 to just six.

- The project team was reduced from over 16 to around ten people.
- The total amount of management time tied up in the process was reduced by over 60 per cent.
- The total cost of steering each individual brand through this process was reduced by $1.2m.

How to streamline an existing process

Step 1: Scope and design parameters

This step focuses on defining the scope and the brief for the process simplification project.

Scope

Your processes will often feed into other processes and many will cross different functions, department or physical locations. Processes connect with each other across functional, departmental and geographic boundaries. They are therefore interdependent, with unseen knock-on effects when changes are made. So defining the start and end points for the process you are redesigning is essential. Your inputs come from someone else's process. Your outputs may be needed by other functions, so these 'touch points' and interfaces must be identified and the scope of the redesign defined accordingly.

Design parameters

At this stage you will also need to identify any key design standards or mandatories that you need to consider when making the process simpler. There are sometimes trade-offs that may have to be considered in redesigning a process. For example, it might be very easy to define a very simple process, but this might lead to lower quality, higher risk and even lower efficiency – although in most cases simplicity and efficiency are aligned. Establishing the fixed parameters of quality, risk, speed and efficiency at the scoping stage gives you the boundaries within which you can change the process. We are often asked about regulatory risk because there is a belief that simplifying the process will increase regulatory risk. In fact, the opposite is true: simpler processes can be safer. If I try and teach you a very complex Argentinean tango, chances are you will trip up during the dance. If I teach you a simple waltz, you'll tend to make fewer mistakes and tread on your partner's feet less often.

STEP 1:
SCOPE AND DESIGN PARAMETERS
What is the scope? Where does the process you are
simplifying start/finish?
Are there any major design parameters that need
to be considered?

STEP 2:
UNDERSTAND
Understand the current process in detail. What is
done at each stage? What are the outcomes at
each stage?
Why is it done at all?

STEP 3:
FOCUS
Now identify the parts of the process that produce
the most pain and most gain.

STEP 4:
RESHAPE
Reshape the process to make it simpler,
without making the outcomes more risky or poorer
in quality.

STEP 5:
PILOT AND LAUNCH
If possible, test the process in a 'safe area', then
communicate and train, and measure outcomes as
part of the launch.

FIGURE 6.2
Five streamlining steps

Right process – wrong inputs

In some instances the process is not the problem – it's just that it is being used for some situations that were never anticipated when the process was created. An example of this might be a driver phoning the sales line of their car insurer to discuss a claim because they know it will be answered quicker than the claims line (which is always busy and probably under-resourced). From the insurer's viewpoint the sales process has been interrupted and sales people are now spending their time re-routing calls. You don't need to simplify the sales process, you just need to restrict the 'claims call' inputs.

Understand the behaviors that will be important

At the scope stage you should also identify if there are any management behaviors or environmental conditions that need to be considered. For example, open collaboration or creative thinking may be essential to the outcome. So the simpler process design must cater for these design parameters as well.

> 'No matter how complicated a problem is, it usually can be reduced to a simple, comprehensible form which is often the best solution.'
>
> *An Wang*

Step 2: Understand the current process in detail

This stage focuses on understanding the current process in detail. What is done at each stage? What are the outcomes at each stage? Why is it done that way? At this stage you are not trying to simplify the process (although you will spot some simplification ideas during this stage) because you will need to have an in-depth understanding of the current process before you start cutting things.

Break it down

The first step is to break the current process down into its major steps/ phases. A picture is much easier than words, so draw it as a flow diagram (see Figure 6.3). In Lean, this will be done in excruciating detail. However, we recommend doing this at a much higher level at first. Big-picture

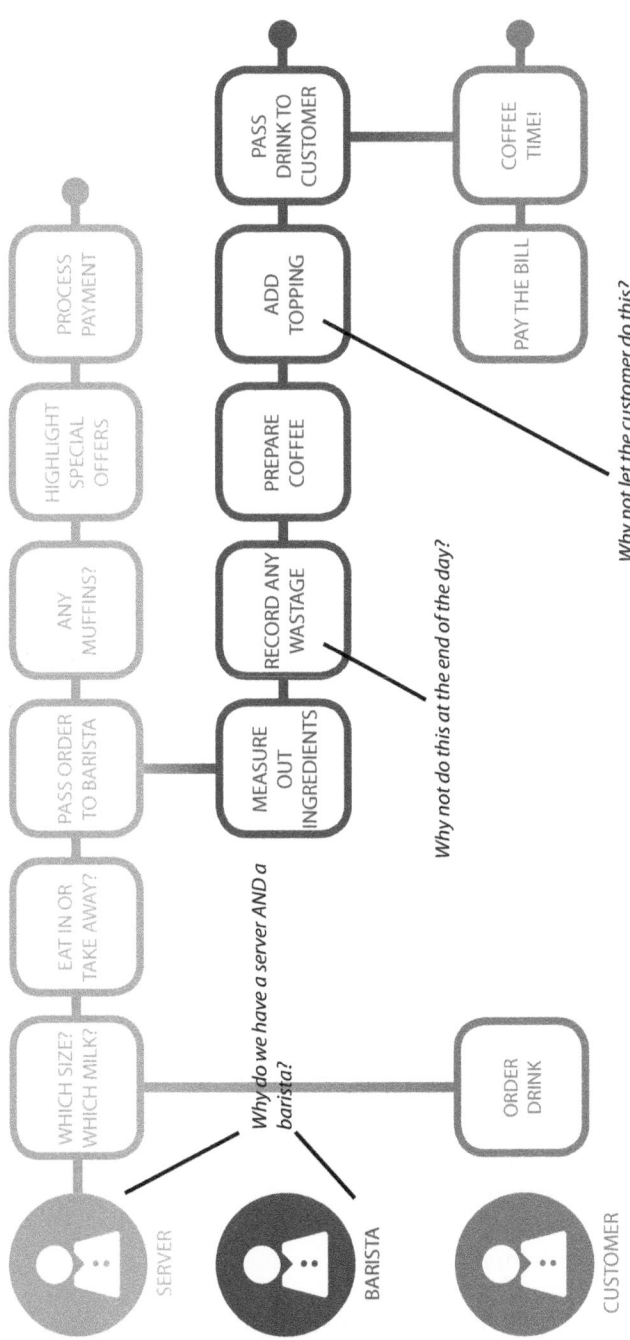

FIGURE 6.3
Break down the process

thinking is more helpful at this stage. Getting lost in the detail too soon can be a barrier to progress. You can always dig into more detail at a later point. Figure 6.3 shows an example of a coffee shop. For each stage/phase, identify the key inputs (what is done by each person involved) and the outputs (e.g. forms, production units, information, order dispatch, other outcomes).

Ask why

The next stage is to understand, in detail, why it is done in that way. Children are great at asking why; as we get older we seem to forget the power of this simple question. Similarly, when we join a new organization we ask why quite a lot, but once we have been there longer we stop asking why. In the Toyota Production System operators were encouraged to ask 'why' five times to really get to the bottom of why something was happening. Persistence on this question will help you understand if there are good reasons for doing things this way or not. Often the answer is vague: 'we've always done it this way!' or 'we don't know why it's done like that'.

Value drivers

The next step is to understand how the process creates value overall and how each major step of the process contributes to this value creation.

- **Overall value creation:** Looking at the process as a whole, does it create value or destroy value? This can be identified by working out the overall value that the process creates for your company and then deducting the total cost of running the process.
  - Overall cost per annum: Calculate how much the process costs your business to run each month/year in terms of management time, operator costs, raw materials, energy, etc. Make sure this is then broken down and allocated by stage.
  - Overall value per annum: Calculate overall how much profit/value you have got from the process. Overall, does this process create value or destroy value? If you can (it is difficult), try to work out the value created at each individual stage.
- **Value creation for each stage:** You should also look at how each major stage in the process creates value. First list what the value drivers for your company are, for example:
  - Speed of problem resolution
  - Low cost per transaction
  - High customer satisfaction rating
  - Regulatory compliance

  Now match up the value drivers to each stage of the process (Figure 6.4): is there a clear link between each step and at least one of the value drivers? If a stage does not directly contribute to value creation, ask why it is done – five times!

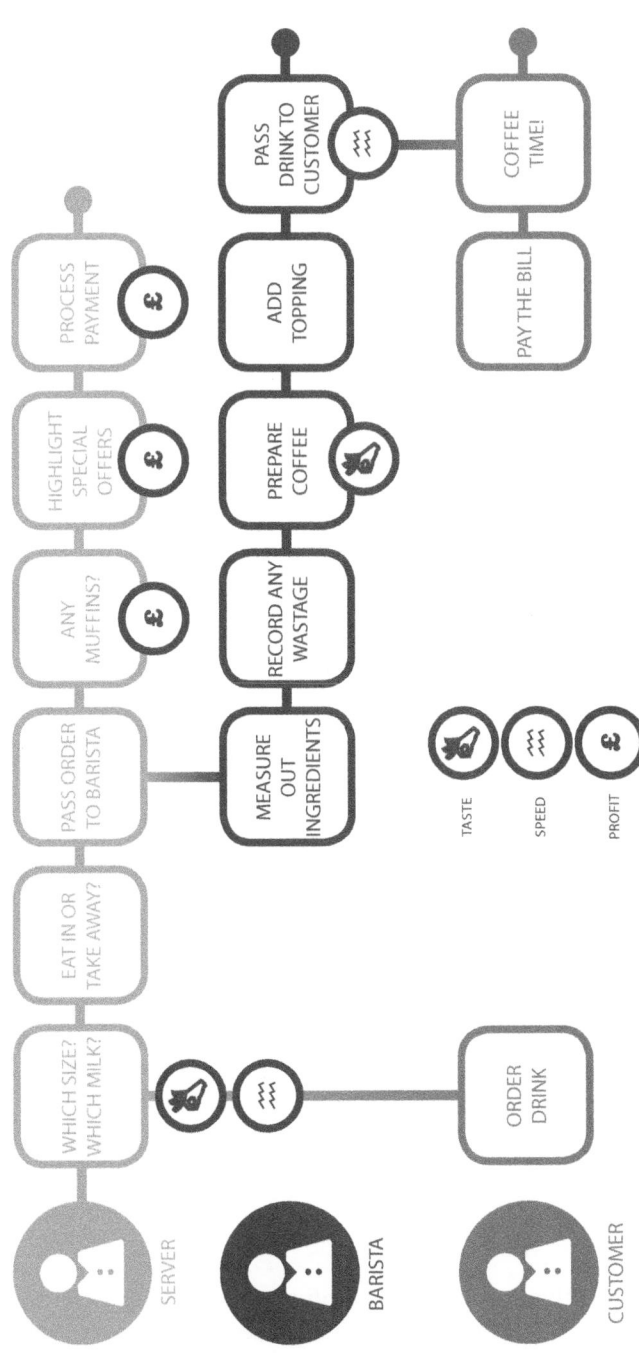

FIGURE 6.4
Value drivers

Step 3: Focus on the gain and pain points

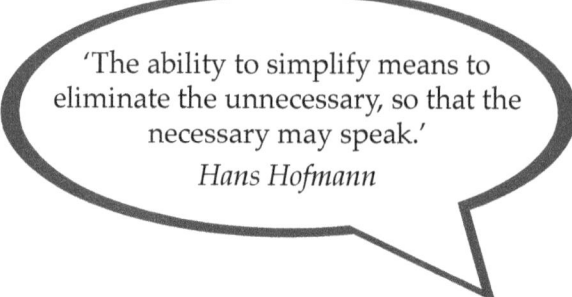

'The ability to simplify means to eliminate the unnecessary, so that the necessary may speak.'
Hans Hofmann

Now you fully understand what is done at each stage, why it's done and how each stage creates value for the company, the next stage is to work out where the focus of your simplification efforts should be.

In simple terms at this stage you need to work out where the biggest pain and gain points are within the current process:

- **Gain:** Where is the most value created in the current process? Which elements of the current process are essential to the overall success of the process? Which steps/elements are non-essential?
- **Pain:** Where is the greatest pain in the process? Which steps cause most downtime, most exceptions, most problems?

Here are some simple tools you can use to help you identify where to focus the efforts of your process redesign.

Pareto
The 80/20 rule predicts that 80 per cent of the value will come from 20 per cent of the process steps. Similarly 80 per cent of the problems will probably come from a small number of process steps. Use the 20/80 rule to identify which steps/elements of the process are most important. Use the 80/20 rule to identify which steps are the most problematic, complex or harmful. This tool is also very useful at the reshape/redesign stage – see Step 4.

Ranking
Again a simple tool, but this can be very helpful in identifying what to keep and what to change. List the stages of the process according to the most important and least important; we suggest using multiple criteria for the ranking.

- How well does this stage currently work?
- How important is this stage for creating value/great outcomes overall?
- How expensive is this stage?
- How complex is this stage?
- How many problems/exceptions currently come from this stage?

Stop/start/continue

Alternatively take each stage of the process and consider the stop/start/continue questions below. The result will be clarity about where to focus the redesign.

- Are there any reasons why I should I **stop** doing this stage?
- Should I **start** doing something different at this stage?
- Are there any reasons why I should I **continue** doing this stage in the same way?

Cluster

The final tool in the focus stage is clustering. This involves looking at all the steps/stages/activities that are similar and then clustering them together. This allows you to quickly see if there is any duplication of work/activities that can be rationalized. It will also identify if there is a more logical order to the process, as clearly there are economies of learning by putting things that require similar skills, resources or decisions into one place.

Step 4: Reshape the process to make it simpler

Only now do you fully understand how the current process works and where the most important pain and gain points are. You can now safely start to reshape the process to make it simpler, without creating a dysfunctional or ineffective process.

Prune

Now you have identified what really matters and what does not matter, you can start to reduce and simplify the process very aggressively. We call it pruning because when you prune a tree you cut off branches/stems very carefully to create a stronger tree, with fewer branches. This is exactly what you are trying to do with process simplification: you simply take the existing process and cut out the all the superfluous stages, connections, people, paperwork, etc.

Zero base

Organizations very rarely redesign their processes from first principles. Instead they take the existing process as a start point and start to tinker with and add to what they already have. Sometimes this means they fail to realize the value from undertaking the redesign or make things more complex not less. Like adding layer upon layer of paint to a door, eventually the paint will look ugly and flakey! Sometimes you need to sand all the way back to the bare wood. Ask the question 'what if we started from scratch and redesigned the process with a blank sheet of paper?' Now you know exactly what matters and what does not, you can create a zero based process option relatively easily – in high level if not in detail. If the current process is very broken or there are no easy ways to simplify it, then this may be the only way forward. People often argue that moving from the current process to the zero based option might also be too expensive or difficult to do. But how will you know that unless you create a model for a zero based option? Even if the zero based option seems impossible, we still recommend that you look at a high-level zero based option, because this approach will provoke new ideas for simplifying the process you currently have. It will also provoke questions about whether you are being brave or radical enough in your redesign of the current process.

Pareto design

Pareto or 80/20 thinking is also very useful here. Focusing just on the 80 per cent of most common situations alone will enable you to radically simplify your process design. Why design a process that caters for all eventualities? It will inevitably be a very complex process designed to cover a lot of quite rare situations/activities/products. Instead, design a process that caters for 80 per cent of the most common situations, then handle the 20 per cent 'rares' off line or by hand. If you include the 'rares' as part of your design brief you will inevitably over-complicate the core process.

Shift

This last tool or approach to process redesign involves looking at all the remaining steps of the streamlined process to identify if some of the steps/activities could be shifted/outsourced to other functions or external companies. How do you decide if something should be shifted?

- Duplication: if the activity is repeated elsewhere, shift it to the best place.
- Non-core: if the activity does not directly create value, but still needs to be performed well (e.g. payroll process) then shift it out of your department/ organization.
- More skilled: if another organization or department is much more skilled than you at this activity/step and you do not need to learn this skill to succeed in your market.
- Cost advantage: if another company or department can do it more cheaply.

Compare

Finally, why not compare how you do something to how other people do things? Really, there's no problem in business that has not been seen and solved by someone else before. If you cannot see how to simplify the process, look for analogous industries, processes or situations and see how they have simplified things. You will be surprised how delighted people will be to share their success stories. So pick up the phone, speak to some of your network or your consultants, and start to look for case studies that you can use to inspire you.

Step 5: Pilot and launch
Documentation
Once you have simplified your process you will need to document it, unless you have already done so during the simplification process. The documentation should be suitable, in whatever form, to allow operators to easily understand what to do and in what order. Making the guidelines simple, visual and short is also essential to ensure the new process is understood and adapted. A simple process with complex instructions is a complex process!

Pilot before full launch
Make your mistakes in private! You should always pilot the new process before a full launch. This might allow a test in a safe area or, if that isn't possible, a like test in a restricted area. If there are any glitches there, they will have no or limited impact on your clients (internal or external).

Support the re-launch
The final part of Step 5 is to consider the communication, training and measurement/feedback that might be appropriate to support the change in process. In some cases you won't need anything – just do it. In other cases you may need to communicate with your operators and clients to explain the changes and the very fact that there is a new process. You may need to train the operators so that they can get used to the process before using it live, and you may need to revisit the measurements and feedback that you have in place to tell you that the process is working efficiently and effectively.

'Simplicity is the final achievement. After one has played a vast quantity of notes and more notes, it is simplicity that emerges as the crowning reward of art.'
Frederic Chopin

FIVE KEY POINTS ON PROCESS COMPLEXITY

1. We highlight three major issues with process complexity in businesses: there are too many processes; there is too much duplication; and many processes are way too complex for their main purpose.
2. We can divide processes into strategic, tactical and basic, as well as 'knowledge-based' and 'machine-based' (more people = more complex and less predictable).
3. Poor-performing firms are 'introverts'; they are overwhelmed by internal sources of costly complexity, particularly process-related complexity.
4. BPR or Lean approaches only help with part of the problem.
5. You need to: eliminate any redundant or unnecessary processes; standardize any processes that are similar/duplicated; and streamline all the remaining processes.

5. From processes to products and services

Although they are essential for a firm to operate effectively, processes have a way of multiplying and eventually getting in the way of value-adding activities. They can evolve from being familiar and efficient simplifying routines to being the jealously-guarded or mindlessly-followed 'way we do things around here'.

Our research highlights two kinds of process complexity that managers say have a big impact on their own productivity and performance: those related to developing strategy – which we dealt with in Chapter 5 – and those related to developing and launching new products and services – which we deal with next, in Chapter 7.

For more on how to cope with process complexity go to: http://www.simplicitypartnership.com/

Chapter 7

How to Simplify: Products and Services

COPING WITH COMPLEXITY: STORIES FROM THE FRONT

Distribution...
Over 100,000 suppliers
147 distribution centers (turning over 80 per cent of their contents every 24 hours)
85,000 employees
53,000 trailers
7950 drivers
7200 tractors

The stores are designed to function more like 'valves regulating flow than reservoirs capturing it'.

Retail...
100 million customers per week (almost one-third of the US population)
3029 supercenters (with 142,000 stock keeping units (SKUs) each)
629 discount stores
611 Sam's Clubs
168 neighborhood markets
= almost 4500 retail locations
= 15,500 acres (larger than Manhattan)
= $400bn of annual revenues
This is Walmart – one of the largest firms in the world, competing in scale with oil firms and the biggest banks. The vast majority of its sales are in the US domestic market, where the complexity of its supply chain has evolved to resemble a highly-developed ant colony or a basic neural network, more than anything man-made.

Walmart employs over 2 million unique individuals ... and yet it all works – predictably and profitably.

1. Why, when and how are products and services a source of costly complexity?

HP is a $100bn+ company with operations in more than 170 countries and dominant global market share in PCs, printers and servers. HP delivers 48 million PCs annually and over 1 million printers weekly. Its product portfolio consists of more than 15,000 server and storage SKUs, over 2000 laser printer SKUs, and over 8 million possible configure-to-order combinations in its notebook and desktop product lines. The knock-on effects for operational logistics, supply chain coordination, distribution, marketing and branding, service and support are mind-bending!

Despite this complexity, HP has a number of simple rules that help it to maintain this product variety and to stay innovative. It focuses its R&D investment and brand development on a specific set of high-potential projects to reduce the complexity of its operations. HP copes well with a high level of complexity as it competes across the fast-moving IT, personal computing and consumer electronics businesses. Most other firms don't.

As markets become increasingly segmented in terms of price, design, reliability and features – by income, interests and preferences, gender, religion, ethics and geographic location – product and service variety proliferates. Consumers have more choice than ever before. As a result, managers have more complex decision-making options than ever before. Led by simple strategies they have to make clear choices about the range of products and services they maintain and develop. If they fail to do this they will be overwhelmed by over-complex portfolios.

> 55% of the firms in our study launch between one and 10 new products every year. 21% launch over 20 (and 5% launch over 100). 17% of firms do not retire any products every year.

Here we look at products and services as a source of costly complexity for managers.

Counting the hidden costs of product complexity

Product and service complexity is a classic example of the Pareto 80/20 rule in practice. That is to say 80 per cent of your margin will probably often come from 20 per cent of your product portfolio. Now imagine how much you could reduce your costs of goods and overheads if you only had to worry about 20 per cent of your products/services.

Unless you are Apple, we are willing to bet that you have too many poor-performing products and services cluttering up your organization.

An example: with just three different mobile (cell) phone handset models in its range, Apple now generates nearly as much revenue from mobile phone handsets as Nokia. If you exclude color changes and memory options, there are just three basic Apple handsets. Contrast this with Nokia, which (at the time of writing this book) has around 30 different models on the market. That's right: five years after entering the market, Apple, with just three handset models, is generating similar sales to Nokia, which has been in the market since 1971! We don't have profit figures for Apple iPhone, but we know that overall Nokia is losing money. To its credit, Nokia are starting to reduce the number of models, but it has a long way to go.

Apple iPhone: $47bn in sales, from three handset models with nine variations (including memory size options and colors)

Nokia: $51bn in sales, from 30+ hand set models with 80+ variations (including color options)

The hidden cost of product/service proliferation is huge. But it is hard to see the complexity costs of poor-performing products/services because many of the costs are hidden from direct view. The more products you have, the more complex the systems for managing logistics will be. Your management reports and financial reports/accounts will be longer and more complex to prepare. More people will be needed in sales, marketing, and customer services. More of your people will be spending their time on products that don't deserve to survive. More, more, more … all because you have too many poor products/services cluttering up your minds, systems, factories, reports and warehouses.

Some firms explicitly make a lean portfolio part of their core competitive advantage against rivals.

The UK DIY chain Wickes has historically operated with a much smaller number of SKUs than its competitors. It focuses on getting the quality, availability and price right on the most important products that DIY customers will need. This smaller product set has enabled it to grow (even in recession) when its competitors have mainly gone the other way, with more variety and lower marginal returns.

The fastest growing burger chain in the US is Five Guys Burgers and Fries. There are 17 things on its menu (and a range of toppings), but in a market where most of the competition is expanding their menu and allowing customization, Five Guys is succeeding through doing a few things well. The knock-on effects from a simple menu in terms of ingredients and logistics are huge, so Five Guys has been able to grow quickly in what many perceive as an already saturated market.

2. What our research shows

Chapter 1 outlines the various research projects we have conducted to understand what sources of complexity damage firms the most, in terms of their efficiency and effectiveness. This includes the Global Simplicity Index (GSI), linking complexity to performance, and our survey of 600 executives in 300 European firms of over 5000 employees.

Table 7.1 shows how managers rate a variety of complexity sources linked to developing, making, distributing and managing products and services, and connecting with their customers.

Creating and launching new products and services is one of the highest-impact sources of complexity in our survey. Alongside this, coping with the sheer number and diversity of customers and their demands is highlighted as a leading source of costly complexity. This clearly emphasizes the dual challenges of managing new product innovation while dealing with the difficulties of managing current customer needs and growing market share. Managing suppliers and distribution channels appears to be less of a complex challenge.

> 47% of our sample takes more than six months to bring a new product to market (19% take more than 19 months).

Our next step was to analyze this data a little differently – by singling out the poorest-performing firms in our survey and comparing their responses to those of managers from top-performing firms. It turns out that a much larger number of the product and service complexity factors appear at the top end of the rankings for these flagging firms. For managers in these weaker firms 'diversity of customer demands' is number two out of over 100 complexity indicators; 'customer interaction with the company' is number three; 'how products/services are presented to customers' and the 'number of suppliers', as well as the 'number of customers', all feature in the top 15.

This means that product and service complexity poses a greater problem for poor-performing firms. To put it another way, there is a clear relationship between failure to cope with these sources of complexity and lost profits.

Several key themes emerge from this analysis – and from other, industry-specific studies we have done. The growing segmentation of markets is having a significant impact on the complexity of the portfolio of products and services that managers have to deal with. This includes the current variety in terms of the range of markets, customers, product features,

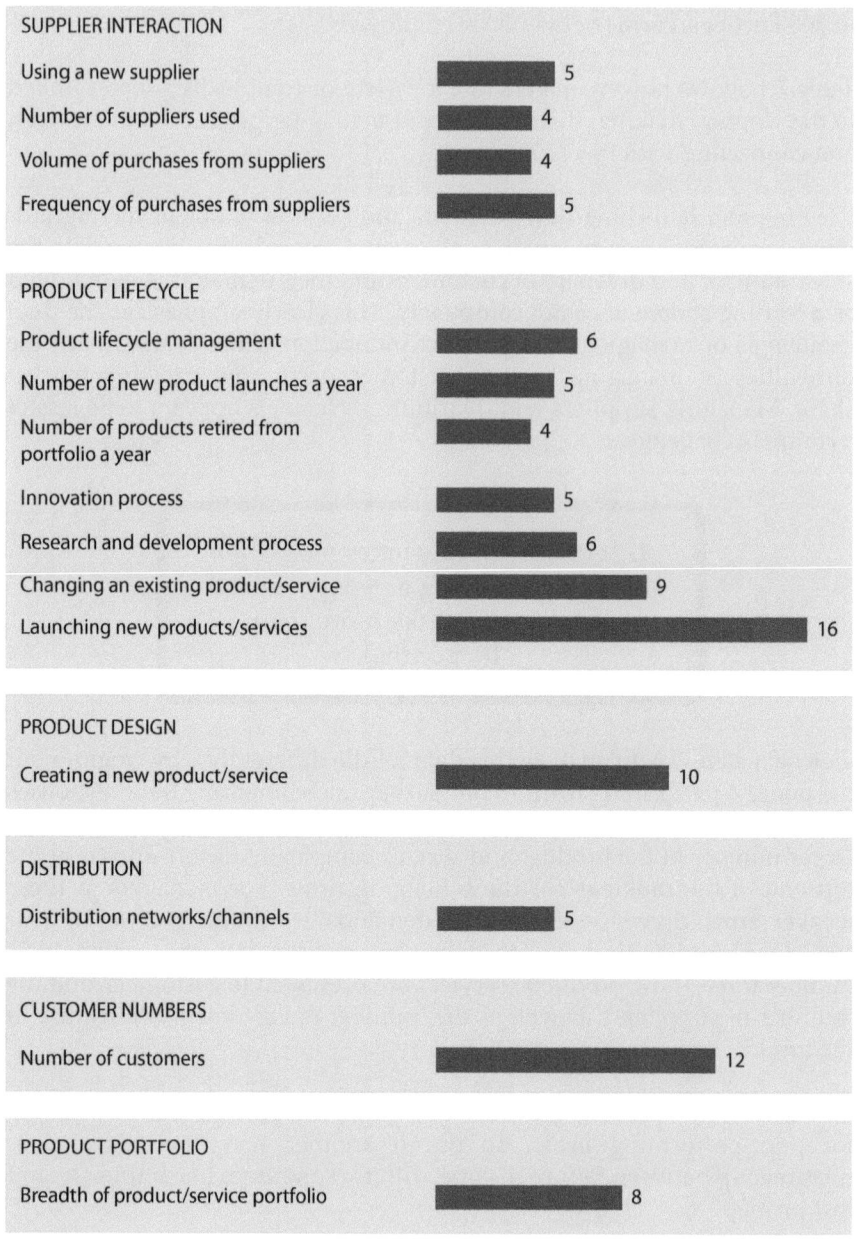

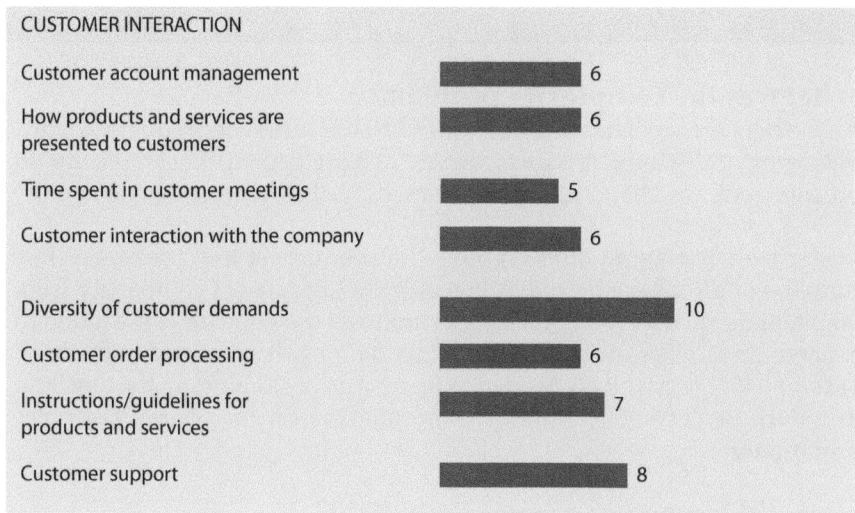

Complexity impact score: low to high

TABLE 7.1
The impact of product-and-services-related sources of complexity on the business
Note: This is a relative measure that combines the frequency with which this source
of complexity was cited by managers in our survey and their rating of the impact
it has on performance.

delivery modes, etc. and decisions about the potential future range of products and services that the firm needs to develop and launch.

All this raises key strategic questions about the diversity of your product and service portfolio – and markets, types of customer, variety of suppliers, distribution channels and, in turn, product divisions, specialist R&D departments and in turn … suppliers, contractors, joint venture partners, retail contracts (etc.) that you can cope with.

TRADER JOE'S: DARING TO BE SELECTIVE

What was the complexity problem?

An average grocery chain carries around 50,000 different product variants. Managing this many products drives a high degree of complexity in procurement, warehousing and logistics, as well as in-store management.

Trader Joe's wanted to offer high-quality products at low prices, but this simply wouldn't have been feasible with the high cost of complexity from maintaining such a broad product portfolio. At the same time, it wanted to expand the number of stores, but that would only have added to the level of complexity. Trader Joe's needed to find a way of simplifying the portfolio to reduce its costs, but without compromising on the overall customer proposition.

How did the power of simplicity help?

Trader Joe's decided to work with a dramatically simplified product portfolio. Today, it carries only 4000 product variants – less than 10 per cent of the number that other players in the grocery industry tend to stock.

To achieve this, it has focused on the core products that appeal to its target consumers. High-quality but unbranded organics give Trader Joe's customers a cheaper alternative to mainstream brands, while a selection of more unusual specialty items can also be offered at lower prices by focusing on own-brand offerings. And since its target consumers lead busy lifestyles, they actually prefer the convenience and simplicity of having fewer options to choose from.

Procurement, warehousing and logistics are all simpler due to the reduced product range. While traditional grocery retailers tend to stock some low-margin products and even some loss-leaders (products sold at a loss to entice customers into the store), Trader Joe's has cut all of these from its stores.

Having fewer products means ordering them can be done at higher volumes, so Joe's can negotiate lower purchasing prices, and there is less wastage due to the high turnover of inventory. And, because it now has fewer suppliers to deal with, it can focus on direct purchasing with the manufacturer, thereby cutting out the distributor in the middle.

What was the impact?

Focusing on simplicity has enabled Trader Joe's to achieve its objective of offering high-quality products at low prices. As a result, it has grown from a quirky regional chain to a national household name. Its limited product portfolio sends out a clear and focused message about the Trader Joe's brand – this has in turn strengthened its customer value proposition, and the retailer now has a highly loyal base of dedicated customers.

3. How to reduce product and service complexity

Some companies have already started to respond to the above challenges. These are normally the ones that have been pushed by a crisis in the business and falling profits to take a serious look at their product portfolio, markets and competitors.

Some focus more on 'upstream' complexity in terms of reducing the complexity of product inputs – materials, technologies, components, packaging and associated suppliers and developers – and moving toward leaner supply chains. Others focus more on 'downstream' complexity in terms of product outputs – models, features, brands and associated marketing and distribution channels, sales contracts, customer interfaces, etc.

We think you should do both of these together. Any extension of the product portfolio has upstream and downstream knock-on effects. So applying our two favorite simplicity principles will benefit the entire value chain:

- **Reduce downstream:** Identify the products and services that have a low marginal contribution to your profit and/or low growth potential. Cut these products/services out and you have dramatically simplified your business.
- **Standardize upstream:** At the component/ingredient end it is relatively easy to see where several products/services share similar ingredients or components. Standardize the components.

If you are in a firm that has already taken steps to simplify upstream and/or downstream the key question for you is probably: how can we go to the next level of sophistication, to squeeze more simplification out of the product and service portfolio?

For others, perhaps those who have not reached (or do not know they have reached) the portfolio complexity tipping point, a more basic starting point is to apply the two simplicity principles above.

> 27% of managers in our
> survey were coping with
> over 50 different suppliers.
> 7% had to deal with over 200!

The key steps to reducing product and service complexity

So how can you reduce product and service complexity? On one hand this is a very simple complexity challenge. Remember the Hans Hofmann quote, '*the ability to simplify means to eliminate the unnecessary so that the necessary may speak*'? Making your products and services less complex is mainly about working out what to keep and what to cut. But this process is often hampered by a simple fear – if I cut out poor performers I will lose revenue and profit.

To overcome this fear we need to work out a way to simultaneously reduce the number of products/services and increase profits. This is possible if you really understand your business well. To achieve this 'holy grail' of portfolio management there are five keys that we would usually focus on:

- Key 1: Understand the true cost of your product/service tail – if you could see the true profitability of your poor performers you would have little hesitation about cutting them.
- Key 2: Drive fixed costs down – when you cut your poor-performing products/services you must always cut fixed costs.
- Key 3: Understand your customer/consumer in more detail. If you do not understand your customers well enough you will end up with too many poorly designed products, and you will not know which products/services to keep. In addition, poor consumer understanding leads to over-engineering of your products.
- Key 4: Be brave enough to cut deeper – trust and bravery are essential because there are risks involved in reducing your product/service lines.
- Key 5: Refocus your energy and resources on your best products/services – you must ensure that you have a strong sales and marketing plan to drive consumers/customers over from the discontinued products/services to your other (better-performing) products/services.

Key 1: Understand the true cost of your product/service tail

The idea of product/service tail analysis is well established in many companies. The principle is very simple: you identify the 'tail' of poor performers in your product/service range and retire them from your product catalogue/range. If you do this well you can dramatically reduce complexity across all areas of your business.

However, there is one major challenge with tail analysis: it is incredibly difficult to calculate the true cost of poorly performing products/services. So many companies simply do not know that they are losing money on many of their products. As a result they think their product tail is more much more profitable than it is.

Figure 7.1 shows the problem more graphically. It is very difficult to allocate all the true cost of a product/service directly to individual products. So many costs are shared out on a percentage of revenue basis. When you do calculate the true cost of each product/service you will often find that your tail is a very expensive one.

Marginal contribution (or 'contribution margin-based pricing') is madness: product/service tail analysis often makes the mistake of only looking at the marginal contribution of each product/service. Under this approach, only variable costs are allocated to individual products/services. The assumption is that if a product/service is making a positive contribution to fixed costs then it deserves to live on.

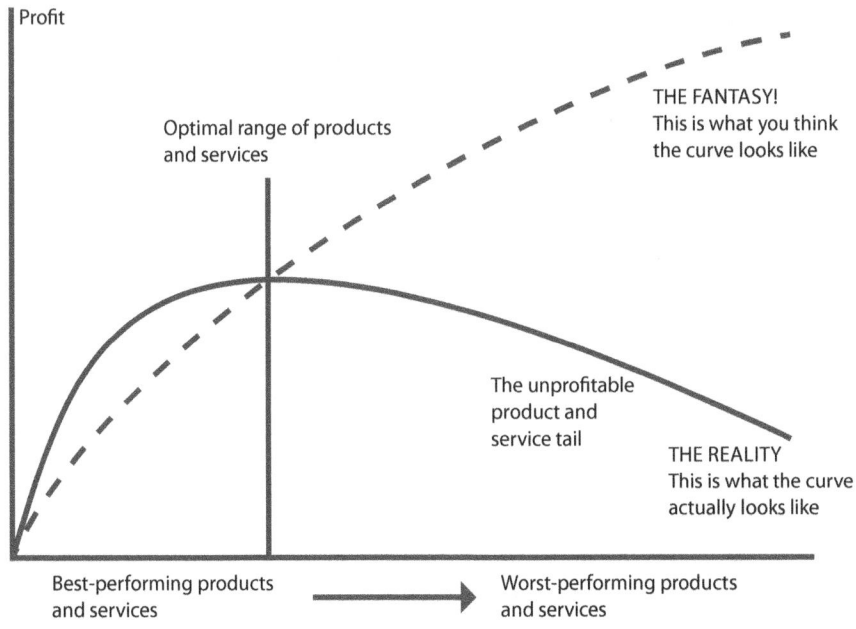

FIGURE 7.1
What your product/service profitability really looks like

When you think about it logically, this makes no sense. The more products/services you have to manage, the higher your fixed costs will be as you will need more people, more space, bigger systems, etc. In addition, more management time is devoted to fixing poor product/service performance than discussing your high performing products/services. Your poor performers take up more warehouse space for longer. You don't have to arrange endless promotions (which further reduce margins) to keep your good performers going. You don't have to argue with your customers that they should keep the good performers in their catalogue or on their shelves. You don't get complaints about good products/services.

So your poor performing products/services need to cover a much bigger proportion of fixed costs than the good performers. Using this marginal contribution approach is clearly going to create a false impression about the value of your tail products. So fixed costs have to be taken into account – and by their very nature they can be difficult to cut. Manufacturing capacity, for example, is 'fixed' because of the size of a plant and individual kit in the plant. Economies of scale are achieved by large-scale investments, but these can then only be cut by large-scale decommissioning and closures. Removing a small bit of your capacity can be impossible in some industries.

Fully costed tail analysis is better, but is still fraught with problems. In this approach you look at the profitability of each product and allocate all variable costs and a share of fixed cost to each individual product/service. Techniques like Activity Based Costing allow you to allocate some fixed costs with a degree of accuracy.

However, many fixed costs (e.g. central management overheads in finance, HR, etc.) can only be allocated on a percentage of revenue basis. These fixed costs are rarely allocated accurately. Poor performers will by definition have low revenues, so in absolute terms they pick up a low fixed cost allocation; but in real terms they will take up more management time and overhead than good performers. In order to justify their existence, poor performers should really be allocated a higher percentage of fixed costs than high performing products.

> One of the divisions of Novartis was responsible for making specialist foods for hospital patients. It was a fast growing and high margin business that looked like a star in comparison to other business units. The case for investing for growth in this area looked very compelling. However, it was a highly specialized area with low volumes, but the products were being made in factories originally designed for high volumes. These products were bulky, and stayed in the logistics system for longer. In addition, the quality assurance costs, regulatory compliance, R&D costs, customer

> *service time and patient support were all on a different scale. The*
> *precision and complexity of these products meant that more management*
> *time was devoted to this business area than to the simpler food products*
> *made for regular consumers. When all true costs were calculated, the*
> *true profitability of this business area was found to be only just above*
> *average for this part of Novartis business. The case for investment was*
> *less compelling and many product lines were not making money at all.*

So make sure that you have an accurate way of calculating true profit at the level of individual products/services. This means the costing and profitability model you use for your tail analysis has to be designed carefully to ensure that all the 'true costs' are allocated against each product/service. It is a good idea to standardize to one product/service profitability model that everyone uses and buys into. This reduces debates around the accuracy of the numbers or debates around the methodology used to assess products/service profitability. Investing in a good 'true cost' financial model will allow you to make better keep/kill decisions.

Key 2: Drive fixed costs down

Many of our clients complain that their tail analysis and cutting exercise has simply resulted in lower profits. They have taken out some poor-performing products/services, revenue has fallen and profit has declined. When we dig deeper into this the reason is often that they have seen a reduction in revenue by removing poor performers, but they have not reduced fixed costs.

As you add in more products/services, your fixed costs will obviously increase. However, portfolio proliferation does not just add to your complexity and costs in an incremental and proportional way. It can be exponential, and even worse, these costs are hidden. Adding one new product to your portfolio, even in a simple scenario, can mean adding one new customer, two new suppliers and three new contracts. Internally, this means one or more new projects for multiple additional decisions and interactions (reports, meetings, emails) between R&D, production, procurement and marketing – with additional work for central accounting and finance, IT and personnel. There will be further work if new people are hired, adding more complexity across many of these departments.

Calculating all of this – even with the most detailed activity based costing approach – is very difficult, if not impossible. We know, however, that this is the kind of step too far that takes firms over the complexity tipping point. As a result your fixed costs grow too fast because you have too many new products and services.

It follows that if fixed complexity costs have increased exponentially as you add new products and services, you will have to remove fixed costs exponentially when you cut out the poor performers. If you don't reduce the fixed costs aggressively, these expenses will simply get reallocated to the remaining good performers, which will now look marginal! This can push you into a downward profit spiral.

As part of your product/service tail review, you MUST also identify how you can reduce the fixed costs. Then you must follow through and make sure the fixed costs are driven out of the business. One way to do this is to ensure that for every $2 in revenue you might lose through tail cutting you find $1 in fixed cost savings. Another way is to look at how the business would be configured and managed if you went from, say, 1000 products to 600. The rationale behind this is simple. Although you can never estimate the benefit of the reduction of one product in terms of costs or organizational design, you can estimate what you could save if you cut 40 per cent of your products.

Write-off costs are also used as a reason for not cutting poor performers, i.e. if we stop this line we will have to write off the costs, which will harm our balance sheet. We appreciate that this is a difficult issue, but again, not making these courageous decisions is hiding the true profitability of your business, which skews decision-making. The write-off cost should also be covered by finding overhead savings that cancel it out.

Clean house: remember that even if you do retire the poor performing products/services, unless you do a proper cleanup afterwards, a lot of the complexity costs that went with these products will stay in the system for many years after.

> One of our clients is a very successful international technology company. In its fast-changing, innovative world it is no surprise that product life cycles are very short. So logically most of its products will be obsolete within a short period of time. The company is pretty good at retiring old products as they decline and become irrelevant to consumers. Some information needs to stay in the systems, as consumers quite rightly expect product support for the life of the product. However, the company also maintains up-to-date records on pricing for all its products, even the ones it doesn't sell. It also keeps details of stockists who no longer sell discontinued products. In three European warehouses, it has $13.2m worth of spare parts for products they no longer support. Presumably these are still recorded as an asset on their balance sheet. Someone somewhere has to manage and update all the information that goes with each old product. It costs you money to store irrelevant data in your systems

and it makes the system more complex and fragile if it is asked to store and manage more information than necessary. So yes, the product itself has gone, but most of the complexity it caused is still cluttering up the company's operations.

Aggressive fixed cost reduction needs to be at the heart of any tail cutting exercise that you run. Otherwise, you will keep products/services that you should be cutting.

Key 3: Understand consumer needs much better

Poor alignment of your portfolio to true consumer needs will also create product/service complexity. In order to make sure you have the right products/services you need to have an in-depth understanding of consumer needs, segments and usage occasions. Having a superficial understanding of the consumer/customer will create additional product/service complexity problems.

1. Duplication of product/service, where several of your products are being bought by the same people.
2. Poor product design and over-engineering of products.

Many companies have products/services that they think are different from each other, but consumers see them as being similar. This means that you will have duplication in your product/service portfolio with several products/services being used interchangeably by the same customer/consumer. What you need, of course, is for each product/service to be playing a different role in your portfolio by appealing to very different types of consumer or situation. If each product/service has a unique consumer proposition, then you can cover the market with a small number of products. Again Apple is the master of this.

For this reason many organizations have now adopted a more sophisticated product/service portfolio approach that ensures each product/service focuses on very specific customer needs or behaviors. In this approach, rather than looking at the products/services across the market as a whole, you break the market down into specific consumers' needs and usage situations or specific customer segments. This requires some sophisticated market research and volume modeling techniques, but the payback on the research costs is usually good.

Once you fully understand the different customer segments and their unique needs, your products and services can easily be mapped against the customer segments or needs that they best meet. What this often shows is that several products which you think are very different are in fact appealing to the same customer.

In Figure 7.2, four different products are being bought by consumers looking for a 'convenient family favorite'. Of these four products, two are performing well, but two are low margin/low potential. If you remove these poor performers from your portfolio, most of the revenue will transfer over to the remaining two products that address this consumer need. A recent example from a breakfast cereal maker illustrates the point. One of its brands is sold in 250g, 500g, 750g and 1000g packs. Now anyone who

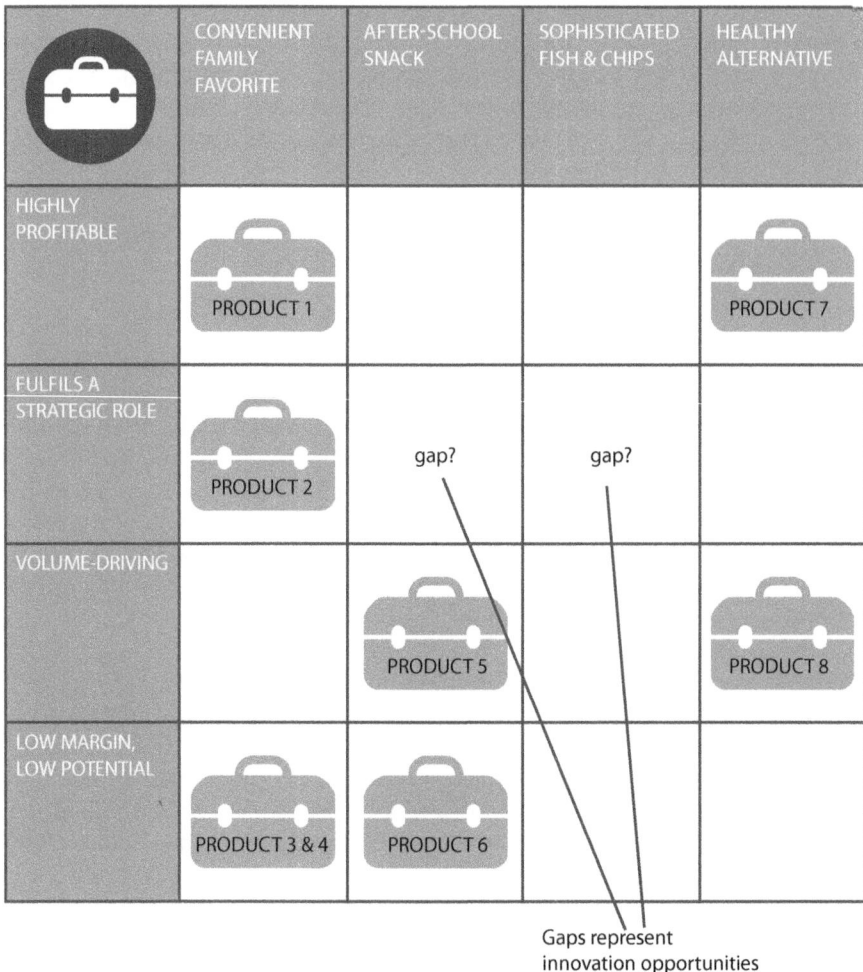

FIGURE 7.2
Customer needs-driven portfolio map

> Most of our respondents
> have one (or even fewer)
> customer meeting each week.
> But 6% have more than 15!

buys a 750g pack must love that breakfast cereal brand very much. If you discontinue the 750g pack, it's very unlikely that they will switch to a completely new brand. The research showed that loyal consumers would trade up to 1000g packs and that revenue would INCREASE by reducing the number of lines.

In summary, having a better understanding of consumer needs means that you can minimize revenue loss by cutting out products/services that are interchangeable for your customers. If you do this and reduce fixed costs, your tail cutting work will always have a positive impact on profit.

Steve Jobs used this approach on his return to Apple in 1995. He drew a simple two-by-two matrix with laptop/desktop on one axis and professional/consumer market on the other axis. To meet the needs of these segments he worked out that the company needed four core products to cover all the key needs in the PC market. This led to a dramatic rationalizing of R&D projects to focus on a smaller number of high-potential PC products.

UNILEVER: FROM 1200 TO 400 BRANDS

What was the complexity problem?

Following a series of major acquisitions during the 1960s, 70s and 80s, Unilever ended up with over 1200 brands in its portfolio.

This made it increasingly difficult to run Unilever efficiently. Having so many different brands reduced the amount of senior management time available to focus on the highest-growth opportunities.

In addition, this massive portfolio made factories complicated to run, and logistics slow and unreliable. Decision-making was slow and convoluted; thousands of relatively low-impact initiatives cluttered up middle managers' time.

How did the power of simplicity help?

Unilever announced that it would cut back its portfolio to less than 400 strategic brands, while at the same time growing its revenue and profit.

No one really believed it could do this, let alone while improving financial performance.

First it identified a small number of brands with global growth potential and developed new brand strategies to drive these assets through a globally focused marketing organization.

In addition, it identified a larger number of 'local jewels'. While these brands didn't possess true global potential, they were strong, growing and profitable in the countries/regions where they competed.

The rest of the brands and products were sold off, discontinued or migrated under the remaining brands.

What was the impact?

- Organizational, product and process complexity were dramatically reduced.
- Unilever managers could now focus their time on a small number of brands with high revenue and profit potential.
- Sales, revenue and profit increased, even though there were 800 fewer brands in the portfolio.

Understanding customer needs in more detail will lead to further product/service simplification benefits.

Better consumer understanding also prevents over-engineering. Another common form of product/service complexity is the over-engineering of products and services. Each additional feature, ingredient or component adds cost, but it also makes your product more complex for customers to use and more expensive for them to buy. So to us it seems there are no winners when products are over-engineered. This is definitely the case with mobile phones and laptops. These products are packed full of expensive features: most customers use less than 90 per cent of the features available in their technology products. One of our clients found that the majority of its new products launches were losing money, because there were too many features that customers simply would not pay for, but they were being given the features anyhow. If you are determined to waste money on unnecessary features, at least take Apple's lead and make it easy and intuitive for your customers to navigate past the useless and find the useful! The best way to avoid over-engineering your products is to understand in detail the real needs of your customers and how much utility they place on each individual feature. This can easily be done using market research techniques like conjoint or 'trade-off' analysis, where customers are asked to trade off different features, in order to understand which features are really important. Since different segments of consumers/customers will have different needs, it is important look at each customer/consumer segment separately. We have successfully done this in mobile phones to identify the optimal mobile phone 'feature bundles' for six distinctively different segments of mobile phone customers.

Better consumer understanding also stops you launching poor products/services: is this too obvious a point to make? Many new products launched are not in response to customer needs, but rather they exist because you missed something important out in the first version you launched. Why does Apple only need to sell three models of the iPhone? Simple: the product is so good they don't need to launch new variants every few months. If you are launching a new product soon after the last version, ask yourself why. Is it because technology is changing that fast or customer needs demand it … or is it because you did a poor job on the original product design?

Understanding your consumers also allows you to design simplicity into all your products/services: 'simplicity inside' should be one of your design mantras, along with simple to use. Without compromising on quality you will find there are many ways to simplify product design. Always challenge the product/service design teams to create simpler products by:

- understanding customer needs in real detail, so they only build in features that customers will pay a premium for;
- using existing standard ingredients/components where possible;
- outsourcing component complexity and assembly to specialist suppliers;
- where complexity cannot be removed, 'hiding complexity' by making products/services intuitive for customers to navigate and use.

Key 4: Be brave and cut deeper

The next reason why you probably have too many poor-performing products and services is that you are not being brave enough. It takes courage to cut your tail and sometimes we don't have enough of that!

- **Risk aversion:** People should be rewarded for their courage in cutting out poor performing products/services. In many cases we see our clients start on the road to cutting significantly, but end up cutting too few, even though they know some products are unprofitable. This is usually because of the fear that profit will be reduced or that they will kill the product before it has had a chance to thrive. Being open and honest about the risks is key, as is then sharing the responsibility.
- **Politics:** We call this chairman's wife thinking – she loves that flavor so he'll never let us cut that product out. If someone senior believes a product/service is very important or good, it's often hard to take it out of your range.
- **Frequency of review:** The process of reviewing and cutting the product tail should be done every year at the very least. This is because during the year you will add more new products/services and others will start to lose share in the market. So you should have mini reviews every six months and full reviews every year as part of your annual planning process.
- **Uncertainty of growth potential:** The final reason for not taking out poor performers is thornier. Something might be small today, but it could be a big seller in the future. The key here is to make sure that you have carefully considered the growth potential of each product/ service as part of your review. Remember every product/service you launched made sense on paper before you launched it. If in doubt, thoroughly test new products/services before launching them. The cost of market research or market testing is usually much lower than the cost of keeping poor performers in your product/service portfolio. Once a product/service is launched it is very hard to take it out again.

In our experience there are five good reasons to hang onto a poorer-performing product/service. If your poor performer cannot PROVE that it ticks one or more of these boxes, then it should be on death row.

Five good reasons to hang onto poor performing products/services

1. **High growth potential:** Is this product/service competing in a fast-growing segment of the market? Is this product likely to benefit from any positive consumer/customer trends? Does this product/service meet a unique consumer need that is not covered by another one of your products? If so then keep it, but be sure it has real growth potential. Often this is just a triumph of hope over reality or good salesmanship!
2. **Too early to tell:** Has the product/service been on the market for long enough for you to assess potential? If it has been on the market for several years and is not performing, you'd need to have some pretty good reasons why this would suddenly change!
3. **Key customer relationship:** The product/service may be critical for maintaining a relationship with a particular customer; taking it out may have a detrimental impact on the relationship and sales of other key products and services. It is easy for the sales team to claim this is the case. Make them prove it beyond doubt!
4. **Holding the shelf/market space** until you can bring out the latest version. In some markets it is very hard to get onto the customers' shelves, or into their product catalogues. In this case you may prefer to keep a poor performer in the range until you can bring in something better to replace it. But make sure you get something better on the shelf before they spot you are underperforming and rationalize you from their portfolio! Good retailers will stop selling your product way before you even realize there is a problem. Each product has to pay a minimum 'rent' for its place on their shelf or in their catalogue. If you don't pay enough rent, you will be out on the street. Retailers are efficient and brutal at kicking out poor performers.
5. **Competitor spoiler:** Finally, a poor performing product/service may be a real thorn in the side of a competitor. In this case, if you can prove it fulfils this role, then you have a strong argument to keep the product/service in your portfolio.

Prove it! The key point it not to let these things become excuses for taking the soft option and keeping poor performers on. If you can prove your product/service fits into one of these categories then fine, keep it. But make your managers prove their case.

Key 5: Refocus your energy and resources on your best products
Products/service rationalization is the perfect excuse to do what you should already be doing anyhow, selling more of your best products/services! What would happen if you poured all your marketing and sales resources behind promoting your best products? You would probably be

able to increase your revenue on those products. Going back to the Apple/
Nokia illustration – all of Apple's marketing might is focused on three
products, while Nokia's is dissipated across over 30.

So part of the portfolio rationalization project should be focused on how you
can redirect resources to growing the revenues from your best products. In
the example of the food company above (see Figure 7.2), any money that
was being spent on products three and four should now be redirected to
growing products one and two.

The most successful portfolio managers we see will always develop a sales
and marketing plan that goes hand in hand with the tail cutting process.
The objectives are simple:

- To actively migrate existing consumers from your old products/
  services to your best ones. This is a clear win/win. The customer gets a
  better product, you still get their money.
- To promote your top sellers more aggressively and bring in new
  customers. Your best products are the best way for new customers to
  experience your company. So now you have cleared some dead wood
  you should have more resources to promote your best products/
  services.

ALLIANCE UNICHEM: RE-PACKAGING THE
OWN-BRAND RANGE

What was the complexity problem?

The range of private-label products had grown significantly in number, but profit and growth were declining.

How did the power of simplicity help?

The company had decided to redesign the packaging, hoping this would resolve the sales problem. However, it soon became clear that this would cost over $3m due to the high number of individual products that needed to be repackaged.

So we recommended that it start by dramatically rationalizing the number of products in its range. This would not only reduce the cost of the packaging redesign, but there would also be massive cost savings throughout the production and logistics chains.

To do this, we revisited the overall positioning of the range, asking the simple question: 'what will make our private label range unique and exciting to our customer?' This allowed us to identify a stronger, clearer purpose for the product range, which was about offering a high-quality, good value alternative to the branded products that its customers bought most frequently. It was not about offering an alternative to every single brand! Once this was agreed, it immediately became obvious which products should be kept and which should be discontinued.

What was the impact?

Having a clear and simple positioning for the own brand lead to a rationalization of the range by 50 per cent. Of the remaining 50 per cent, about 50 products accounted for circa 80 per cent of the revenue generated by the range. These were identified as the candidates for re-packaging. The sales force were refocused on the own brand, with the simple, clear purpose for why you would stock it, and sales of the 50 core items grew by 17 per cent in the first year.

Other ways to reduce product/service complexity

Simplicity sells – be simple to choose and simple to do business with
There is a growing body of research that proves customers prefer companies that are simpler to do business with and will choose less complex products and services over apparently better products/services that are more complex.

In their recent study of brand simplicity Siegel+Gale conclude that customers are now saying, with an ever louder voice, 'If you want our business keep it simple. Be straight. Be clear. Be quick and be real.'

In the same study, they provide some powerful data to support their findings:

- Price premium: They estimate that consumers will pay a price premium of between 5 and 6.5 per cent for simpler brands or services that are simpler to buy.
- Brand loyalty: 82 per cent of consumers are more likely to recommend a simpler brand. Simpler brands are easier to understand and live longer in the memory as a result.

This makes absolute sense to us. People's lives have become more and more hectic and complicated. Going shopping is confusing to the point of distress, with a plethora of choices but very little true differentiation between products. People simply don't have time to deal with complex customer service processes: they will go elsewhere. They will not work hard to try and find your product; they do not have time and why should they? If it takes ten minutes to resolve a simple query when they phone you you'll probably be talking to them for the last time.

Zurich has made 'being easy to do business with' one of its major initiatives to strengthen its relationships with the brokers it depends on to sell its insurance projects. Which company will the broker favor? The one with the great products he/she does not understand, or the one with simpler insurance products? Similarly, will the broker prefer the simpler IT system provided by Zurich over a more complex one from its competitors? Which insurance company will the customers favor? The one that resolves their claim simply and effectively or the one that makes them fill in a long, complicated claim form and jump through 100 process straps before they eventually get their money?

Similarly, Vodafone has made simplicity one of its core values, which covers not only its internal operations but also how it can make mobile technology and customer interactions as simple as possible.

The simplicity-sell principle can be applied to pretty much everything you do to promote your:

- simpler product/service/brand strategies
- simpler product design
- simpler product/service manual
- simpler websites

- simpler positioning statements
- simpler advertising
- simpler shelf layouts in store
- simpler promotions, etc.

This point extends into the relationship between suppliers and customers.

- Companies that are complex to do business with will not get the lowest prices from their suppliers. The cost of doing business is now added into the prices you are charged.
- Suppliers that have complex ordering, delivery and invoicing systems will quickly find that no one is placing orders with them.

Remove 'same but different' local variations

In many multi-product companies we often see that there are several products that are very similar to each other in different countries, but local marketing teams claim that the small differences, which complicate the product portfolio, are the key to success in their country. If you changed my logo from light blue to dark blue I would lose 100 per cent of my sales. This is rarely true: increasingly consumers are becoming less different as the world of products and services globalize. Many products/services can be harmonized across national boundaries to reduce complexity dramatically. So you should push hard to harmonize recipes and products/services across national boundaries.

Cut your customer tail

As we have identified, the hidden cost of poor-performing products and services is significant. The same is true of poor-performing customers. Most of the true cost of supplying your products/services to them is hidden. So even if you are sophisticated enough to have a customer profitability model in your company, it is still likely that the true cost of doing business with small customers is hidden. They take up a disproportionate share of fixed costs.

So the same principles as the 'product tail process' should be applied to regularly reviewing your customers and cutting out tail customers.

Where you cannot risk losing the customer all together you can do several things.

- Get the customer to work with you to increase volumes, so you can make them worthwhile.

- Increase prices.
- Create a separate business unit or sales organization to focus just on the tail customers.
- Outsource management of these customers to a specialist outsourced sales organization.

Reduce component/ingredient complexity

Many products/services have different ingredients/components even though they could easily share one common ingredient or component. We recently spoke to a food company who had undertaken a major review of ingredients used in their product recipes. They discovered that they had 13 different specifications of onion flavor, which was used as a minor ingredient in several different products they made. They rationalized it to two different onion flavor products. Their product scores improved, as they rightly decided to use the best onion flavor out of the 13 available. This one small change saved them $2m each year and reduced complexity immediately. It is often the case that standardizing to the best single ingredient/component results in a simplification of the product and an improvement in quality. You should regularly review all product component/ingredients lists to identify opportunities to simplify your product specifications.

> Over half of the firms we surveyed (51%) are dealing with over 10,000 sales transactions each and every day (22% are coping with over 1 million!). 34% manage over 10,000 purchasing transactions each day and 10% over a million.

Contract manufacturer

Increasingly clever companies are focusing on the parts of the value chain where you can add most value, e.g. customer insight, product design, sales, marketing and distribution. They use contract manufacturers to design components and assemble/manufacture the final product.

'Special' products group

Some companies are setting up special business units to manage their non-strategic/tail products with efficiency in mind. AstraZeneca has successfully done this for many drugs approaching the end of their patent life.

Sell them to a competitor/specialist

Finally consider selling your tail products to a competitor or to a specialist third party 'multi product' marketing and sales organization. To a competitor? Yes, let them carry the cost of poor performers!

> 'Fools ignore complexity.
> Pragmatists suffer it. Some can avoid it.
> Geniuses remove it.'
> *Alan Perlis*[1]

FIVE KEY POINTS ON PRODUCT AND SERVICE COMPLEXITY

1. Product and service portfolios can grow in range and diversity to the point that they take firms over the complexity tipping point.
2. Launching new products and services is one of the most complex things that managers do. Coping with the diversity of customer demands is also a key challenge.
3. Removing poor-performing products and reducing upstream and downstream complexity should be the targets when streamlining product portfolios.
4. Cutting the poor-performing tail is not straightforward. It needs to be done with a full understanding of the cost–benefit trade-offs and the real preferences of customers.
5. Simplicity sells.

---

4. From products and services to simplifying – everyday

Product portfolios can grow to become large and diverse in a good way, adding profitability by serving a range of market segments. But they can also take firms over the complexity tipping point by becoming too big and diverse, creating upstream and downstream complexity and hiding loss makers alongside profit leaders.

A firm's range of products and services need to be managed and developed in conjunction with a close understanding of changing customer needs. Cut out the redundant tail and keep adding only the versions, features, bells and whistles that customers will really pay for. This way added value is maintained.

As we said in Chapter 1, one of the most common problems brought about by complexity in business is the disconnect between added value in products and services and the individuals who sit at the heart of the firm working away on a daily basis. The ideal firm involves everyone simply adding value through everyday actions and activities, and this is where we focus next, in Chapter 8.

For more on how to cope with product and service complexity go to: http://www.simplicitypartnership.com/

Chapter 8
How to Simplify: Everyday

COPING WITH COMPLEXITY: STORIES FROM THE FRONT

Over-the-top management reporting

In the European region of a large global original equipment manufacturer, a campaign to simplify regular reports was initiated, since it was felt that some redundancy had accumulated over the years. The Vice President of Manufacturing decided on a radical approach. First, he pinned up all known regular reports on the wall in a conference room. To his team's amazement, nearly all the wall space in this sizeable room was covered.

Next, he instructed his organization to stop sending all reports, including those to the global center, and wait for the reaction. A report that was missed by a recipient could be reinstated with the authority of one of the VP's next in command.

After four months, there was no reaction from the usual recipients of no less than 60 per cent of the reports! At this point, the VP and his team reviewed the 60 per cent and only two of these reports were reinstated. Two large boxes were filled with the monthly volume of eliminated reports. Examples of the redundant reports:

- Daily absentee report from each manufacturing plant.
- Monthly report from each plant to split headcount into defined categories, e.g. hourly/salary; hourly by skilled/unskilled; skilled by multi/electrical/mechanical; health restricted employees; male/female, etc. This report had initially been done for a one-off benchmarking exercise but had never gone away.
- Daily Accident Report by plant with description of any reported incidents including cuts and bruises. This had been introduced to increase the focus on safety at the workplace. Reported incidents had reduced by over 90 per cent with serious incidents almost eliminated. Decision taken was to trust the well-ingrained processes, to report only serious incidents and to make one overall annual report by plant. The result was no increase in incidents and a reduction of 99 per cent of the reports.
- Monthly report to monitor purchases and stock levels in Expense Stores. Decision was to trust plant management and processes and to carry out an annual audit.

1. Simply add value – everyday

It would be wrong to read this book and conclude that attacking complexity is only about setting up projects to re-engineer processes, redesign your global organization design or rationalize product/service portfolios. The average manager spends the majority of her/his day in meetings, writing emails, reporting on results/KPIs or progress on major projects/issues, discussing and agreeing important decisions, preparing briefing documents and presentations, working on project actions and talking to customers, colleagues, regulators, etc. There is significant complexity in all these day-to-day activities, so attacking this everyday complexity is a critical battle in the overall war on complexity.

One of the central themes of this book is that firms and the people in them need to make every effort to focus on 'simply adding value'. By doing this not only will the firm perform better, but the individual efficiency gains mean that people will have more time, i.e. they can add the same value in less time or more value in the same time. This gives them more choices in terms of their work–life balance and this generally makes everyone happier.

Asking these two questions can help you be more effective everyday (Figure 8.1):

- Am I doing the right things?
- Am I doing things in the right way?

Wasting the work day is bound to make everyone unhappy – in the short term or the long term, as inefficiencies begin to mount.

For those very (rare) people who don't want to spend time on value drivers, here's ten great ways you can waste your day! This is deliberately provocative, but who can say that they never do any of these things in their work day?

Ten ways to waste your work day
1. **Work really hard going in the wrong direction**
    - Devote as much of your day as possible to projects or activities that have limited impact on the real value drivers in your business.
    - Spend your time on really urgent things, even if they are not important to success in the long term.
    - Try and reverse all the decisions you made yesterday.

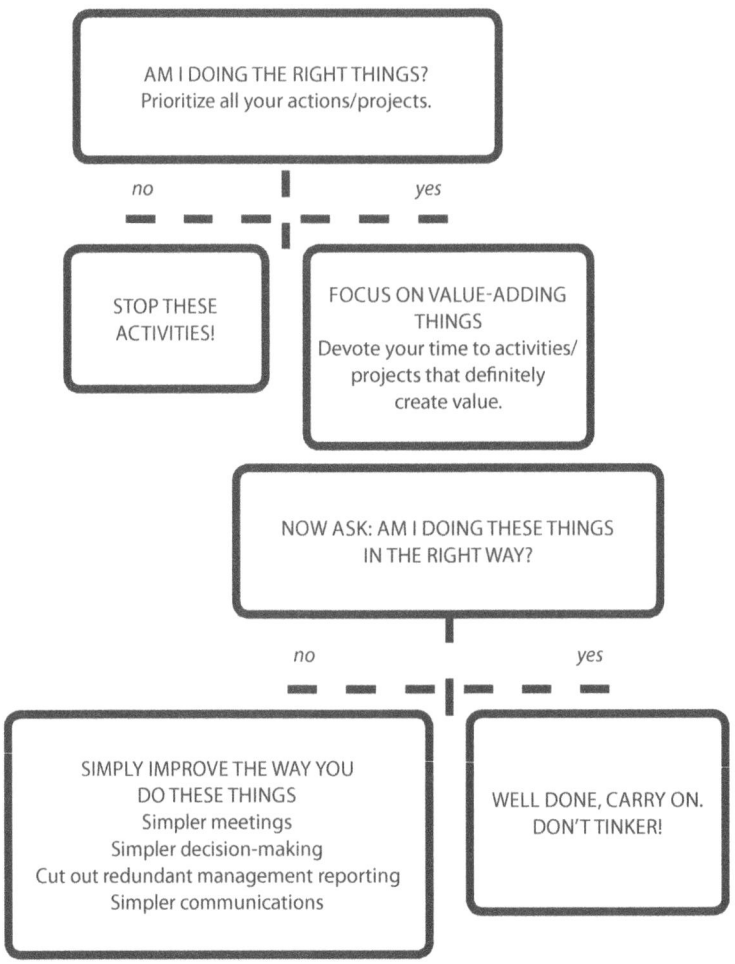

FIGURE 8.1
Am I doing the right things in the right way?

2. **Learn rocket science**
   - Don't delegate things that you are no good at to the real experts. Just try and do them yourself; you'll get there eventually.

3. **Pontificate**
   - Defer all important decisions until you have some more useless or unobtainable information, and then delay the decision for another month.
   - Talk around the subject as much possible, but don't talk about the real issues or move things forward.

- Repeat what the last person said, but don't use the same words as them. That way it will sound like you are actually making a different point.
- Overintellectualize and overcomplicate absolutely everything you can.
- Focus on the politics; don't worry about truth or action.

4. **Involve everyone in everything**
    - Have as many points of view as you possibly can, as it's great to hear 100 people's identical perspectives, all expressed in subtly different ways.
    - Try to involve people who don't have the experience/skills to add value, and then listen to them all really diligently and try to implement all their suicidal suggestions.
    - Try to spend as much time as possible aligning people on issues that don't affect them or they cannot contribute to.

5. **Focus on the process, not on the action/issue itself**
    - Spend your days agonizing over the process; don't worry about getting things done when there's a process to be embellished or discussed!

6. **Perfect absolutely everything**
    - Make sure you get everything 100 per cent right all the time, even if it's not particularly important.
    - Don't worry about spending your time perfecting everything to the point where it's two years too late!

7. **Reinvent the wheel**
    - Change/amend everything that comes across your desk to reflect your personal views or preferences. Don't worry about whether your changes are substantive; just make sure it's done your way!
    - Revel in the joy of reinventing something that exists, or repairing something that works really well already!

8. **Make email the focus of your entire day**
    - Log on to your email at 6am the morning, then spend all your time working on your email inbox.
    - Respond immediately and start working on anything unimportant or humorous. Defer anything important to another day.
    - Send as many emails to as many people as possible, making sure that your ass is fully covered by copying everyone in the company into every email.
    - If you don't have access to your computer, check your phone every three minutes.

- Don't bother with the phone and don't walk ten meters to talk to the person next to you, just send them another email.

9. **Duplicate, duplicate**
   - Don't waste time doing your own job, spend your time doing someone else's work, or even better do exactly what another person/department does but in a slightly different way.

10. **Do everything you can think of**
    - Develop a list of 100 projects/ideas that you think might be good.
    - Don't prioritize the projects/ideas that will have the biggest impact on your company's performance; instead divide your day into 100 individual slots and devote six minutes (1/100 of your working day) to each idea.
    - This is great because you will never achieve anything, so you won't make any mistakes, so you won't get fired.

In order to effectively reduce overall business complexity your organization will need to bring the power of simplicity to all of your daily work activities. There is a huge range of everyday activities that cause complexity, so for the purposes of this chapter we have focused on the ones that come up the most often with our clients.

1. Prioritize rigorously.
2. Simplify meetings.
3. Simplify communications: email, documents, presentations.
4. Streamline management reporting.

Not all of these things will be broken in your organization. So use your complexity diagnosis to identify which things are the biggest problems for your organization, then focus on improving the forms of everyday complexity that are the biggest drag on your success. Some of you may also feel that the guidelines that follow are patronizing or even obvious, but you only have the right to be offended if you can honestly say that you always do these things well! Sometimes stating the obvious clearly, simply and somewhere visible is all you need to get back on track.

If you would like to simplify your everyday work life, there are four overarching 'simplicity principles' that you can use:

- **Prioritize:** There is plenty of evidence to suggest that the more things you try to do, the less you will achieve. The brain and body have limits: when you try to do too much you end up failing to achieve both the big and the small things you have set out to do.

- **Reduce:** The unnecessary things will always get in the way of progress. So the simplest way to reduce complexity is to remove everything that is unnecessary from work life. You should focus only on what really matters and reduce/remove everything else. Once you have identified the top priorities in your day, or the most important meetings or projects, then it should be easy to cut out the less important things.
- **Standardize:** Make things as similar as possible, and remove any duplication. This allows people to become familiar with how things are done, reducing complexity and increasing efficiency.
- **Clarify:** Make it clear how things are done, what you really mean, who is responsible and visualize complex ideas/components. Anything that is unclear will create complexity, while people try to work out what is required.

To make these principles real and tangible, it is useful to introduce some supporting rules and guidelines for attacking everyday work complexity. The following few pages will, we hope, be helpful.

2. Prioritize rigorously

Simplify your weekly to-do list by clarifying, prioritizing and reducing. Most of you know that focusing on fewer bigger things will mean you have a better chance of delivering the big ticket items. As we have already mentioned, the average manager spends 40 per cent of his/her time on activities that have no real value to the organization's success, so a lot of our work is simply not useful! Even when all the activities we have on our list are adding value in some way, there is too often not enough time in the day to-do them all, so prioritizing your to-do list and pruning it down to a manageable number of items is critical. Very few managers do this routinely well.

- You should start each week (or day if you prefer) by listing all the activities that need to be completed that week/day. Don't forget to allocate time for thinking, planning and developing ideas where necessary. These tasks can be even more valuable than formal meetings or workgroups.

Once you have your list, review the activities that are planned and ask which activities will have the biggest impact on the success of your company/ department today. Which will have little or no impact?

Now create a prioritized activity list for the day/week. It is important to carefully consider the criteria you will use for prioritizing. Here are some suggested prioritization approaches:

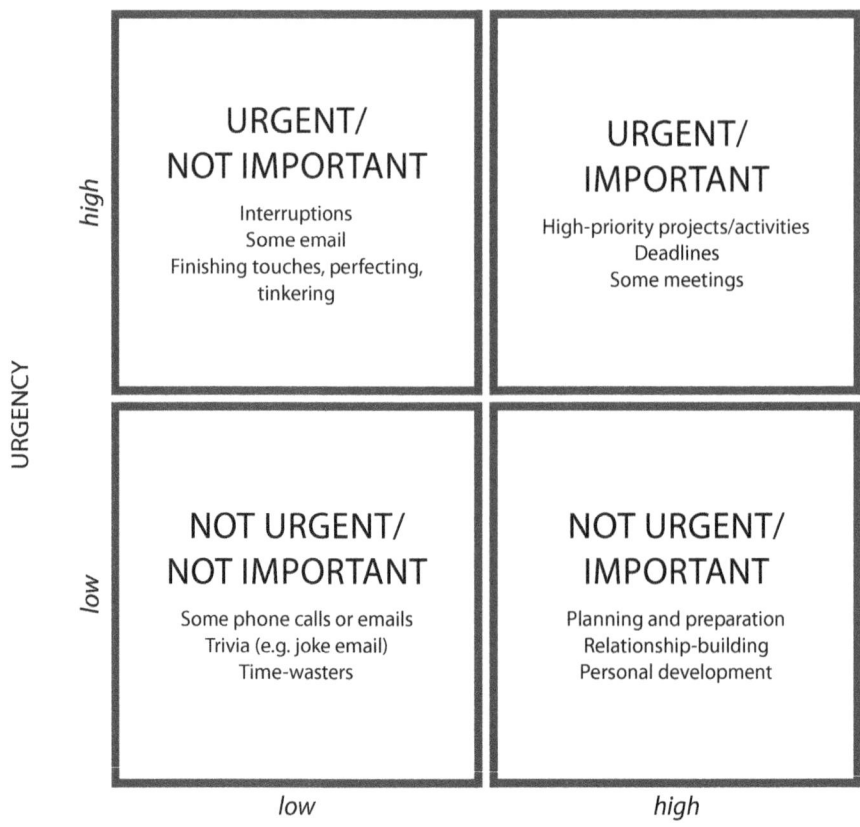

IMPACT ON VALUE DRIVERS/STRATEGY

FIGURE 8.2
Value/urgency matrix

- Rank items according to the level of impact each item will have on value drivers or achievement of your strategy.
- Use the value/urgency matrix in Figure 8.2 to help you prioritize the most important activities each day. Only allow a maximum of three tasks in the top right box at any one time – if you add in something new, you must move one of the existing tasks into a different box.
- Look for the 80/20 opportunity. Pareto's 80/20 rule tells us that 80 per cent of your success will come from 20 per cent of your projects, so try to identify the 20 per cent of your projects/activities that will give you 80 per cent of your results.
- If your work is closely linked with other people, consider the dependencies other people have on you and schedule your tasks accordingly.

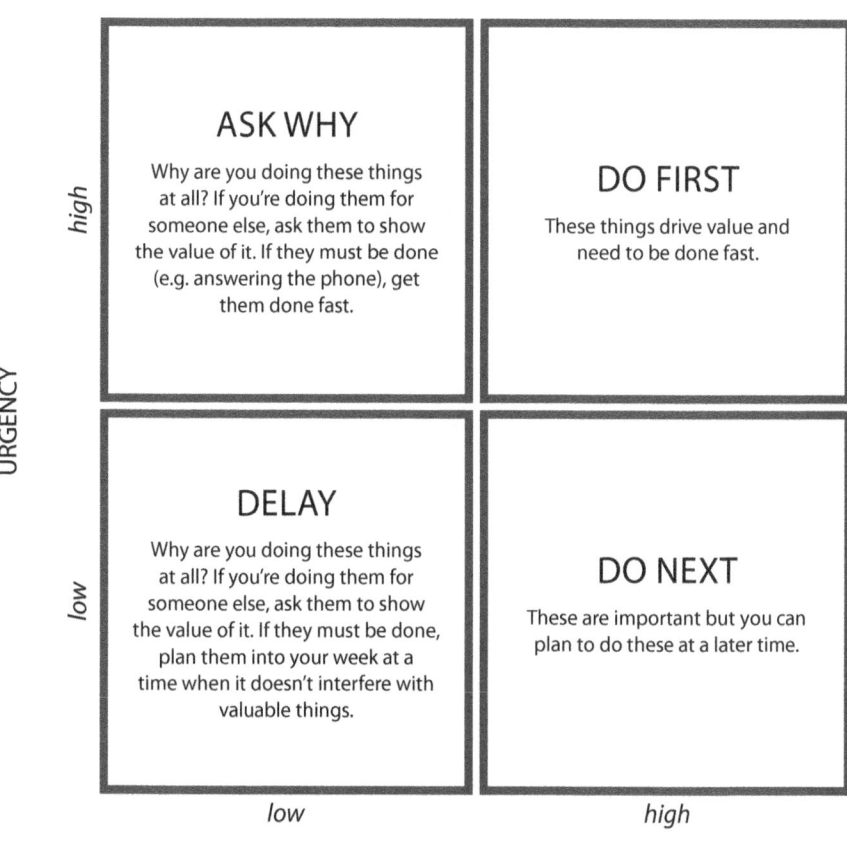

IMPACT ON VALUE DRIVERS/STRATEGY

- Challenge/stop doing the 'low impact' activities or push back and challenge the originator of the request by asking why they need you to do this. Challenge them to prove that their request is linked to one of your company's value drivers. If it must be done, seek the simplest and most effective way to do it, then move on to a real value driver!
- Shift: Trying to do activities that are way beyond your experience/skill set will increase complexity. Shift activities that do not fit with your department's role/value drivers to other departments or external suppliers who will be better than you at doing this.
- Time-box your activities in advance, and challenge yourself to stick to the timings as closely as you can. This will reduce the overall time spent on activities by cutting out the final tweaking/embellishing stage that you may spend an extra hour on in order to avoid moving onto the next, more difficult task!

Regularly prioritize company/departmental projects. Your people will be working on several major projects. Market information will be changing constantly and your people will be learning new things about the project as it progresses. This constant flow of new information needs to be fed back into the debate on which projects to prioritize. So you should revisit project priorities each month/quarter to check that there are not too many and to reprioritize them as necessary. Don't change priorities unnecessarily, as this will add complexity.

3. Simplify meetings

Most businesses have meetings at the core of everyday activities, but most people don't stop to think about the cost associated with having a meeting. It seems like an easy way to solve a problem, but if you add up the cost of all the people in the room, does that always justify the added value that results from the meeting?

Reduce the number and length of meetings

Most companies/departments have a monthly/weekly/annual cycle of regular meetings that people attend. At the time these schedules were created (sometime in the distant past) each of these meetings was probably necessary. But the chances are when they stopped being necessary they were never taken out of the calendar, or other similar meetings have been added to the schedule. So you should start by reviewing all the regular meeting that your department runs or attends.

- List all the meetings your department regularly runs or attends. Show them on a calendar or diagram so you have a simple overview of them all.
- Which are the most important meetings for your team/department? Rank each meeting in terms of the impact each meeting has on your company's value drivers. Or use the 80/20 rule to identify the most important meetings for your overall success.
- Now look for opportunities to reduce everything.
  - Set a stretch target to reduce the number of meetings by 50 per cent.
  - Stop/kill any meetings that do not have a clear value in helping to deliver your strategy or don't help to improve your profit.
  - Reduce the number of people attending the remaining meetings.... Make sure that the people who are ESSENTIAL are DEFINITELY THERE – otherwise the meeting will not deliver the outcomes you need. Make sure anyone who is NOT NEEDED is definitely NOT THERE.

   – Reduce the number of regular agenda points to reduce the length of the meetings.
   – De-dupe: Are any of the meetings duplicating what happens at other meetings? If so either cut out one of the duplicates or combine them into one meeting.
   – Reduce the amount of information that is shared before/during the meeting. My old boss used to say meetings are for conversations, not presentations. If you want me to sit and read something send it to me by email. If we need to talk, let's meet!

Improve meeting management skills and behaviors

The other way to simplify meetings is to improve your basic meeting management skills. Again you might think this is already common in most companies, but surprisingly it is not! Or if it is common knowledge, it is not used! Often there are pockets of good practice in meeting management, but these are not being followed company-wide. Standardizing your approach to meeting management across the company is a great way to ensure that everyone is running simple and effective meetings.

To refresh your memory here are some of the basic rules of good simple meetings:

- Structured agenda: Always send an agenda when you book the meeting (see Figure 8.3). People can then see if they need to attend. The agenda should have no more than five items in total. Under each agenda item provide the following information :
  - Value driver: Say explicitly which company value driver this agenda point contributes to.
  - Purpose: Be clear on why you are putting this point on the agenda: This could be to get everyone's input/ideas, to make a decision on something important, to share critical information on something (but make sure a meeting is the right way to communicate).
  - Outcome: What outcome, action or decision do you want from each agenda item?
  - Information: What information will be needed to make this decision/ agree this action?
- Estimate the cost of the meeting and put this cost on the agenda. People are often blissfully unaware of the costs of a meeting. So we recommend that each meeting that lasts more than 60 minutes has a cost associated with it and that the participants are told how much it is costing for them all to be there. Work out the number of hours the meeting will take, multiply by the number of people in the meeting and then multiply by the average hourly cost of the people in the room. For ease of use

TIME	9:00–10:15	10.15–12.00
AGENDA ITEM	Review of NPD pipeline	Customer review
VALUE DRIVER	Customer-centric innovation	Focus on top 10 customers
PURPOSE	Discuss NPD priorities for the rest of the year	Share learnings for pilot project in Germany
DESIRED OUTCOME	Agree to reduce the number of NPD projects further	Agree how best to share learnings from this with other countries
INFORMATION	PRE-READ: full recommendation from J. Smith. AT MEETING: summary of pre-read.	PRE-READ: top-line summary of successes and failures to-date.

FIGURE 8.3
Example of best practice agenda structure

we use a departmental average cost per person/hour. (I.e we use the roughly right principle.) Now add travel costs for getting everyone in the meeting. We recently attended a two-day meeting with 15 people that cost $75,818. Throughout the meeting we reminded everyone that we needed to find $75,000 in complexity reduction savings just to pay for the meeting itself.

• Prepare carefully: Make sure any information that is needed is prepared well in advance and circulated at least three days before the meeting. Make sure participants understand that they MUST read the information before you meet. Name and shame people who don't provide the required information in time or who don't read information before the meeting. Do not allow pre-read information to be more than five pages long.

- Time: Allow a sensible amount of time for each agenda item.
- Have a chairperson: one person whose sole role is to chair the meeting, nothing else. This person ensures that: everyone has a chance to make their point; you stick to the agenda; you stay on time; and any conclusions/actions are recorded.
- One-page meeting minutes: Meeting minutes can vary depending on the formality of the meeting, but this is another area where simplicity will pay dividends. Even if you need more detailed meeting minutes for governance/regulatory reasons, always send a simple one-page version of the meeting minutes the day after the meeting. The simple one-pager should just summarise the key decisions made, actions agreed and responsibilities for the actions. If you do need to record full proceedings of the meetings for regulatory or compliance reasons, then separate the actions/conclusions from the more detailed full meeting notes, so that participants do not need to read everything to get an overview of the key decisions and actions.
- Score the meeting at the end: Scoring the meeting enables everyone to take feedback and improve their contributions to meetings:
  - Did this meeting create value or contribute significantly to the delivery of our organisation's strategy?
  - Was this meeting worth the cost of having the meeting?
  - Did we stick to the time available?
  - Did we stick to the agenda?
  - Was the pre-reading and preparation good enough?
  - Did we make good decisions?
  - Did we re-visit decisions we have already taken?
  - Any side conversations?
- Be a good meeting participant: Finally you should take personal responsibility to be a good meeting contributor and attendee:
  - Stop attending meetings where you have little to contribute, or where someone else from your team can represent your views.
  - Do your meeting preparation on time.
  - Listen more than you talk.
  - Think before you speak: Work out what your point is and the simplest/clearest way to say it is. Throwing a badly thought out or confusing comment into the room will create complexity.
  - Focus on the agenda items and encourage others to do the same; don't drift off the point.

– Say less, mean more:
  ■ If you have nothing to say then say nothing.
  ■ Don't repeat/duplicate a point that someone has already made.
  ■ Be relevant: make sure what you say is relevant to the meeting/ issue.
  ■ Be insightful: make sure your contribution brings something new and valuable to the discussion.

Keeping meetings simple
Are you the meeting host?

You have the **responsibility for keeping it simple**. If you achieve this, the meeting will be shorter, more effective and more enjoyable for you and everyone else.

Consider the **type of meeting** you are holding, as the content and format will be dependent on this – is it an information update meeting, a regular project meeting, a problem-solving meeting, a meeting to take a decision?

You may want the group to agree some **meeting rules** up front and then put them on the wall and make everyone stick to them – for example, no mobile phones, no checking emails, no side discussions.

✓ DO prepare the meeting properly with a clear, concise agenda, the right people there and all the information available for a productive meeting.
✓ DO keep things moving along by intervening if contributions are too lengthy or going off topic.
✓ DO milestone the discussion by visually capturing decisions and outputs along the way, to show progress and to resist U-turns.
✓ DO actively acknowledge good contributions and allow the speaker time and space to develop the idea or argument.
✓ DO recap all decisions and actions at the end of the meeting, and distribute simple, clear minutes if needed.
✓ DO stick to the agenda and keep participants on track.
✗ DON'T be tempted to dominate the discussion just because you are hosting the meeting.
✗ DON'T dwell too long on trivial points – make sure you start with the substantive issues that are outlined in the agenda and don't sweat the small stuff.

Are you a meeting participant?
Each and every participant in the meeting can have an impact on keeping it simple, and can **take personal responsibility** for not falling into complexity traps.

- ✓ DO your meeting preparation really well, read the pre-reads, think about the issues on the agenda, make notes on key points and information you will mention.
- ✓ DO be concise when making your point.
- ✓ DO keep up – follow the direction of the discussion and avoid repeating what's already been said.
- ✓ DO actively listen to what others are saying and take time to digest before responding.
- ✓ DO call out if you think the meeting is veering off track.
- ✗ DON'T have side conversations that distract the focus of the meeting.
- ✗ DON'T say anything if you have nothing new to add.
- ✗ DON'T keep quiet if you don't agree.

4. Simplify your daily communications: email, documents, presentations, etc.

Communication between people in companies is a subject that could fill a book by itself. In fact, by popular demand, we now run a one-day training program specifically to address the major challenge of how to communicate simply.

Here's how you should think about it:

- Every time you communicate with someone, you create work and complexity for both yourself and for them. If your communications are unclear, verbose, ambiguous or irrelevant then they create even more confusion and complexity.
- The more people you communicate to the more work you create. On average each work email that is read creates two minutes of work simply to read the email, more if you send attachments. So if you send one email to ten people, you have created at least 20 minutes of reading work for other people, more if they have to take action as a result of your email.

So you should always apply the following overall rules to your daily communications with other people:

- **Reduce:** Write less and to fewer people. Only create work for them by communicating when it is essential. When you do communicate say less, so you can mean more. Write shorter presentations. Some companies have set a maximum of ten pages for PowerPoint presentations. Others have introduced email-free Friday or email rationing so that one person can only send 30 emails each day.

- **Clarify:** Make sure everything you communicate is simple and clear to understand. Imagine that the audience has a below-average intellect and you have 30 seconds to get your key messages before moving on. Make sure what you say is clear. To explain is to fail.
- **Have an impact:** Make sure you are communicating things that are essential and valuable for people to know and will have an important impact on them and their role. One way to do this is to use the following checklist of questions to test if a point deserves inclusion:
  - **Is this relevant?** All communications should link to a company value driver, key strategy or project. Is your message/information really relevant to your audience? They should not be thinking 'why are you telling me this?' or 'I don't need to know that'.
  - **Is this new?** Equally the audience should not be thinking 'I already know this'. Focus on what is new or what has changed significantly.
  - **Is this information actionable?** Emphasize points that require immediate action in order to improve your business or reduce risk.
  - **Is this point insightful?** Good key messages provide new insight or deeper understanding about the subject or issue at hand. Don't tell them what they already know, tell them something that provides a new angle or perspective.
  - **Is this information compelling?** Good communications should also be compelling, or inspiring or engaging to your audience. They should want to remember and to act on what you have said.

5. Streamline management reporting

Each day vast numbers of highly detailed reports are created and sent to vast numbers of people who don't read them, or take any meaningful action as a result. This could be one of the biggest sources of wasteful complexity in your company. In our work we have measured the reporting waste and in some companies up to 50 per cent of management reports are unread and/ or result in no meaningful action. In many cases the report was relevant at some point in the past, but the report is still produced even though there is no longer any need for it.

Step 1: Audit Stage
Start by drawing up a complete list of all the management information/ reports produced by your department. The key information you need to gather at the audit stage is:

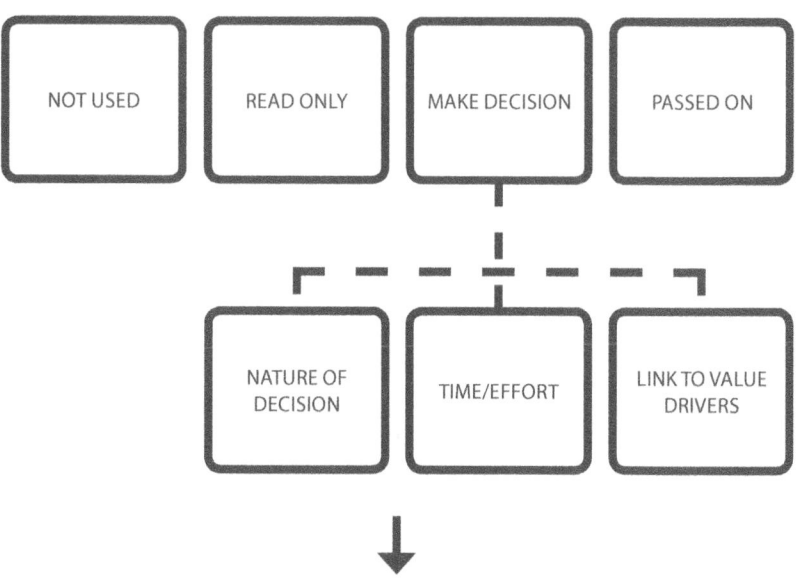

UNDERSTAND WHAT INFORMATION IS CREATED,
WHY, AND HOW MUCH IT COSTS TO CREATE

UNDERSTAND HOW
THE RECEIVER USES
THE REPORT

| NOT USED | READ ONLY | MAKE DECISION | PASSED ON |

| NATURE OF DECISION | TIME/EFFORT | LINK TO VALUE DRIVERS |

LESSEN THE BURDEN OF MANAGEMENT
INFORMATION BY REDUCING,
STANDARDIZING, AUTOMATING AND
CLARIFYING

FIGURE 8.4
Steps for streamlining reporting structures

- Title of the report
- Purpose/objectives of this report/information: what is the objective or purpose of this report?
- Who creates this report?
- How long is the report in total pages/number of words?
- How much does it cost to create this report?
  - Time cost: How many hours of management time X average hourly cost of employment of the people who create the report

- – Input costs: Identify any other costs, e.g. purchase of market data, IT costs etc.
- Importance of this report/information: Make an initial assessment of how important you think this report is to the delivery of your strategy and/or to creating value at your company. Score each report 1 to 5 for importance: 1 = very low importance, 5 = very high importance.
- Identify which reports take up most time/resources and focus on these ones at the next stage.

Step 2: Receiver Use Analysis

Next you need to speak to the people who receive the report. Using a structured one-to-one interview approach, or a self-completion questionnaire, you can determine how they actually use your report – if at all.

- List the people that the report goes to and then arrange interviews with a sample of them (or send them a short questionnaire).
- What do they do with this report when they receive it? How does the report help them with the delivery of your organisation's strategy? Which value drivers does the report contribute to? By this we mean does this report/information help them to make decisions or take actions that will create value/profit for the company?
- Do they really need it, or is this report just a management comfort blanket? Challenge them to prove to you that they really need your report and that they use it to make decisions that drive value for your company. Ask them to provide concrete examples of the key decisions, actions or processes that this information is used for. Make sure that this is the only (or the best way) for them to get this information.
- Find out what the most/least important parts of the report are – some parts might be critical, others might be useless?
- Ask for their ideas on what could be done to make this report simpler and or better.
- Calculate the 'cost of readership' for each major report: Estimate how long it takes each receiver to read the report on average. Then multiply this average reading time by the average hourly cost of their time and then multiply by the number of people the report goes to.
- Receiver reprocessing: Find out if the report/information is used as an input into another report or process. Then follow the report along to the next set of users and ask the same questions.
- Now rate the importance of the report again. Based on the receiver use analysis, score this report again on the 1 to 5 importance scale. If you are unsure, stop sending the report out. This is a great way to work out who needs your report, as they will soon be calling you to see where it is.

Step 3: Streamline

The final stage is to use the results above to dramatically streamline your management reporting / information.

Prioritise: You probably cannot (and don't need to) attack every single report. So at this point it is helpful to prioritise the reports that you are going to work on. Use the 80/20 rule to identify the 20 percent of reports which cause the most complexity or cost. Or plot the reports on the value/ cost grid in Figure 8.5.

Now you should have a list of around 10 key reports that you are going to attack.

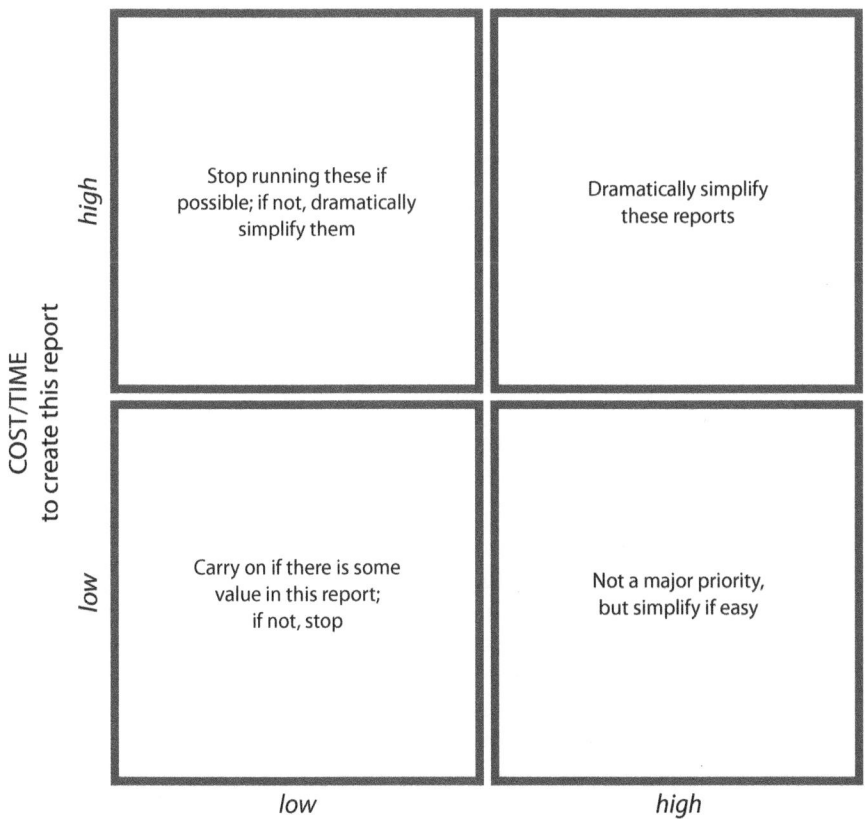

FIGURE 8.5
Importance versus cost/time

- Reduce vigorously: Set a stretch target to reduce management reporting and information by 50 percent. To do this you will need to radically reduce everything you can.
  - Reduce the number of reports by killing the ones you don't need
  - Reduce the frequency with which the reports are written/produced
  - Reduce the number of pages/volume of data
  - Reduce the number of people involved in writing the reports/generating the information
  - Reduce the number of people the report is sent to
- Can you simplify the production process? Map out the process/steps used to create the report. Then identify ways to reduce the number of steps/stages, the number of people involved and the volume of inputs that are used to create the report.
- Standardizing things is a great way to make life simpler. Can you standardize the layout, the content, the source of the information or the production process?
- Combining can be useful – if used with care. Can you combine two reports into one? But be careful not to create a Frankenstein report that is even more complex!
- De-dupe: Are any of the reports duplicating information which is also provided in another report/system? Can the information be obtained more easily from another source? If so, remove any duplication of effort.
- Make the report simpler to read/use. Many management reports are used to make important decisions, but this useful information is often presented in a complex or confusing way, with too much data, too few diagrams/graphs, too little relevant insight. You should work hard to re-design each management report. Here are a few simple pointers:

  - Think about how the information can help with one of your company value drivers or monitor the delivery of your strategy. Focus only on information that has a connection to a value driver.
  - Minimize the amount of information that goes into the report by focusing on the key points only. Use the rules of 'Communicating Simply' to test the importance of the information you are including. Make sure each point ticks at least one of the following boxes (as in Section 4):
    - Is this information **relevant** to the receiver?
    - It this **new** information?
    - Is this information **actionable**?
    - Is this information **insightful**?
    - Is this information **compelling**?
  - Simplify the layout of each report: use layering, diagrams, images and graphs to make things clearer for the reader and more engaging to read.
- Can you automate the production of the report (or parts of it)? Remember you should always simplify before you automate. Otherwise

the automation project and the final report will be far more complex than you need.

- Establish good housekeeping rules: Things always seem to evolve over time to become more complex, not less complex! If left unchecked, complexity will creep back into your management reporting over a short space of time. New data/reports will be requested. People will forget that they can get certain measures/results from existing reports, so new reports will be created that duplicate existing ones. Things will go wrong, so new ways of measuring will be created to address the problems/contain risk. It is also important that you create a minimalist culture which encourages people to challenge requests for new analysis or new reports that are not essential to the running of the company. Some businesses have created a gatekeeper for reporting who has to authorize changes to the reports that are produced (and won't do so without a sound business case). If you are asked for a new report, challenge the request using these questions:
  - What action will flow from the person receiving this information; i.e do they really need it for strategic or value-generating reasons?
  - Is this information already available somewhere?
  - Review circulation lists on a regular basis – challenge when new names are added.
  - If you add something – take something else away.
- Take personal responsibility: If you are the receiver of any management reports, then take personal responsibility and challenge yourself on whether you need it. If the report is unclear, incomplete, over-engineered or unhelpful, then be honest: feed those points back to the people that created the report. Take yourself off the copy list if you possibly can.

Simplifying everyday underpins everything we have said in this book

As we said at the start and throughout: people – you! and specifically your behavior – lie at the heart of the business and behind all sources of both good and bad complexity.

You are the cause and effect. You are also the solution. You create complexity and suffer from its impacts – and only you can simplify every aspect of the firms we have covered in our book: the processes, the organization, the product and service portfolio, and the strategy.

As with most aspects of life, changing your behavior is the simple key to success and the biggest challenge to overcome. But the rewards are not just greater profitability. In the end, simpler businesses are better places – for you and everyone you work with. So why not make a start – now!

Costly Complexity in the Pharmaceutical Sector

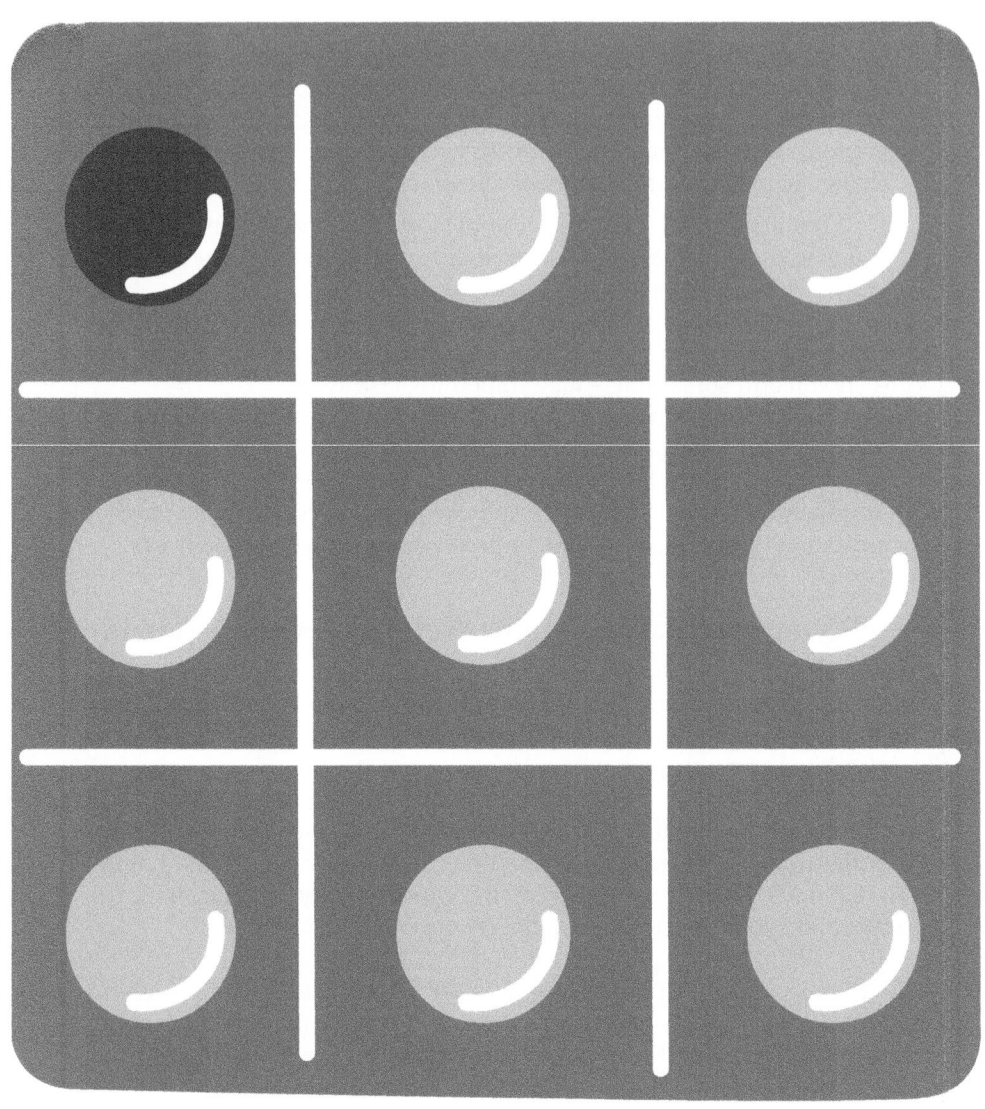

In Chapter 1 and throughout this book we talk about our research and the Global Simplicity Index (GSI), which we created from a study of the largest 200 firms in the Global Fortune 500.

Eleven of the firms in the GSI are pharmaceutical giants, and the pharmaceutical industry is the fourth most complex and the highest-performing industry sector in this study.

Increasing patient and physician demands, stronger regulation and the growing diversity of regulatory regimes, dramatic changes in government funding, growing competition from Asia, declining R&D productivity and new technologies all combine to make the pharmaceuticals industry an increasingly turbulent place to operate. Coping with these challenges will require pharmaceuticals firms to be more agile, able to navigate in and adapt to their changing operating environment, and to do so better than their competitors.

This appendix provides a more detailed analysis of the extensive data set we now have on the causes and consequences of complexity in pharma. At the end of the review, we also identify what actions big pharma must now take in order to reduce the effects of costly complexity on profitability.

Pharmaceutical industry complexity: summary of our key findings

Pharma is the fourth most complex industry to operate in and the highest-performing sector, on average, compared to 11 other industry sectors

External sources of complexity are rated as high-impact sources in pharma, more so than in other industries; however, some pharma companies are managing external complexity better than others. With highly technical R&D programs, strict regulation and sophisticated products, it is tempting to argue that complexity is an inevitable consequence of operating in the pharma industry. But if this were true, all pharmaceutical companies would have similar levels of complexity. Our study shows a wide variation, with some pharma companies managing complexity much better than others.

The poorer-performing firms in the pharmaceuticals sector are too internally focused: our study looks at over 100 specific forms/types of complexity to see how these specific drivers of complexity can impact a company's financial performance. The low performers suffer more (relative to the high performers) from internal complexity drivers, particularly people complexity factors and internal process complexity. The more successful companies are externally focused, i.e. they focus more on the market, competitors and customers than on internal factors.

In many cases M&A activity has increased overall complexity in pharma, destroying value for shareholders, rather than creating value. Better management of the integration process is clearly needed to ensure that M&A activity is implemented without increasing harmful complexity levels.

There are four distinct complexity drivers that pharma companies need to focus on in order to reduce harmful complexity.

Strategic complexity

The complex and rapidly changing competitive environment presents a particular challenge to pharma firms and places a premium on efficient and adaptive internal strategic and decision-making practices. Our study suggests that managing strategic complexity is a bigger problem in pharma relative to the other 189 companies in the GSI.

Complexity of the innovation process

Changing customer behavior, cost-cutting by governments, growing numbers of competitors, new product development challenges and the need to react increasingly quickly to external change all drive up the need to innovate efficiently and the complexity of doing so. Our study suggests that the complexity of the innovation process is a bigger issue in pharma than in other industries.

Technology-related threats and opportunities

New technologies offer opportunities for more effective product innovation and more efficient process innovation. But new competitors are also riding these waves. The results of our work suggest these factors are driving high levels of complexity in pharma.

Organization design

More than for other industry sectors, the recruitment, direction and coordination of a wide diversity of specialists lies at the heart of the internal value chain in pharma, including and beyond the R&D pipeline. Our study suggests that organizational complexity is an even bigger issue in pharma than it is in other industries.

1. How are the world's largest pharmaceuticals firms ranked on the GSI?

The GSI ranks 200 companies according to their complexity and performance over 2005–10. There are 11 major pharmaceuticals firms in the GSI.[1] If we compare these firms against those in other industry sectors, we find that this is, on average, the highest-performing industry and the fourth most complex industry in the study (see Figure A1.1).

When we examine individual pharma firms using the GSI, we can classify companies into the four major typologies shown in Figure A1.2. In the high performance/low complexity quadrant, pharmaceutical giant GlaxoSmithKline (GSK) outperforms rivals such as such as Pfizer, Roche

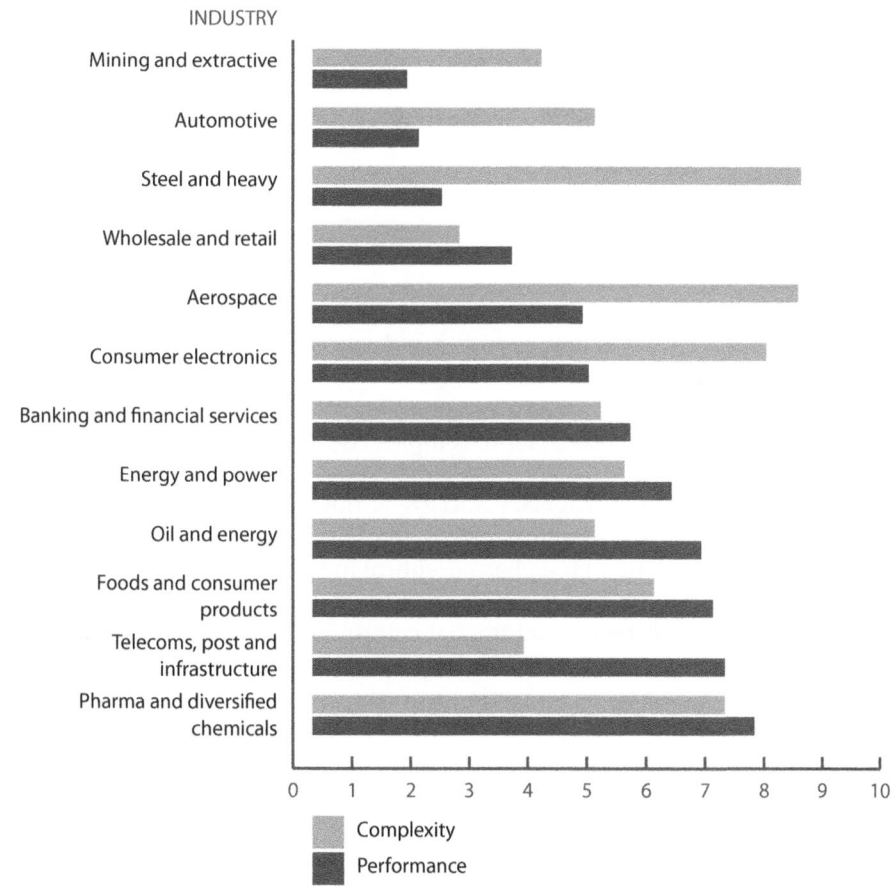

FIGURE A1.1
Average performance and complexity rankings of the GSI 200 by industry sector

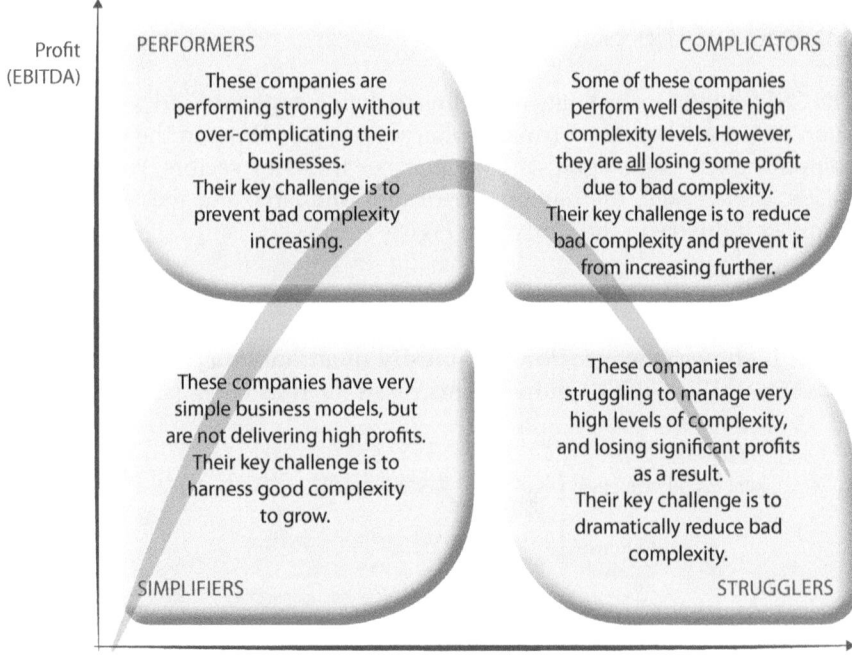

FIGURE A1.2
Four firm types based on high and low complexity and performance scores

and Novartis, and achieved an impressive profit level of 19.5 per cent of sales in 2009, well ahead of more complex competitors.

An important factor in GSK's success is how it copes strategically and operationally across two dimensions that can create bad complexity for companies operating in the pharmaceutical industry in particular: the R&D pipeline and M&As. Extending each adds new sources of diversity and turbulence, which require additional control and coordination. A pharma company that over-extends itself along either dimension can create harmful complexity, reducing its strategic focus, the efficiency of its coordination, and the careful balancing act between too few and too many strategic options orchestrated by senior management.

GlaxoSmithKline spends over $4.6bn on R&D each year, but manages a tightly focused product development strategy and has developed an efficient structure for its research organization. Similarly, GSK frequently acquires partners and competitors, as it did with Stiefel Laboratories, which specializes in skin health, and Pfizer's HIV business, among others. This could easily create an overload of restructuring initiatives, but so far GSK has managed to derive maximum value with minimal disruption.

Figure A1.3 shows the specific positions of all 11 pharmaceuticals firms on the performance–complexity matrix.

Pressures for consolidation in the pharmaceuticals industry have driven up the level of M&A. This reduces the number of competitors in the sector, but presents additional complexity challenges for the remaining firms. Our study suggests that in many cases M&A activity has increased overall complexity, destroying value for shareholders, rather than creating value. Better management of the integration process is clearly needed to ensure that M&A activity is implemented without increasing overall complexity levels.

The Novartis acquisition of Alcon in early 2011 provides lessons for others. This was one in a long line of acquisitions in the pharmaceuticals industry that

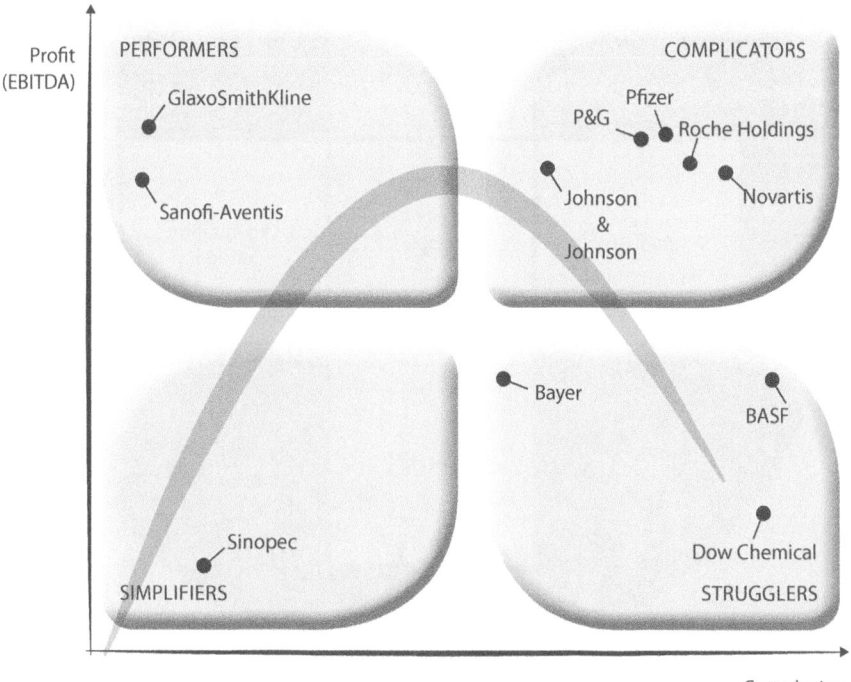

FIGURE A1.3
Eleven pharmaceuticals firms on the performance–complexity matrix

left the acquirer with the challenge of integrating another equally complex firm into its operations. With a presence in over 140 countries, Novartis was already a massive business, and merging with Alcon added further complexity to the firm. In a drive to overcome the declining productivity of R&D pipelines and achieve even greater economies of scale from R&D to marketing, firms like Novartis are multiplying their strategic and operational complexity, rather than simplifying down to their core competences.

The GSI categorizes Novartis as a 'complicator'. Our study suggests that much of Novartis' costly complexity has been driven by previous acquisitions, as well as high R&D intensity, over-engineering of processes and a wide portfolio of operations, across a large number of therapeutic

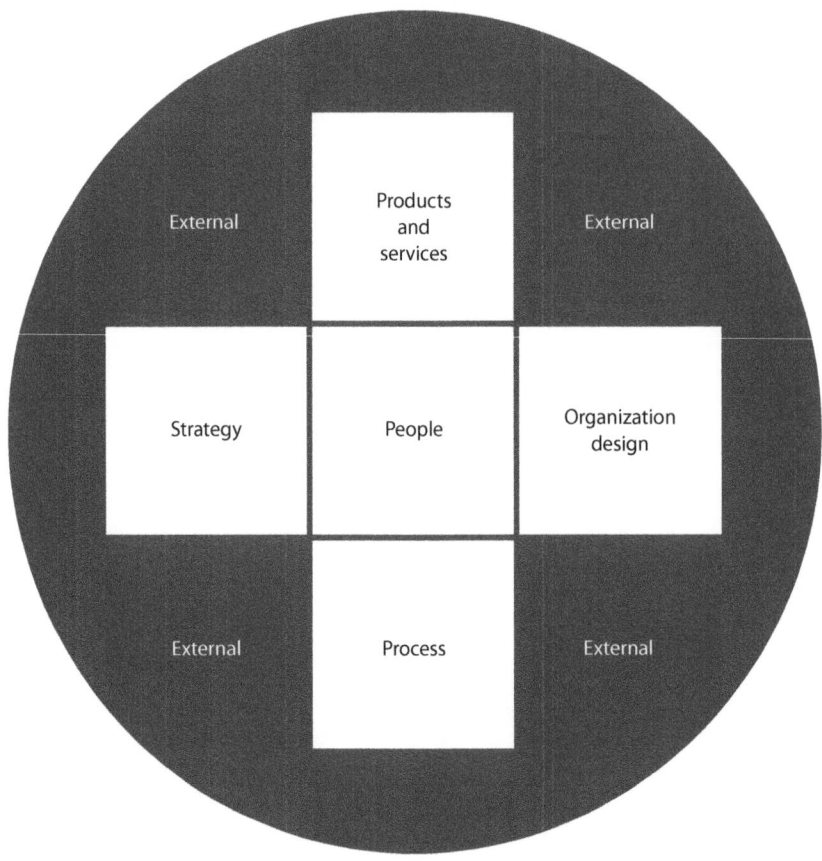

FIGURE A1.4
The six major sources of complexity

areas. Such acquisitions may initially appear to add value, but often result in increased complexity, strategic misalignment and poor organizational coordination between sub-divisions.

In order to improve profits, complexity reduction needs to take center stage within the pharmaceutical industry. It is vitally important for pharmaceutical firms to view complexity more holistically. Although closing factories and R&D centers will reduce operating costs, it will not be enough to reduce the stifling levels of complexity within the industry. This requires complexity to be reduced in strategy, organizational structure, process and many other areas of the business. Additionally, it requires a change in management behaviors to ensure that complexity does not creep back into the organization.

2. What are the most harmful sources of complexity for pharma companies?

Our survey of management complexity – described in Chapter 1 – captured the views of 600 managers on the forms of complexity that had the highest impact on the performance of their firms, across our six dimensions.

When we analyzed the relationship between performance and specific sources of complexity, we found that lower-performing firms in the pharmaceuticals sectors suffer more (relative to the high performers) from internal sources of complexity, particularly the **people**, **organization** and **process** forms. Respondents in high performing firms are more concerned about external sources of complexity. As we have emphasized throughout the book, the poorer performers are more 'introverted' – overwhelmed by internal complexity and distracted from external strategic threats and opportunities. This trend is strongly emphasized in the pharmaceutical industry.

When we break down these internal sources of complexity we find clear industry differences. Figure A1.5 shows the relative importance of these different kinds of complexity on respondents in different industry sectors.[2] First, note in this survey that only automotive and instruments manufacturers report higher levels of overall complexity than PLDC (see note 2) firms (contrasting the GSI analysis). Second, the Strategy and External categories dominate the responses from managers and employees in PLDC firms, with People complexity sources coming third.

A more detailed breakdown of the sources of complexity for pharma firms is provided in Table A1.1. This table identifies the top 25 sources of complexity.

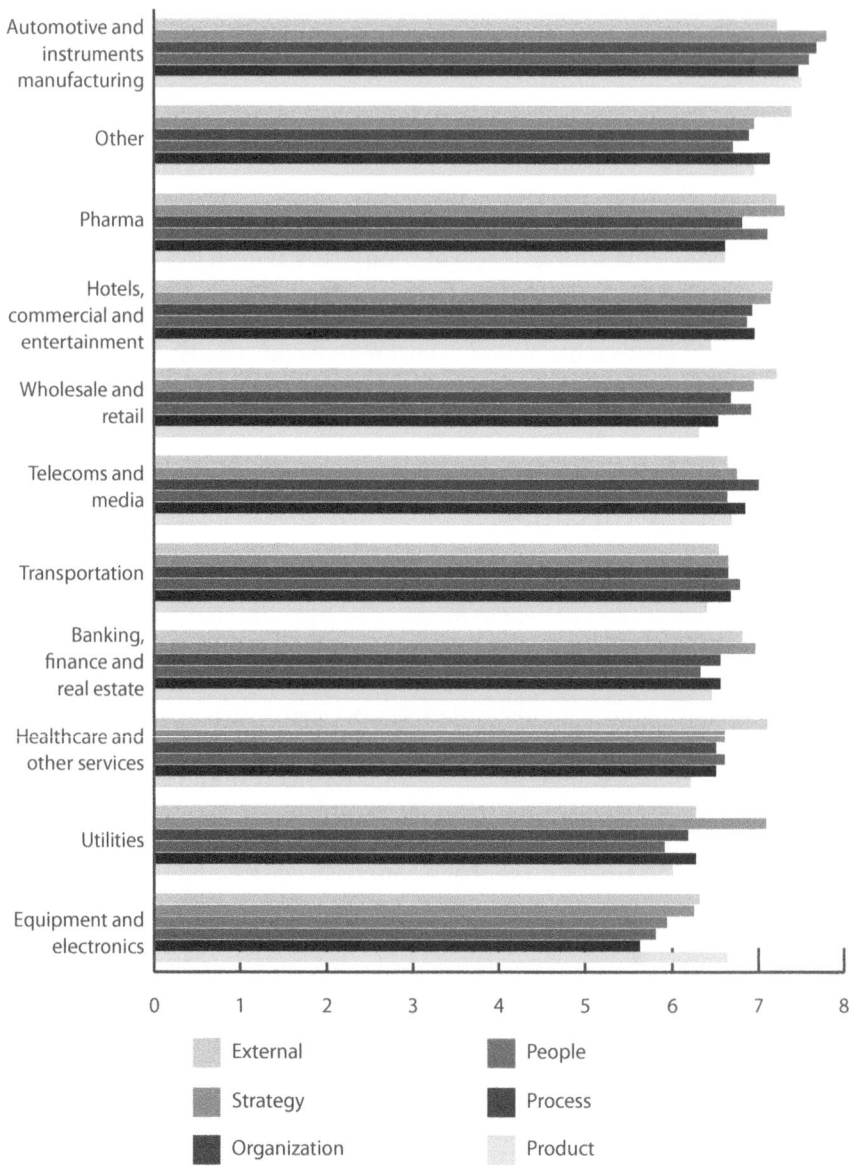

FIGURE A1.5
Industry sectors compared across the six types of costly complexity

#	THE LEADING PHARMA COMPLEXITY SOURCES
1	Changes in customer behavior
2	Fluctuations in the performance of the economy
3	Changes in company core strategy
4	Launching new products/services
5	Use of the internet and online technologies
6	IT systems
7	Changing technology within your market
8	Number of new hires made a year
9	Changing an existing product/service
10	The core business strategy itself
11	Internal communication processes
12	Number of strategic initiatives pursued
13	The number of competitors in your market
14	Clarification of roles and responsibilities
15	Diversity of customer demands
16	Measuring and reporting on KPIs/balanced scorecard objectives
17	Annual budgeting process
18	Hiring staff
19	Creating a new product or service
20	Inter-firm networks (e.g. suppliers, customers, etc.)
21	Number and variety of specialist roles
22	Customer support
23	The amount of innovation launched into your market
24	Making capital expenditure decisions
25	Major project processes

TABLE A1.1
The top 25 sources of complexity for pharmaceutical companies

The sources listed in Table A1.1 come from across our six dimensions, but there are some specific patterns relative to other industry sectors. We can analyze these as 'clusters' of complexity sources that most strongly affect the productivity and performance of managers and employees in pharma firms.

External complexity

External sources of complexity are identified as being the biggest drivers of overall complexity in pharma. These include 'changes in customer behavior', 'fluctuations in the performance of the economy', 'changing technology within your market' and 'the number of competitors'. However, some companies in this sector are managing these external forces well, while others are too internally focused to successfully manage these external complexity forces.

Technology-related complexity

Technology-related opportunities and threats are seen to be a key source of external complexity, given that 'use of the internet and online technologies', 'IT systems' and 'changing technology within your market' are all rated high. This highlights the importance of, and complexity challenges related to, biotechnologies, new drug delivery and gene therapy technologies, for example. But it also points to the significance of 'enabling technologies', including IT systems and the internet, to support productivity improvements in intelligence gathering, drug discovery and testing.

Strategic complexity

'The core business strategy itself', 'changes in company core strategy' and 'the number of strategic initiatives being pursued' are big sources of harmful complexity for pharma firms, according to respondents. This is exacerbated by the complexity of the processes that are used to create the strategy in the first place. This clearly indicates that some pharma firms are struggling to develop and implement clear, focused and consistent business strategies.

Complexity of the innovation process

The challenges inherent in the process of 'launching new products/ services' and 'changing an existing product/service' are one of the biggest drivers of overall business complexity for the 200 companies in the GSI; this appears to be an even bigger problem in the pharma industry. The internal processes are, it seems, distracting from a more market-focused/ market-led approach, which is necessary for innovation to be successful and efficient. Potentially the overall approach to innovation in big pharma needs to be refocused on a simpler, more market-led approach.

Organizational complexity

'Clarification of roles and responsibilities', the 'number of new hires made a year' and the 'measuring and reporting on KPIs/balanced scorecard' are all rated as bigger drivers of complexity in pharma than in other industries. Coordinating, directing and monitoring the diversity of specialists are also complex challenges in pharma. This suggests that organizational complexity is a significant problem. Any inefficiency in the structures and processes underpinning related functions in pharmaceutical firms will be particularly frustrating for employees. These will either distract them from value-adding activities, or make decision-making and action slower than needed for responding to the changing competitive environment.

3. How should pharma industry executives respond to the complexity challenge?

The findings of our two large-scale studies, the GSI and the management survey of complexity, lead to some clear recommendations for pharma sector executives. A larger-than-average number of pharma firms are in our 'complicator' category of the GSI. They are currently performing above average in profit, but are in danger of falling over the tipping point and becoming overwhelmed by the complexities described throughout this book.

Our study proves that, over time, the 'complicators' will continue to add harmful complexity. As Edward de Bono points out, things very rarely evolve to become simpler. The result is that the complicators will continue to waste resources and reduce profits – and many will end up as 'strugglers'. The inevitable result will be a loss of agility, significant destruction of profit and reduced motivation as even simple things become increasingly difficult to achieve.

So what actions should pharma companies take?
Increase external focus
Pharma companies need to identify the key drivers of customer value, i.e. the activities, processes and projects that will have the biggest impact on long-term customer satisfaction and demand. Internal business processes should then be simplified by removing any steps that are not clearly and directly related to creation of customer value. This means also removing steps/activities that are duplicative or focused more on departmental hand-overs than on customer drivers. Pharma firms should also delayer organization to put leaders closer to the customer, and refocus peoples' roles and responsibilities to emphasize external customer focus. Firms should also start the process of developing an externally focused culture, encouraging everyone (not just sales and marketing) to be more in tune with their customers' needs and concerns.

Clarify strategy and devolve strategic decision-making

Despite the diversity of external threats and opportunities and the high level of economic, market, competitor and technological turbulence, senior executives need to simplify, communicate and then stick to a core strategy for the firm. This should be more about **what** needs to be achieved than **how** managers should achieve it. The days of top-down command-and-control organizations are gone. Adaptive strategies need to be developed and implemented by those further down the management hierarchy in response to the market conditions they face. Managers throughout the organization need to develop the capability and assume the responsibility for strategic decision-making, but with full knowledge of the firm's prime objectives and within clear boundaries set by the leadership. They can then be responsible for simplifying the range of initiatives followed and focusing on the core business strategy.

Develop a simpler, more market-led innovation approach

Market-led innovation lies at the heart of the industry value chain, and a range of sources of complexity, from customers to competitors, make this strategic remit challenging. Pharma firms need to simplify their R&D pipelines and reconfigure them to be user-led, emphasizing market-pull instead of science-push. The processes and decision-making structures for selecting, prioritizing and allocating budgets for new product development projects have to reflect market drivers and be sensitive to changing customer needs. Strategic ambiguity confuses employees and convoluted processes distract them from added-value activities. A greater emphasis on marketing, both in terms of gathering market intelligence and enhancing your own brand image, is necessary.

Harness new technologies more efficiently

Complex opportunities and threats stem from the emergence of new technologies. These raise the difficult strategic questions of whether to pursue development and exploitation in-house or via inter-firm joint ventures and alliances. Some technological capabilities sit within the core competences of pharma firms and should be retained in-house. Others need to be left to the market or specialist partners. Senior executives need to clarify the strategic boundaries between these kinds of technology and direct R&D efforts towards proprietary technologies that will yield future advantage. Simplifying the relevant selection processes and aligning these with recruitment and HR management practices will help pharma firms handle the kinds of complexities associated with new technology.

Manage the M&A integration process to minimize complexity

M&A activity is significantly increasing complexity in the pharma industry. Once the deal is done, the emphasis moves onto the integration; in the desire to do this quickly and realize the synergies identified in the M&A strategy, the opportunity to simplify the business is often missed. In fact, poor management means that complexity increases as organizations, product portfolios and processes are smashed together without adequate thought about the complexity costs attached to the integration process. Simplicity should be a core principle that guides how you manage the integration process. Table A1.2 gives some ideas on how you can prevent complexity increasing as a result of M&A.

	WHAT YOU CAN DO
STRATEGY	• Establish a clear, shared vision and direction for the new organization. • Map your strategy simply on one page and share this with everyone: clear statements of where you play and how you win in the new organization.
PEOPLE	• Establish a set of simplicity principles (e.g. standardization, prioritization), which staff should adhere to as the two organizations are integrated. • Create a single, concise set of KPIs, aligned with the strategy, which should feed directly into performance metrics and discussions.
ORG DESIGN	• Set unbreakable principles for organizational design: spans of control, number of matrix or indirect reports, maximum number of organizational designs, etc. • Identify your strategic processes and create simple RACIs to clarify accountabilities for key decisions. • Audit your reporting to identify the reports you actually need, and eliminate the others. • Identify the appropriate model for each function (acquire model? best of both? complete transformation?). • Maintain distributed power and authority as much as possible – managers use M&A as an excuse for decision inertia.
PRODUCT	• Map your markets and the products/services that serve them, then identify and eliminate overlapping products or over-serviced markets.
PROCESS	• Identify and amp your core processes. Pinpoint common or duplicated processes and use the simplest one, or create a new process that's even simpler.
EXTERNAL	• Align views of the merging companies on external complexity sources and how to best handle them post-merger.

TABLE A1.2
Practical steps for reducing harmful complexity resulting from M&A

Simplify organization design

Lack of role clarity, duplication of responsibility and ambiguity around decision-making processes and rights are now very common problems in big companies; however, these issues seem to be hampering pharma much more than other industries. In addition, many people are unclear how their role creates enduring value for the company, which means they may be busy, but they are probably not creating economic value on a day-to-day basis. The solution to this is to simplify your organization by:

- delayering – there should be no more than eight layers from the CEO to the customer;
- focusing everyone's role on activities that are clearly related to creation of customer value; and
- clarifying roles and removing matrix or geographical duplication of responsibility.

4. Conclusion

It is easy for pharma managers to say that they have to work in a complex business sector, that it is inherent to their industry and that there is nothing they can do about it. The fact is that some firms are coping better with this complexity than others. Weaker-performing firms are losing more than our average of 10.2 per cent EBITDA to costly complexity. The evidence suggests that managers in these firms have to cope with too much internal complexity and are distracted from focusing on the significant competitive opportunities and threats outside their firms.

Our analysis pinpoints the specific complexity problems that pharma companies should focus on and gives some ideas about the actions that pharma executives can take. By systematically attacking these identifiable sources of complexity, pharma companies can become more agile and better able to navigate in – and adapt to – their changing operating environment, and do so better than their competitors. Bayer and others have already started to successfully do this through a global complexity reduction program, designed to address many of the issues highlighted above. Others would do well to follow.

Costly Complexity in the Banking Sector

Of the 200 companies in our Global Simplicity Index (GSI), 26 are banks.

Would the global financial crisis of 2008 have been less serious if the banks had been less complex? In 2008, the crisis led to the collapse of financial institutions such as Lehman Brothers and the financial bailout of many more. The complex interconnections between institutions and the complex nature of the products was undoubtedly part of the reason for this failure. If anyone had understood the nature of the structured products they sold and the network of interdependencies linking the portfolios of the various institutions, then Lehman Brothers would arguably not have failed. Unfortunately, this form of connected, systemic complexity was invisible to even the protagonists themselves.

Three years on, the GSI, conducted in 2011, tells us that the banking industry is still one of the most complex industries in the GSI, and the reaction of governments to the crisis has been to significantly increase regulatory oversight, which has further added to the complexity of operating in this sector.

In 2004, well before the financial crisis, the Royal Bank of Scotland (RBS) had released a report entitled 'Managing Complexity', telling us that it was important for firms to get a grip on this important issue in order to avoid major shocks in the market. Four years later, the crisis showed us the critical importance of simplicity and transparency in this industry. RBS was one of the major casualties of this crash, relying on public money to bail it out. It failed to follow its own advice – and our GSI study shows that it has long been more complex and less profitable than most of its competitors.

Banking industry complexity: summary of our key findings
The financial services sector is the sixth most complex industry to operate in and the sixth highest-performing sector, on average, compared to 11 other industry sectors. Banks had higher levels of complexity than other firms in the financial services industry.

The majority of global banks are close to or beyond the complexity tipping point
Our data shows that excess complexity is already destroying shareholder value in over 40 per cent of the banks but, in addition, nearly 20 per cent of the world's biggest banks are dangerously close to the complexity tipping point.

Geographical diversity has a negative impact on the banks

Top-performing firms within the banking sector are operating in fewer countries compared to their poorer-performing rivals. Banks with a wider geographic spread found it harder to manage the complexity, suggesting that geographic diversification is not as helpful as a hedge against risk as the banks may claim.

Product and service diversity improves performance

Although product and service factors were identified by banking executives as a major source of complexity, our data shows that the banks with a wider diversity of products/services have performed better than their more focused rivals.

Internal forms of complexity are more harmful than external sources

Internal sources of complexity (organization design, processes and the other sources discussed in this book) have a bigger impact on the banks' performance than external forces like regulation and economic turbulence.

Strategic complexity is a major problem

As with the pharmaceutical industry, the banking industry appears to be suffering heavily from multiple and/or unclear strategies, alongside the problems of over-complex strategic decision-making and strategy communication processes.

Organizational complexity

Our detailed analysis of the banking sector indicates that excessive organizational complexity is reducing the agility of the major banks.

Interactions with customers

Interactions with customers and the challenges of customer-led product innovation rank highly in the complexity factors identified in our survey.

Process complexity

Despite the wide application of Lean, process complexity, particularly in knowledge-based processes, is still too high in banking.

1. How are the world's largest banks ranked on the GSI?

The GSI ranks 200 companies according to their complexity and performance over five years. There are 48 major financial services firms in the GSI. If we compare these firms against those in other industry sectors we find that financial services in general is the sixth highest-performing industry and the sixth most complex industry in the study (Figure A2.1).

Figure A2.2 shows the specific positions of 26 banks on the performance–complexity matrix. While we note that ten of the banks are already beyond the tipping point, many of the ones in the 'performers' category (e.g. Santander) are very close to the tipping point. Since most organizations evolve to become more complex, not less complex, over time, all of the companies close to the tipping point are at significant risk of seeing complexity increase at the expense of performance.

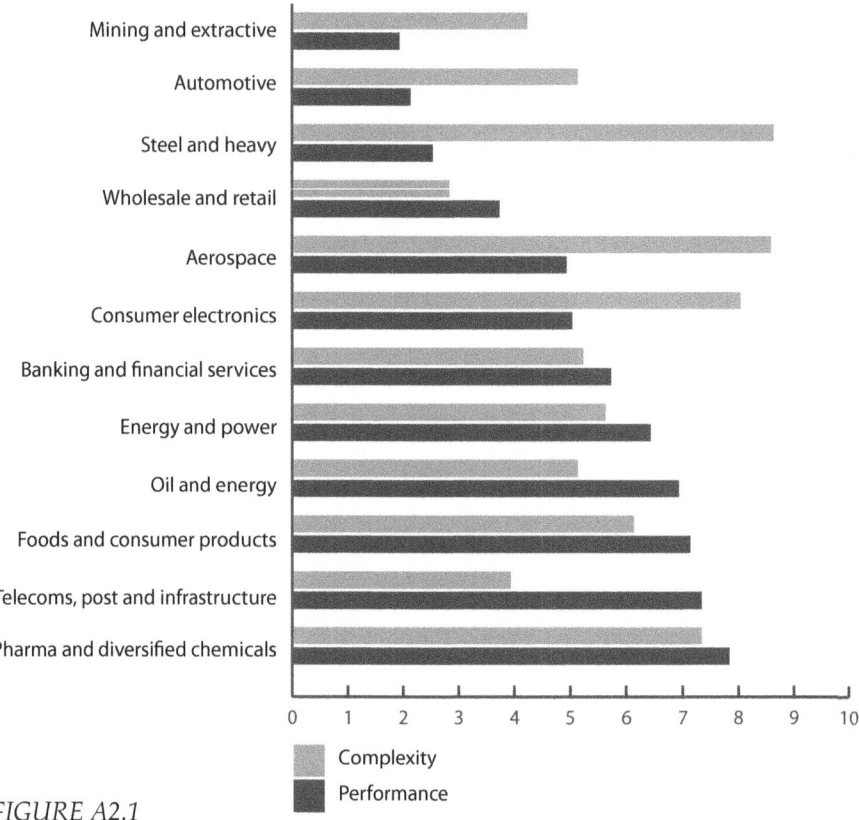

FIGURE A2.1
Average performance and complexity rankings of the GSI 200 by industry sector

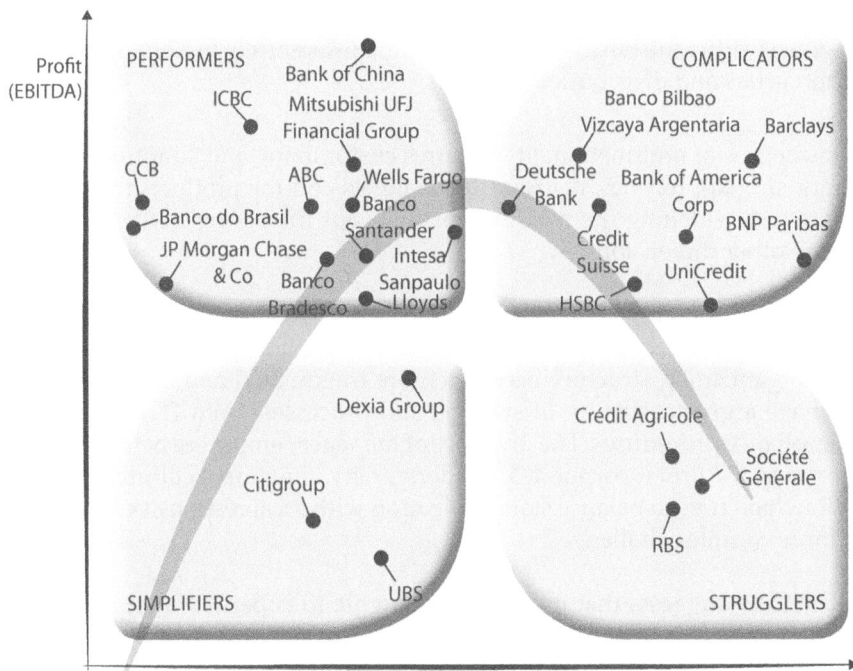

FIGURE A2.2
The Twenty-six banks on the performance–complexity matrix

Many of those in the 'performer' category are simpler in terms of their geographic spread. Chinese banks in particular, but also the Brazilian and Japanese banks, are less multinational than their Western counterparts and often backed by the state. State support lifts their performance 'artificially' and protects them against some global financial risks.

2. What are the most harmful sources of complexity for banks?

Asked whether he thought the global banks were too big, the former Lloyds CEO Eric Daniels famously stated 'I don't think it's a big-ness issue; it's a complexity issue'. He was right: banking is one of the most complex industries and our data suggests the industry is struggling to manage this complexity.

Operating across too many geographical territories has a negative effect for banks. This one factor was a far higher indicator of negative performance than any other factor in banking. Operating in more countries requires banks to deal with different capital markets, institutions and regulatory regimes; different business cultures; and different customers, marketing approaches and distribution channels.

This degree of multinationality requires customizing and adapting brands, marketing approaches, distribution channels and the products themselves – not just widening the product portfolio but increasing diversity across many other dimensions.

Different strategies are required for different markets, and cost–benefit trade-offs and resource allocation decision-making gets more complex. The organization structure becomes more fragmented and the firm has to manage a greater variety of systems and processes, from IT platforms to compliance procedures. The diversity of manager / employee behaviors also grows as the firm incorporates a wider variety of national cultures. Central HR, which tries to balance standardization with local responsiveness, faces a more complex challenge.

Our study suggests that most banks struggle to cope with these forms of complexity. This indicates that the priority of firms should be to obtain extensive knowledge of fewer geographical markets, rather than spreading operations across too many different geographical regions, each with different customer needs, competitors and regulatory environments. Alternatively the banks need to become much better at managing geographical diversity than they are at present.

Maybe surprisingly, having a wide range of products and services across different market segments didn't have a strong negative impact on the performance of banks. In other words, the benefits of having a broad portfolio of products and services, with segment branding and common back office platforms, seem to outweigh the costs of the additional complexity. This suggests that the ability for banks to cross-sell products and services and meet the needs of multiple client segments is at least equal to the costs of the additional complexity that it brings.

Again, surprisingly (particularly as this contrasted the findings in other sectors), the highest-performing firms in the industry were those that undertook the most M&A activity. Generally, high levels of M&A are associated with poorer performance, so this finding suggests that firms in the banking industry are able to integrate acquisitions more effectively than companies in other industries. It is also important to note that all M&As within the industry have not had successful outcomes. RBS's acquisitions of Charter One and ABM Amro over-stretched the firm's global structure, with a large number of subsidiaries and divisional offices across a wide

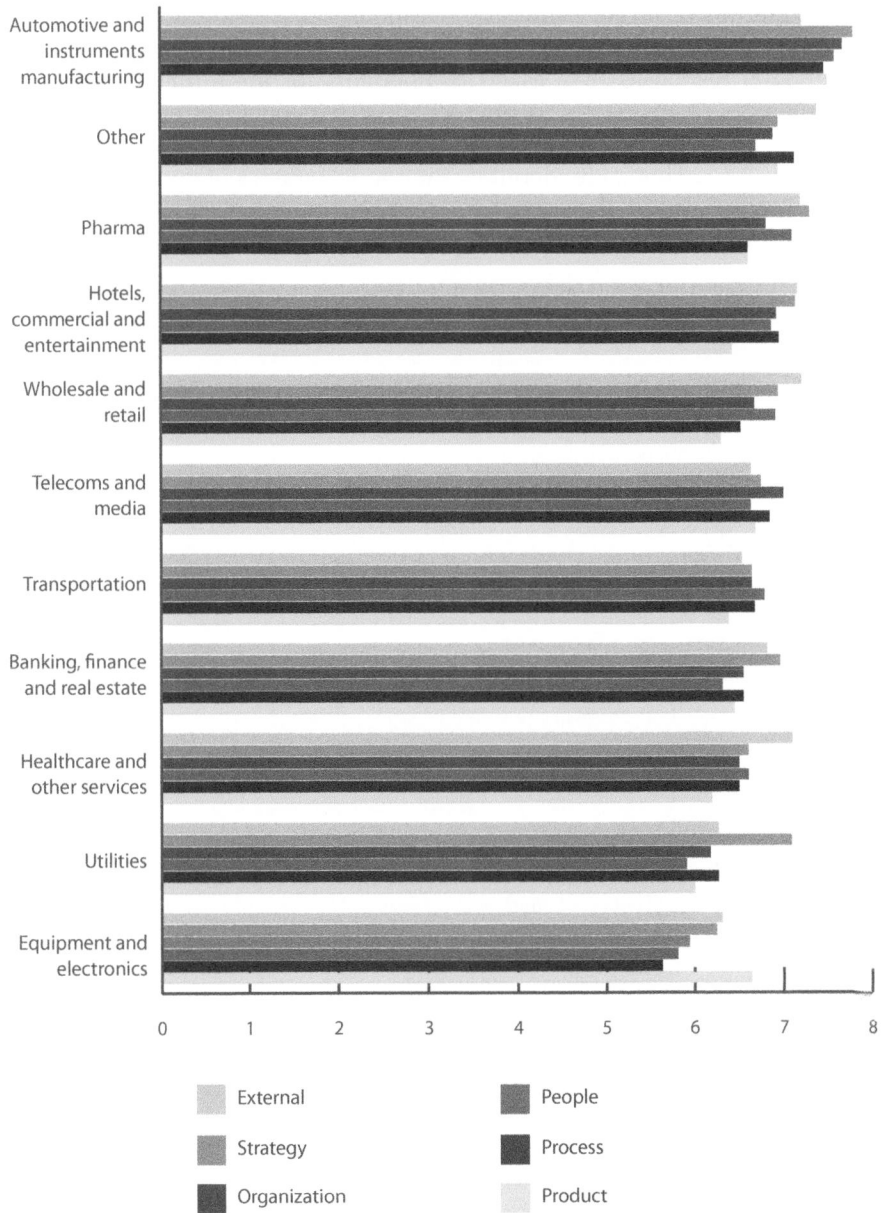

FIGURE A2.3
Industry sectors compared across the six types of costly complexity

range of overseas locations. This adds coordination costs as well as the complexities of operating in many different institutional environments and across a variety of business cultures.

The Complexity Survey captures the responses of 600 executives across 300 European firms of over 5000 employees (and further expanded captures over 1200 responses). We asked respondents to rank different forms of complexity according to the impact these had on their productivity. A detailed breakdown of the major sources of complexity for banks is provided in Table A2.1. This table identifies the top 25 sources of complexity. This table can be used by these firms to identify where they should focus their complexity reduction efforts.

#	THE LEADING BANKING COMPLEXITY SOURCES
1	Changes in core strategy
2	Launching new products
3	Annual budgeting process
4	Number of competitors in your market
5	The core business strategy itself
6	Levels of management/organization structure
7	Fluctuations in the performance of the economy
8	Number of strategic initiatives pursued
9	Amount of innovation launched into your market
10	The pressures of regulatory compliance
11	Understanding and following process guidelines
12	Operating in multiple markets
13	Moving into a new industry sector
14	How products/services are presented to customers
15	Making overall expenditure decisions
16	The challenge of globalization/international expansion
17	Changes in customer behavior
18	Changing technology within your market
19	Measuring and reporting on KPIs/balanced scorecard objectives
20	Number of customers
21	Creating a new product/service
22	Customer account management
23	Instructions/guidelines for products/services
24	Changes in environmental policy
25	Customer interaction with the company

TABLE A2.1
The top 25 sources of complexity for banks

Internal forms of complexity are more harmful than regulatory oversight

The survey results suggest that the banking sector has become relatively introverted and is struggling to deal with the level of external change because of inherent complexity in its strategies, its organization designs and its process designs. Regulatory oversight is often stated as a key driver of complexity in banking; however, our data suggests that this may be an excuse rather than a real reason for complexity. Although the regulatory and competitive environment for banks does add to the complexity of the banking system, internal forms of complexity are having a bigger impact on the overall complexity and corresponding performance of the banks.

Strategic complexity is a major problem

Just as in the pharmaceutical industry, the banking industry appears to suffer heavily from complexities that result from a lack of clarity in the core strategy being pursued, plus the wide variety of strategic initiatives that senior executives are trying to implement. Frequent changes in strategy exacerbate these problems.

Organizational complexity is seen as a major factor by managers

The sixth highest driver of complexity, identified by banking executives, was the number of layers of management and the overall complexity of the organizational structure. Decision-making in general was seen as a significant source of harmful complexity. This is significant given the increased premium that will be placed on clear and effective decision-making as competition grows in the banking sector.

Interactions with customers

Interactions with customers rank highly in the complexity factors identified in our survey. As customer choices and behaviors change, banking technologies evolve and a growing variety of channels to the customer (online, mobile phone, smart cards, etc.) appear, it will be firms that are able to adapt their customer offering that will have the biggest advantages. In an era where customers have more choice, global competition between the banks gets tougher. Those who are able to offer simple propositions and easier interactions with customers will find themselves obtaining a competitive advantage over their peers.

Process complexity

The banking industry has been an avid exponent of Lean, which has been widely and in some cases successfully applied to many of the core processes in the banking industry. Despite this, process complexity is still having significant impact on the banking sector, with core processes and 'following guidelines' being cited as major drivers of overall complexity. In our experience this is because Lean is a less effective tool when applied to knowledge-based processes (see Chapter 6 for a fuller explanation). So Lean will not be the right tool for streamlining the types of banking processes that are characterized by high levels of human interaction, human skill and experience.

3. Banks appear ill-equipped to cope with future increases in complexity

As we have seen, the majority of banks are either very close to the tipping point or already past the tipping point. This is particularly concerning since there are many forthcoming changes in the banking industry that will significantly add to the complexity of this industry. Based on the GSI's 2011 findings, we doubt that banks will be able to successfully manage these future complexity drivers unless they dramatically reduce their overall complexity levels. In other words, in our view, the banking industry does not have the agility it will need to respond to the turbulence to come.

Even greater regulatory oversight

As governments continue to seek measures that will prevent another collapse in the global financial system, regulatory oversight will continue to increase above recent levels and above those existing when our GSI study was conducted. Although it is not yet clear how governments will implement banking reform, it is clear that the agenda set out by the G20 and the Basel Committee will have far-reaching consequences and this will permanently change the way global banks do business.

Greater liquidity

The major impact of Basel III is that banks will need to increase their capital and liquidity requirements, which will impact on firms' profitability. In turn, the need to accurately report on and adjust liquidity levels will place additional stress on systems and processes within the banks. The accountancy firm Ernst & Young suggests that the result of Basel III could be a push to re-evaluate legal entity structures and cross-entity activities. Any decisions to untangle these entities and their constituent structures and processes will be challenging, but probably necessary to reduce the overall complexity of banking operations.

Heightened risk management

On the face of it, managing risk better is not really a driver of complexity, and it is something that most people would say is an absolute must for global banks. However, our research shows that excessive risk management, or over-complex due diligence and compliance processes, can consume businesses and the people working within them. Not only does it suffocate agility – as people procrastinate or explore every eventuality for even the most trivial decisions – it also so often leads to risk avoidance, which means decisions aren't just late, they may never be taken at all.

4. What can banking professionals do to reduce complexity?

Reduce geographical complexity

It may be very difficult for the major banks to reduce the number of countries across which they operate; however, a review of their geographic portfolio to focus on fewer key countries would be advisable for the majority of the global banks. Where this is not possible, it is absolutely necessary for multinational banks to review their organizational structures, and redress the global/standardized versus local/customized balance. This does not necessarily mean that centralized, top-down command-and-control decision-making structures are appropriate. It does mean that careful restructuring is needed.

Increase external focus

The overt focus on internal organization, process and decision-making structures has reduced the agility and competitiveness of many banks. The banks need to refocus their energies on the external factors like changing customer needs, competitors and technological change. They should consider delayering to put leaders closer to the customer and refocus people's roles and responsibilities to emphasize external customer focus. They should also start the process of developing an externally-focused, customer-facing culture, encouraging everyone to be more in tune with the markets and customers' needs and concerns.

Reduce organizational complexity

A fundamental review of banks' organization design is essential to enable the external focus we have discussed above. Chapter 4 provides clear guidance on this, but in short, we think delayering, optimizing spans of control, reducing matrix complexity, devolving control to local or customer-facing managers, and simplifying decision-making will all be required to achieve the new level of organizational simplicity needed in banking. Without these changes the banks will not have the agility they will need to adapt to the future.

Increase strategic focus and communication

It is also clear that lack of strategic clarity is harming banks' performance. This may come from being unclear on what the core strategy is, from trying to do too many things, or from constantly changing the strategy. The development, communication and implementation of a simple and consistent strategy will enable the highly talented managers in the banking industry to identify and realize the very rare growth opportunities that do still exist.

Streamline knowledge-based processes

Many of the more transactional and systems-based banking processes have already been transformed using Lean. Attention should now focus on the more knowledge-based banking processes, which can be streamlined using the steps outlined in Chapter 6.

5. Conclusion

Three years on from the global financial crisis, as credit and liquidity pressures ease, the major banks remained highly complex and were clearly struggling to find ways to reduce overall complexity levels.

The future of the industry will be characterized by trends such as: the end of declining interest rates; more (and more changeable) regulation; diverging growth rates between developed and emerging (and developing) markets; aging populations; a growing range of channels to the customer; and a growing variety of customer preferences.

In order to thrive or survive, the major banks must become more externally focused and must simplify their operations, organizational structures, processes and strategies in order to improve their performance.

Appendix 3

Costly Complexity in the Insurance Sector

Of the 200 companies in our Global Simplicity Index (GSI), 19 are insurers.

Insurance firms are currently facing a range of new threats and opportunities in their external competitive environment, including: growing economic instability; market differentiation and the need to customize customer relationship management (CRM) approaches; emerging markets; new competitors, including those from emerging economies; and a range of new technologies for managing and delivering products and services.

For the 'strugglers' in our study, these challenges add to an already high level of complexity brought about by an era of M&As and a proliferation of product portfolios. The financial crisis has revealed a number of vulnerabilities in these insurance firms; life and pension insurance are particularly exposed in a post-crisis era of restrictive capital requirements and transparency regulations. New restrictions on the management of distribution channels, specifically affecting remuneration and contracts, will also push up costs and force a streamlining of these channel arrangements.

The growing variety of regulatory requirements, many designed to prevent a future financial crisis, will alone increase the pressure on insurance firms to simplify their operations and their product portfolios. Additional regulatory reforms tend to give rise to additional internal organizational complexity in insurance firms, reducing efficiency and damaging profits. Therefore, in the build-up to this new wave of legislation, it is vital that insurance companies review the levels of complexity within their firms, and where possible look to remove unnecessary and value destructive complexity. This will ensure that insurance companies are well placed to manage the impacts of these regulatory changes.

Insurance industry complexity: summary of our key findings

The insurance industry can be divided into three very distinct clusters of companies:

- **Local simplifiers:** Firms that are overly simple, that tend to operate in one geographic region and that only offer a limited range of product and services.
- **Regional performers:** Firms that also tend to operate in one geographical region, but tend to have a larger, but still focused, portfolio of products and services. These companies tend to be the highest performing in the industry.

- **Global strugglers:** Firms that operate in multiple geographical markets, as well as offering multiple products and services. This causes high levels of costly complexity, in turn causing them to have below average performance. Harmful complexity is reducing annual profits by between 10 per cent and 40 per cent in this sub-group of insurers.

Geographical complexity has a negative effect on performance
Dealing with a wide geographical diversity of markets, institutions, cultures and regulatory environments clearly takes its toll on profitability.

Product/service complexity also has a negative effect
The majority of high-performing firms within the industry tend to have one major product or service line that accounts for the bulk of their revenue (a focused portfolio), with other supplementary products or services accounting for smaller revenue shares. Product design is too complex within insurance.

IT systems and strategy issues are major sources of complexity
As with most industries where there is a high reliance on complex IT systems, this form of complexity has a large impact on productivity in the insurance industry.

Strategic complexity also needs to be reduced in the large global insurers.

1. How are the world's largest financial services firms ranked on the GSI?

Mapping each of the 19 insurers on the GSI matrix shows an interesting polarization between the local insurance giants and the globally diverse insurance giants (Figure A3.1).

Mapping the insurers on the GSI matrix reveals three very distinct clusters.

Local simplifiers
The first are those with low complexity and low performance. This group consists of Nippon Life Insurance, Sumitomo Life Insurance, The Dai-ichi Life Insurance, Meiji Yasuda Life Insurance and State Farm Insurance companies. These firms tend to operate within one country and offer one

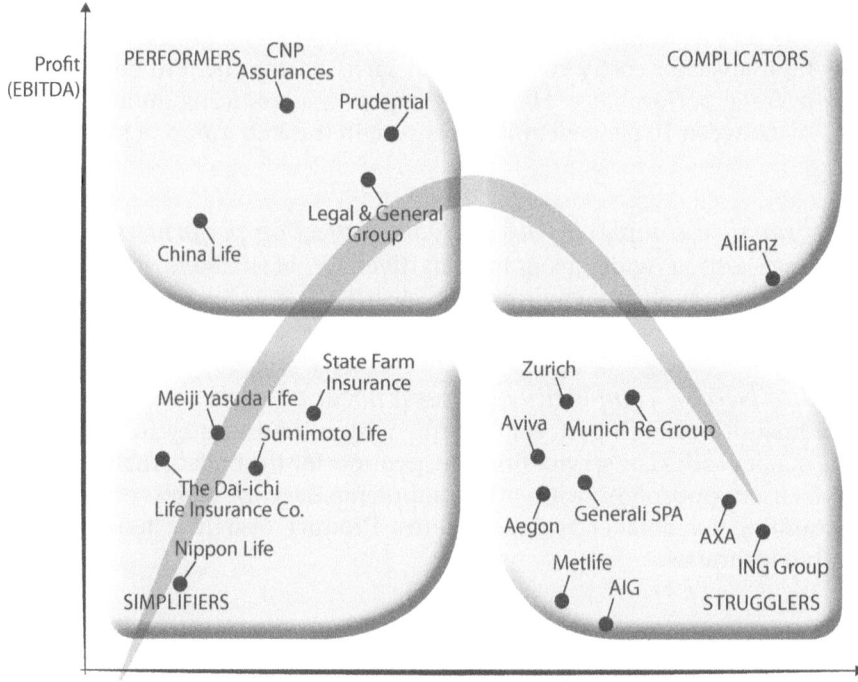

FIGURE A3.1
The 19 insurance companies on the performance–complexity matrix

product or a very limited variety of products (the majority being Japanese life insurance firms).

Regional performers

The second group are those with slightly higher complexity than those in the local simplifiers group. This group includes China Life Insurance, Prudential, Legal and General, and CNP Assurances. These companies are the highest-performing in the industry. They tend to have the majority of their operations within one geographical region, reducing their exposure to regulatory changes and increasing their knowledge of the market. They also tend to have a fairly limited number of products and services.

Global strugglers

The final group consists of those companies with high complexity and poor performance. The insurance industry has an unusually high proportion of strugglers. Excess complexity in this group of companies will be costing them anything between 10 and 40 per cent of their annual profits. This group includes Aegon, AIG, Allianz, AXA, Aviva, Generali SPA, Metlife, Munich Re and Zurich. The vast majority of these firms have below average levels of performance (only Allianz has slightly above average performance in the industry). These companies tend to be diversified, both in their product portfolio and in their geographical spread. This additional complexity outweighs its performance rewards.

2. What are the most harmful sources of complexity for insurance companies?

As with the banking industry, operating across too many geographies has a negative effect for the global insurance companies, with the benefits of diversification being cancelled out by excessive complexity. Operating in more countries requires the insurers to deal with more external complexities like different regulatory regimes, different customer types and different local competitors, many of whom have much simpler business models.

Our study suggests that the insurers are not good enough at managing these external forms of complexity. This indicates that the priority of firms should be to obtain extensive knowledge of fewer geographical markets, rather than spreading operations across too many different geographical regions each with different customer needs, competitors and regulatory environments. Alternatively, the insurers need to become much better at managing geographical diversity than they are at present.

The second important finding from the GSI is that product/service diversity is harming the performance of the global players in this market. The majority of high-performing firms within the industry tend to have one major product or service that accounts for the bulk of their revenue (a focused portfolio), with other supplementary products or services accounting for smaller revenue shares. The global insurance strugglers have much wider product/service portfolios, but because they are too broad, the overall impact of having more products/services has a negative effect on performance.

Separate research by the branding experts Siegel+Gale identified that customers perceive brands from the health and general insurance sectors to be more complex than those in other industries, so there is a clear need to reduce overall product/service complexity, which will improve customer satisfaction with insurance products.

The Complexity Survey captured the responses of 600 executives across 300 European firms of over 5000 employees (and we have extended it since, to capture over 1200 responses). We asked managers to rank different forms of complexity according to the impact these had on their productivity.

When we break down these internal sources of complexity we find clear industry differences. Figure A3.2 shows the relative importance of these different kinds of complexity on respondents in different industry sectors.

A more detailed breakdown of the sources of complexity for insurance companies is provided in Table A3.1, which shows the 25 greatest drivers of complexity. Ranked in order of importance, these are the sources of complexity that have the greatest impact on productivity, according to respondents of our survey working in this sector.

The information in Table A3.1 can be used by insurance companies to identify where they should focus their complexity reduction efforts.

We can analyze these as related clusters of complexity sources that most strongly impact the productivity and performance of managers and employees of insurance companies.

Technology-related complexity
The insurance industry depends heavily on IT systems for its day-to-day operations. From the survey results it is very clear that the industry is struggling with the levels of complexity driven by IT systems. Respondents stated that introducing major IT systems, changing departmental software and specialist IT/software systems were the three largest sources of complexity within their working lives. This is a striking finding, suggesting that there are considerable opportunities to reduce complexity in the insurance industry through rationalization and simplification of IT systems.

Legacy IT systems (and legacy portfolios) are a major part of the problem for some firms, alongside the difficulties of dealing with multiple systems that do not connect with each other, accumulated through acquisitions. These complexities add to the infrastructural costs of administering policies, which can increase by 35–40 per cent during the lifetime of the policy.

Regulatory complexity
Complying with regulations is also a major source of complexity for insurance companies, suggesting that increased oversight and additional restrictions have made a complex industry even more complex.

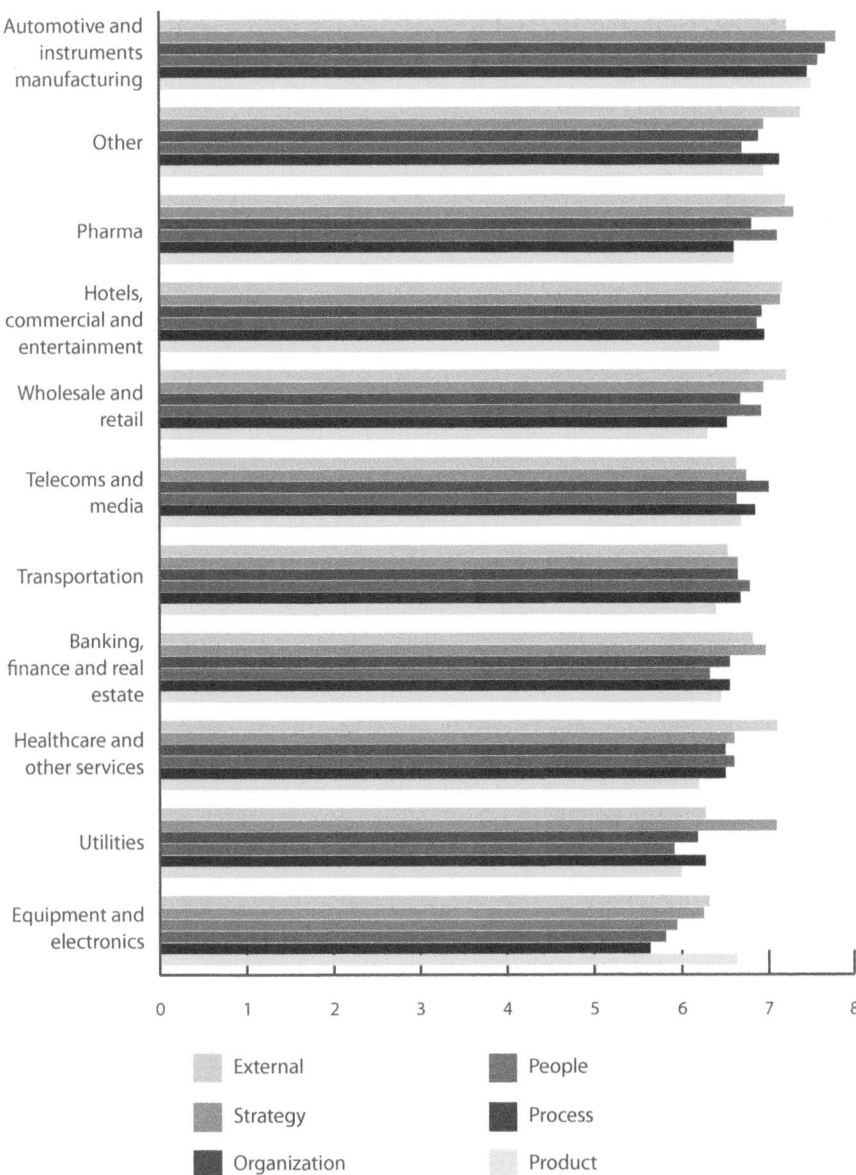

FIGURE A3.2
Industry sectors compared across the six types of costly complexity

Strategic complexity is also a concern

Like the pharmaceutical industry and the banking industry (see Appendices 1 and 2), the insurers appear to be suffering heavily from complexities driven by frequent changes in strategy.

#	THE LEADING INSURANCE COMPLEXITY SOURCES
1	Introducing major IT systems
2	Changing departmental software
3	Specialist IT/software systems
4	Measuring and reporting on KPIs/balance scorecard objectives
5	Pressures of regulatory compliance
6	Number of IT systems
7	Changing business strategy
8	Changing existing products or services
9	Major project processes
10	Fluctuations in the performance of the economy
11	Use of the internet and other online technologies
12	Operating in multiple markets
13	Time spent dealing with email
14	Content and politics of meetings
15	Using IT Systems
16	Changes in the regulatory environment
17	Number of strategic initiatives pursued
18	Annual budgeting process
19	Levels of management/organizational structure
20	Number and variety of specialist roles
21	Number of competitors
22	The challenge of globalization and global expansion
23	Launching new products and services
24	Creating a new product/service
25	Clarification of roles and responsibilities

TABLE A3.1
The top 25 sources of complexity in the insurance industry

3. How should insurance industry leaders respond to the complexity challenge?

Advice for the strugglers
For these companies, complexity reduction should take a high priority. Complexity is having a major impact on profits and is also reducing their agility, thus making it hard for them to respond to market and regulatory changes.

- Rationalize product/service portfolios: Chapter 7 gives some simple advice on how the insurers might rationalize their tail of poor performing products and services.
- Review geographic priorities: While exiting some markets may seem extreme, given the high cost of complexity there is a clear need to review geographic priorities. Where it is not practical to exit a market then product/service portfolio rationalization is critical. This will at least ensure that geographic complexity is not further compounded by product/service complexity.
- Rationalize IT systems: There is a clear need to reduce the number of different IT systems and to ensure that each IT platform is simple for managers/staff to use and integrates well with other IT systems. Bundling portfolios on to a smaller number of platforms while consolidating and standardizing the back office infrastructure should be a priority.
- Simplify product design: Significant improvements can be made by addressing the complexity of the services and experiences that the insurance industry provides to customers. The brand research conducted by Siegel+Gale has identified that customers perceive brands from the health and general insurance sectors as more complex that those in other industries. This suggests that there is significant room for insurance companies to differentiate themselves from their competitors by reducing product complexity for their customers.
- Simplify the overall strategy: There is a clear need for these companies to develop a clear and consistent strategy and communicate the strategy more effectively to their employees.
- Finally, developing a simpler organization design to support the above strategy will help improve overall performance. Less ambiguity in organizational structure and processes means more effective risk management and compliance.

Advice for the simplifiers

These firms should look to carefully add new services to their portfolio, ideally within their core geographical region, while diagnosing and reducing existing value-destructive complexity within their organizations. Many of the Japanese insurance firms in our study are the simplest of the Fortune 200 examined within the GSI, but they suffer from low performance and are trapped in a flat market. Growth in the Chinese mainland market and across Asia in general should represent a good opportunity for Japanese firms to expand across the region, although the pace of deregulation in the Chinese domestic market is a key limitation on access to this market.

Advice for the performers

These companies need to refrain from adding complexity while identifying and reducing value-destructive complexity within their firms. These firms need to be aware that regulatory changes may add complexity, and should therefore react to make changes to their internal processes and external interactions as simple as possible.

4. Conclusion

Four years on from the global financial crisis the global insurers remain highly complex and are struggling to find ways to reduce overall complexity levels.

Most of the global insurance companies are classified as complexity strugglers, indicating that value destruction from harmful complexity is destroying 10–40 per cent of their annual profits. Bold leadership is needed now to dramatically reduce complexity and improve profits.

References and further reading

Anderson, P. (1999) Complexity theory and organization science, *Organization Science*, 10 (3), 216–32.

Ashby, R. (1956) *An Introduction to Cybernetics*. London: Methuen.

Ashby, W.R. (1958) Requisite variety and its implications for the control of complex systems, *Cybernetica*, 1 (2), 83–99.

Ashkenas, R. (2007) Simplicity-minded management: A practical guide to stripping complexity out of your organisation, *Harvard Business Review*, 85 (12), 101–9.

Ashkenas, R. (2010) *Simply Effective: How to Cut Through Complexity in Your Organization and Get Things Done*. Boston, MA: Harvard Business School Press.

Ashkenas, R. (2011) The C-level job for everyone: Reducing complexity, HBR Blog network. Available at: http://blogs.hbr.org/ashkenas/2011/02/the-c-level-job-for-everyone-r.html (last accessed 1 September 2011).

Ashkenas, R. (2011) When managing complexity, less is more, HBR Blog network. Available at: http://blogs.hbr.org/ashkenas/2011/05/when-managing-complexity-less.html (last accessed 1 September 2011).

Boisot, M. and McKelvey, B. (2010) Integrating modernist and postmodernist perspectives on organizations: A complexity science perspective, *Academy of Management Review*, 35, 415–33.

Bozarth, C.C., Warsing, D.P., Flynn, B.B. and Flynn, E.J. (2009) The impact of supply chain complexity on manufacturing plant performance, *Journal of Operations Management*, 27 (1), 78–93.

Brown, S.L. and Eisenhardt, K.M. (1997) The art of continuous change: Linking complexity theory and time-paced evolution in relentlessly shifting organizations, *Administrative Science Quarterly*, 42, 1–34.

Brown, S.L. and Eisenhardt, K.M. (1998) *Competing on the Edge: Strategy as Structured Chaos*. Boston, MA: Harvard Business School Press.

Chandler, A.D. (1962) *Strategy and Structure: Chapters in the History of Industrial Enterprise*. Cambridge, MA: MIT Press.

Child, J., and Rodrigues, S.B. (2011) How organizations engage with external complexity: A political action perspective, *Organization Studies*, 32 (6), 803–24.

Cilliers, P. (1998) *Complexity and Postmodernism*. London: Routledge.

Collinson, S.C. (2011) Is complexity killing pharma profits? *Pharma Mag*, May/June 2011. Available at www.pharma-mag.com.

Collinson, S.C. and Jay, M. (2011) Complexity kills profits – CEOs need to simplify their businesses, *European Business Review*, November/December 2011, 35–8.

Collinson, S.C. and Jay, M. (2011) The Complexity Challenge, Advanced Institute of Management (AIM) research, Executive Briefing, London. Available at: www.aimresearch.org/index.php?page=executive-briefing (last accessed 5 May 2012).

Collinson, S.C. and Jay, M. (2011) Is complexity stifling mobile innovation at Nokia?' *Mobile News*, 6 June 2011.

Collinson, S.C. and Morgan, G. (eds.) (2009) *Images of the Multinational Firm*. Oxford: Wiley.

Collinson, S.C. and Pettigrew, A.M. (2009) Comparative International Business Research methods: Pitfalls and practicalities, Chapter 27 in Rugman, A.M. (ed.) *The Oxford Handbook of International Business* (2nd edition). Oxford: Oxford University Press.

Collinson, S.C. and Rugman, A.M. (2008) The regional nature of Japanese multinational business, *Journal of International Business Studies*, 39(2), 215–30.

Damanpour, F. (1996) Organizational complexity and innovation: Developing and testing multiple contingency models, *Management Science*, 42 (5), 693–716.

D'Aveni, R.A. (1994) *Hypercompetition: Managing the Dynamics of Strategic Manoeuvring*. New York: Free Press.

Davis, J.P., Eisenhardt, K.M. and Bingham, C.B. (2009) Optimal structure, market dynamism and the strategy of simple rules, *Administrative Science Quarterly*, 54, 413–52.

de Bono, E. (1998) *Simplicity*. London: Penguin Books.

Dooley, K.J., and Van de Ven, A.H. (1999) Explaining complex organizational dynamics, *Organization Science*, 10, 358–72.

Eisenhardt, Kathleen M. and Brown, Shona L. (2003) *Competing on the Edge: Strategy as Structured Chaos*. Boston, MA: Harvard Business School Press.

Eisenhardt, Kathleen M. and Sull, Donald N. (2001) Strategy and simple rules, *Harvard Business Review*, Reprint R0101G, 106–16.

EIU (2011) *The Complexity Challenge: How Businesses are Bearing Up*. London: Economist Intelligence Unit.

Fried, J. and Heinemeier Hansson, D. (2010) *Re-Work: Change the Way You Work Forever*. London: Vermilion.

Garud, R., Gehman, J. and Kumaraswamy, A. (2011) Complexity arrangements for sustained innovation: Lessons from 3M Corporation, *Organization Studies*, 32, 737–67.

George, M.L. and Wilson, S.A. (2004) *Conquering Complexity in Your Business: How Walmart, Toyota, and Other Top Companies Are Breaking Through the Ceiling on Profits and Growth*. New York: McGraw-Hill.

Haldane, A. (2009) The basis for a speech given at the Marcus-Evans Conference on Stress-Testing, 9–10 February 2009, posted

13 February 2009. Available at: www.bankofengland.co.uk/ publications/speeches/2009/speech374.pdf (last accessed 5 May 2012).

Hayek, F. (1989) *The Collected Works of F.A. Hayek*. Chicago, IL: University of Chicago Press.

Hayles, K.N. (ed.) (1991) *Chaos and order*. Chicago, IL: University of Chicago Press.

Helfat, C.E., Finkelstein, S., Mitchell, W., Peteraf, M., Singh, H., Teece, D. and Winter, S.G. (2007) *Dynamic Capabilities*. Oxford: Blackwell.

Heracleous, L. and Collinson, S.C. (2009) HSBC's strategy and leadership, in Singh, K., Panagarkar, N. and Heracleous, L., *Business Strategy in Asia* (3rd edition). Singapore: Cengage.

Hutzschenreuter, T. and Guenther, F. (2008) Performance effects of firms' expansion paths within and across industries and nations, *Strategic Organization*, 6 (1), 47–81.

Jason, D., Eisenhardt, K.M. and Bingham, C.B. (2009) Optimal structure, market dynamism, and the strategy of simple rules, *Administrative Science Quarterly*, 54, 413–52.

Kim, W.C. and Maubourgne, R. (2005) *Blue Ocean Strategy: How to Create Uncontested Market Space and Make the Competition Irrelevant*. Boston, MA: Harvard Business School Press.

KPMG (2010) *Confronting Complexity: Research Findings and Insights*. KPMG.com.

Lawrence, P.R. and Lorsch, J.W. (1967) *Organization and Environment: Managing Differentiation and Integration*. Boston, MA: Harvard Business School Press.

Leavitt, H.J. (2005) *Top Down: Why Hierarchies are Here to Stay and How to Manage Them More Eeffectively*. Boston, MA: Harvard Business School Press.

Lumpkin, G.T. and Dess, G.G. (2006) The effect of 'Simplicity' on the strategy–performance relationship, *Journal of Management Studies*, 43 (7), 1583–604.

Luhmann, N. (1984) *Soziale Systeme – Grundriss einer allgemeinen Theorie*. Berlin: Suhrkamp. English translation (1995) *Social Systems*. Stanford: Stanford University Press.

March, J.G. and Sutton, R.I. (1997) Organizational performance as a dependent variable, *Organization Science*, 8, 698–706.

Martin, J.A. and Eisenhardt, K.M. (2010) Rewiring: Cross-business-unit collaborations in multi-business organizations, *Academy of Management Journal*, 53 (2), 265–301.

Mariotti, J.L. (2008) *The Complexity Crisis: Why Too Many Products, Markets, and Customers are Crippling Your Company – and What to Do About it*. Avon, MA: Adams Media.

McKelvey, B. (1997) Avoiding complexity catastrophe in co-evolutionary pockets: Strategies for rugged landscapes, *Organization Science*, 10 (3), 294–321.

McMillan, E. (2008) *Complexity, Management and the Dynamics of Change: Challenges for Practice*. Oxford: Routledge.

Miller, D. (1993) The architecture of simplicity, *Academy of Management Review*, 18 (1), 116–38.

Moldoveanu, M.C. and Bauer, R.M. (2004) On the relationship between organizational complexity and organizational structuration, *Organization Science*, 15 (1), 98–118.

Morin, E. (2008) *On Complexity*. Cresskill, NJ: Hampton Press.

Novak, S. and Eppinger, S.D. (2001) Sourcing by design: Product complexity and the supply chain, *Management Science*, 47 (1), 189–204.

O'Connell, F. (2008) *Simply Brilliant: The Competitive Advantage of Common Sense*. (3rd edition). Harlow, UK: FT Pearson.

Patel, P. and Pavitt, K. (1997) The technological competencies of the world's largest firms: Complex and path-dependent, but not much variety. *Research Policy*, 26, 141–56.

Perrow, C. (1967) A framework for the comparative analysis of organizations, *American Sociological Review*, 26, 854–66.

Piscitello, L. (2004) Corporate diversification, coherence and economic performance, *Industrial and Corporate Change*, 13 (5), 757–87.

Porter, M.E. (1985) *Competitive Advantage*. New York: Free Press.

Richard, P.J., Devinney, T.M., Yip, G.S. and Johnson, G. (2009) Measuring organizational performance: Towards methodological best practice, *Journal of Management*, 35 (3), 718–804.

Richardson, K. (2008) Managing complex organizations: Complexity thinking and the science and art of management, *E:CO*, 10 (2), 13–26.

Rivkin, J.W. (2000) Imitation of complex strategies, *Management Science*, 46 (6), 824–44.

Rivkin, J.W. and Siggelkow, N. (2003) Balancing search and stability: Interdependencies among elements of organizational design, *Management Science*, 49, 290–311.

Rugman, A.M. and Collinson, S.C. (2012) *International Business* (6th edition). Harlow, UK: FT Pearson/Prentice Hall.

Rycroft, R.W. and Kash, D.E. (1999) *The Complexity Challenge: Technological Innovation for the 21st Century*. London: Pinter.

Schmidt, T. (2009) *Strategic Project Management Made Simple: Practical Tools for Leaders and Teams*. Chichester: John Wiley & Sons.

Schwandt, A. (2009) Measuring organizational complexity and its impact on organizational performance – A comprehensive conceptual model and empirical study, PhD dissertation, Technical University of Berlin.

Schwandt, A. and Franklin, J.R. (2010) *Logistics: The Backbone for Managing Complex Organizations*. Berne: Haupt Publishing.

Siggelkow, N. and Rivkin, J.W. (2005) Speed and search: Designing organizations for turbulence and complexity, *Organization Science*, 16 (2), 101–22.

Steger, U., Amann, W. and Maznewski, M. (2007) *Managing Complexity in Global Organizations*. Chichester: John Wiley & Sons.

Tatikonda, M.V. and Rosenthal, S.R. (2000) Technological novelty, project complexity, and product development project execution success: A deeper look at task uncertainty in product innovation, *IEEE Transactions on Engineering Management*, 47 (1), 74–87.

Thomas, M. and Singh, N. (2006) Complexity reduction in product design and development using Design for Six Sigma, *International Journal of Product Development*, 3 (3), 4.

Tidd, J. (1997) Integrative themes of research on the management of innovation: Complexity, networks and learning, *International Journal of Innovation Management*, 8, (1), 59–69.

Tsoukas, H. (2005) *Complex Knowledge*. Oxford: Oxford University Press.

Vasconcelos, F.C. and Ramirez, R. (2009) Complexity in business environments, *Journal of Business Research*, 64, 236–41.

Vesterby, V. (2008) Measuring complexity: Things that go wrong and how to get it right, *E:CO*, 10 (2), 90–102.

Waldrop, M.M. (1993) *Complexity: The Emerging Science at the Edge of Order and Chaos*. London: Viking.

Westney, D.E. (2009) The multinational firm as an evolutionary system, in Collinson, S.C. and Morgan, G. (eds.) (2009) *Images of the Multinational Firm*. Chichester: Wiley & Sons.

Whittington, R. (2002) Organizational structures, in Faulkner, D.O. and Campbell, A. (eds.) *Oxford Handbook of Strategy*. Oxford: Oxford University Press.

Wilson, S.A. and Perumal, A. (2009) *Waging War on Complexity Costs: Reshape Your Cost Structure, Free Up Cash Flows and Boost Productivity by Attacking Process, Product and Organizational Complexity*. New York: McGraw-Hill.

Winter, S.G. (2003) Understanding dynamic capabilities, *Strategic Management Journal*, 24, 991–5.

Notes

Chapter 1
1. From *Search for the Real and Other Essays*, Sara T. Weeks and Bartlett H. Hayes (eds.), MIT Press.

Chapter 3
1. For clarity when we use the term 'leaders' we do not mean just 10–15 board members, or the 'C-suite'. In this context we mean the 'leadership team' (the most senior 10–20 per cent of your managers) but we also include change agents/influencers who may be less senior, but are nevertheless very influential. These 'change agents' or influencers have a big impact on many people in your organization, because your managers/staff naturally look to them for confirmation of ideas and follow their lead without being told to.

Chapter 7
1. ACM SIGPLAN Notices, 'Epigrams on Programming', September 1982.

Appendix 1
1. Defined broadly as firms whose primary sales are within the 2800–2900 range of the Standard Industrial Classification (SIC) code. Of these 11, GSK, Roche, J&J, Pfizer, Novartis, Sanofi-Aventis and Bayer are classed as SIC 2834 and are therefore most directly comparable.
2. (1) This study is separate from the GSI analysis described above and a different range of industry sectors were examined. (2) For statistical robustness we have combined several SIC sub-groups into the Pharmaceuticals, Life-sciences and Diversified Chemicals (PLDC) industry group (represented by 'Pharma' in the relevant tables). The GSI uses proxy measures and secondary data, while the survey captures the impact of various kinds of complexity as reported by managers and employees in 300 firms.

Index

3M 152
80-20 rule *see* Pareto
  Analysis
360 surveys 76, 83, 90

active listening 126
Activity Based Costing
  212
adding value 6, 9, 12, 13,
  148–9
cost vs. value creation 51
  disconnect dilemma 13,
    33, 228
  everyday 231–5
  products and services 12,
    226, 228
  value creation 194
  value driver analysis
    44–5, 194, *195*
Aegon 281
agility 34–5, 95, 99, 264, 275,
  276, 284
AIG 281
aimlessness 62, 144
Alcon 23, 255, 256
Alliance Unichem 223
Allianz 281
Apple 24, 25, 65–6, 100,
  203–4, 215, 217, 219, 222
AstraZeneca 226–7
AT&T 16
automotive industry 3, 20,
  179, 181
Aviva 281
awareness, raising 55, 70,
  73, 79
AXA 281

banking sector 16, 17–18,
  265–76
  complexity drivers 267,
    269–74, 272
  complexity tipping point
    266, 268, 274
  customer relations 267,
    273
  external complexity 18,
    267, 273
  geographic diversification
    17, 267, 269–70, 275
  GSI ranking 268, *268*
  liquidity requirements
    274–5
  organizational complexity
    267, 273, 275–6

performance–complexity
  matrix 17, 268–9, *269*
process complexity 267,
  274
regulatory oversight 273,
  274
response to complexity
  challenge 275–6
risk management 275
strategic complexity 267,
  273
Barclays 17
Basel III 274–5
Bayer 23, 75
Beckhard's Change
  Equation 70–1
benchmarking complexity
  levels 40, *43*, 44
best practice, sharing 87,
  174, 187
Boston Box 153, 159, *159*
BPR *see* business process
  re-engineering (BPR)
brain, lazy 155, 180
brainstorming 44, 117, 158
brand differentiation 152, 159
brand loyalty 224
brand positioning 223
brand simplicity 224
branding
  global brand strategy 65,
    189–90, 218
  'local jewels' 218
budget planning 149, 155
bureaucracy 34, 64, 155,
  184, 188
business process re-
  engineering (BPR) 99,
  174, 179, 181, 231
business processes *see*
  processes

call centers 107–8
capital markets crises 8,
  17, 266
capital projects 166
Carrefour 19
Chandler, Alfred 94, 96
change agents 75
change management 70, 75
change, resistance to 79, 84
China Life Insurance 280
China Mobile 16, 26
CNP Assurances 280
command-and-control
  hierarchies 64, 122, 262
  see also bureaucracy
communications
  clarity 244

communicating strategy
  167–71
complexity driver 83
Complexity Impact Score
  (CIS) 32
diagnosis questions 46
everyday 243–4
overload 28, 31
simplifying 243–4
transparency 127
company value, simplicity
  as 74–5, 81–2, 94, 224
competitive environments,
  turbulent 2, 7, 64, 99,
  151
competitor spoilers 221
complex adaptive systems
  3–5, 60
  characteristics 5
  complex and complicated,
    distinguished 5, 94
  components 4, 5, 6, 123
complexity
  bad complexity 7, 9, 10,
    11–12, 13, 14
  complexity–performance
    relationship 9, 14–15,
    15, 17
  defining 3–5, *4*, 59, 99
  diagnosis 38–50, *39*
  dimensions of 28–9, *29*
  drivers *see* external
    complexity; internal
    complexity
  duty to fight against 8,
    35
  good complexity 9, 11,
    13, 14
  impacts of 2, 14, 33–5,
    33, 58
  quantifying cost of 14,
    50–3
  reduction strategy *see*
    simplification strategy
complexity behaviors
  identifying 42
  leadership 43, 64, 67,
    83, 90
  personal 43, 58–63
  see also people complexity
Complexity Curve 14–15,
  15, 63
complexity diagnosis survey
  42
complexity diaries 42
Complexity Impact Score
  (CIS) *30*, 32
complexity tipping point
  see tipping point

compliance 8, 18, 177, 241, 275, 285
  see also regulatory oversight
complicators *21*, 23, 24, 34, 261
ConAgra 118
conjoint analysis 219
consumer electronics sector 24, 25, 65–6, 98, 100, 148, 179, 181, 202–4, 215, 217, 219, 222
contagion effects 17–18
contract manufacturers 226
contribution margin-based pricing 211, 212
core competencies 156, 157, 256, 262
core simplicity principles 54, *55*
Costli Coffee 11–12
crowdsourcing 151
customer relations 19, 205, 221, 225–6, 267
  banking sector 267, 273
  Complexity Impact Score (CIS) *32*
  customer relationship management (CRM) 278
  customer service 31, 105–6, 108, 179
  key relationships 221
  understanding customers 210, 215–18, 219–20
customer segmentation 160
customer value, creating 261, 264
customization 9, 19, 151, 160

Dai-ichi Life Insurance 279
De Bono, Edward 58, 261
decision accountability 109, *113*
  clarifying 112, 121
  final 47
  matrix decisions 125, 128
  right level of 121
  unclear 116
decision committees 101, 116, 117
decision-making 104
  complexity driver 83
  complexity impact, building in 87
  Complexity Impact Score (CIS) *32*
  complexity, symptoms of 115–17

matrix decisions 125–6, 128
simplification of 115–23: accountability, clarifying 112, 121; accountability, level of 121; committing to decision 123; critical information needs 121; 'decision lock' points 122, 23; optimizing who is involved 119–21; process standardization 122; rational decision-making model 121–2; speed–accuracy trade-offs 119, *120*; what you are deciding 119
  strategic 30–1, 142, 172, 178, 262
  styles: autocratic 122; collaborative 101, 119, 122; consultative 122
demotivation 68, 78, 129
developers 138
diagnosing complexity 38–50, *39*
  complexity behaviors, identifying 42
  external sources, diagnosing 38
  gain, calculating 42
  key questions 45–50: organizational complexity diagnosis 47; people complexity diagnosis 46; process complexity diagnosis 47; product/service complexity diagnosis 46–7; strategic complexity diagnosis 46
  management/staff involvement 38, 40
  prioritizing objectives 40–1, *48–9*
  quantifying cost of complexity 50–3
  root causes, understanding 40
  tools 42–7: complexity diagnosis survey 42; complexity diaries 42; feedback tools 43; management report use analysis 45; one-to-one interviews 44; value driver analysis 44–5

differentiators 152, 156
dimensions of complexity
  see external complexity; internal complexity; organizational complexity; people complexity; process complexity; product and service complexity; strategic complexity
disempowerment 121, 182
distribution networks 46
downstream complexity 209
drivers of complexity *see* external complexity; internal complexity
Drucker, Peter 96
due diligence 17, 275
  see also regulatory oversight
duplication 123, 234
  activities 110, 128, 129
  management reports 248
  meetings 239
  processes 174, 186, 189, 198
  products/services 215
  roles 109, 128, 129, 264

EBITDA (earnings before interest, taxes, depreciation and amortization) 14, 264
economies of scale 23, 95, 187, 212
Eisenhardt, Kathleen 15
email 46, 233–4
  overload 68, 69, 243
  rationing 244
empowerment 81, 84, 106, 112, 121, 189
enabling *55*, 62, 71, 72, 82, 89, 90
enabling leadership style 64, 76
enabling technologies 260
  see also IT systems
enterprise resource planning (ERP) 187
everyday complexity 83, 85, 230
  wasting the work day 232–4
everyday simplification 229–49
  adding value 231–5
  communications 243–4

doing the right things
in the right way 149,
231, 232
management reporting
244–9
meetings 238–43
prioritizing 234, 235–8
reduce/clarify/
standardize framework
55, 123, 235
external complexity 2–3,
6–7, 12, 14, 28, 29, 30
banking sector 18, 267,
273
diagnosis 38
insurance sector 278, 281
internal complexity driver
3, 7, 8
pharmaceuticals sector
259–60
top three drivers 30
external focus, increasing
33, 155–6, 261, 275
Exxon Mobil 16

feedback 43, 73, 76, 83, 86,
90, 199, 241
firm, types of 21–7, *21*
complicators *21*, 23, 24,
34, 261
performers 21–2, *21*, 269,
278, 280, 286
simplifiers 20, *21*, 278,
279–80, 285
strugglers 17, *21*, 24–5,
27, 261, 278, 279, 280–1,
284–5, 286
Five Guys Burgers and Fries
204
fixed costs
allocation 212, 214
reduction 213–15
flat organizations 65, 105
food and drink sector
11–12, 118, 128, 204, 208–9,
212–13, 226
Ford 3
From/To tool 162, *162*

Galbraith, J.R. 96
Gazprom 16
General Electric (GE) 81–2
General Motors (GM) 3, 96
Generali SPA 281
geographic diversification
14, 17, 19, 20, 24, 99, 100,
166, 267, 269–70, 275
banking sector 17, 267,
269–70, 275

insurance sector 279, 281,
285
Gerstner, Louis, Jr. 148
GlaxoSmithKline (GSK) 16,
20, 21–2, 23, 253, 254, 255
global financial crisis 266
Global Simplicity Index
(GSI) 13–16, 50, 155, 205,
251
banking sector 266,
268–9
complicators *21*, 23, 24,
34, 261
insurance sector 279–81
performance–complexity
rankings 268, *268*
performers 21–2, *21*, 269,
278, 280, 286
pharmaceuticals industry
253–7, *253*
simplifiers 20, *21*
strugglers 17, *21*, 24–5,
27, 261, 278, 279, 280–1,
284–5, 286
globalization 7, 99
Goldman Sachs 16, 20
group think 116
growth-share matrix *see*
Boston Box

Haldane, Andrew 17
headcount, reducing 79–80,
111, 137, 148
health, safety and security
procedures 176, 230
Hitachi 27
Home Depot 18
HP 202–3
HR processes, building
simplicity into 86
HSBC 17, 139
Hyundai 16

IBM 15, 24, 148
impacts of complexity 2,
33–5, *33*
on agility 34–5
on motivation 34
on profits *33*, 34
resources, waste of 33–4,
33
inertia 95, 125, 126, 176
information and
communication
technologies (ICT) 99
information overload 116
email 68, 69, 243
management reports 31,
101, 121, 230

innovation 19, 27, 51, 99,
105, 108, 136, 151, 152,
160, 161, 205
clusters 134–5
innovation portfolio tool
160, *160*
innovation-generating
routines 152
market-led 262
pharmaceuticals sector
252, 260
process complexity 252,
260
telecoms sector 26, 27
see also new product/
service launches;
research and
development (R&D)
input–output predictability
99, 100, 179, 180, 181, 186
insurance sector 18, 152,
224, 277–86
complexity drivers 279,
281–4, *284*
external complexity 278,
281
geographical complexity
279, 281, 285
global strugglers 279,
280–1, 284–5, 286
GSI ranking 279–81
local simplifiers 278,
279–80, 285
performance–complexity
matrix *280*
product/service
complexity 279, 281, 285
regional performers 278,
280, 286
regulatory complexity
278, 282
response to complexity
challenge 284–6
strategic complexity 283,
285
technology-related
complexity 282, 285
Intercontinental Hotels 154
internal complexity 2, 3, 6, 7,
9, 12, 28, 29, 30–1, 32, *32*, 45
banking sector 18, 267,
273–4
drivers 30–1, *30*, *32*, *258*
see also organizational
complexity; people
complexity; process
complexity; product
and service complexity;
strategic complexity

insurance sector 282–4
pharmaceuticals sector
257
internal politics 31, 34, 62,
67, 68, 79, 181, 220
internationalization *see*
geographic diversification
introverted firms 32–3, 179,
200, 257
IT systems
complexity diagnosis
questions 47
complexity driver 187, 279
rationalizing 285
see also technology-related
complexity

job descriptions 47
simplifying and clarifying
129, 138
job rotation 115
Jobs, Steve 65, 217
Johnson & Johnson 23, 177

keep/kill decisions 213,
214, 220
key performance indicators
(KPIs) 12, 31, 47, 67, 101,
104, 109, 126, 231, 260
knowledge-based processes
51, 99, 155, 179, 180, 181,
276
knowledge-based services,
shift to 99

leadership
alignment behind
simplicity cause 74–6
autocratic 64, 122
complexity behaviors 43,
64, 67, 83, 90
decision authority 121
enabling style 64, 76
micro-management 64,
83, 84
modeling behaviors 75,
76
reporting requirements
67
roles: change management
75; clear boundary
setting 64, 66;
communications 67,
76, 78, 83, 87, 168; goal
setting 67; strategy and
planning 67, 168
self-awareness 76, 83
simplicity behaviors 75–6
spans of control 112, 136

leadership programs 54, 75,
76, 84
Lean 99, 137, 179, 274
portfolio 65, 204, 208–9,
217, 218
problems with 180–2, 274
user resistance 182
legacy systems and
processes 95, 154, 174,
230, 282
Legal and General 280
Lehman Brothers 17, 266
live action learning 72, 73,
84–5
Lloyds 17
local responsiveness 5, 19
Lowes 18

machine-based processes
99, 179, 180, 181
major projects
costing 53
prioritizing 238
management
complexity behaviors 31,
40, 43
matrix roles 124–5
non-value-adding
activities 51, 52, 132, 235
self-awareness 83
spans of control 47,
109–10, 111, 136
see also leadership
management layers 18, 28,
104, 110–11, *113*
complexity diagnosis
questions 47
Complexity Impact Score
(CIS) 32
de-layering 109, 111, 112,
114, 261, 264
optimization 108–9
management reporting
audit 244–6
complexity diagnosis
questions 47
complexity driver 31,
67, 179
Complexity Impact Score
(CIS) 32
costing 53
housekeeping rules 249
overload 31, 101, 121, 230
receiver use analysis 45,
246
report use analysis 45
streamlining 244–9, *245*
value/cost analysis 247,
247

marginal contribution
process 211, 212
market attractiveness 156,
159
market positioning 151
market segmentation 99,
203, 206
Maslow's hierarchy of needs
60–2, *61*
matrix organizations 95,
98, 104
accountability 125
ambiguity, inherent 124,
125
benefits 124
complexity diagnosis
questions 47
divided loyalties 124
matrix/collaboration
model 135–6
simplification 123–7:
connections,
minimizing 124; goals
and measures 126;
good matrix behaviors
126–7; matrix decision
processes 125–6, 128;
matrix operational level
124–5; reduce/clarify/
standardize framework
123; reward structures
126–7
measures 107–8, 153, 179
activity-based 107, 108
matrix organizations 126
outcome-based 107, 108
simpler 108, 126
see also management
reporting
meetings
agenda structure 239, *240*
chairperson 241
complexity driver 68,
69, 83
costs 53, 239–40
good participants 241–2,
243
management skills and
behaviors 239–42
minutes 241
number and length of
238–9
preparation for 240–1
rules 242
scoring 241
simplifying 238–43
Meiji Yasuda 18, 279
mergers-and-acquisitions
(M&As) 9, 25, 26, 35

banking sector 270–1
harmful complexity, reducing 263, *263*
pharmaceuticals sector 21, 23, 252, 254, 255–6, 263
Metlife 281
Metro AG 19–20
micro-management 64, 83, 84
Microsoft 15, 65
mission 78, 156
mistrust 62, 84, 116
motivation 2, 34, 35, 42, 54, 59, 74, 84, 107, 261
multinationality *see* geographic diversification
Munich Re 281

net present value (NPV) 153
network externalities 17, 26
new markets 9, 93, 151, 160, 164
new product/service launches 31, 171, 203, 219, 220, 227
Complexity Impact Score (CIS) 32
Nippon Life Insurance 279
Nokia 2, 9, 24–5, 26–7, 34, 35, 119, 203–4, 222
Non-Production Procurement (NPP) 183
Novartis 23, 212–13, 254, 255, 256
organization design 94–7, 100
activity and skill clusters 110, 113, 114, 115, 135, 136–7, 197
capabilities 96, *96*, *102*, 138
components 95–6, *96*
culture 96, *96*, 102
design pyramid 96, *96*
divisional hierarchy 95
frequent changes in 99
functional structures 95
good design definition 97
governance 96, *96*, *102*
layers 18, 28, 46, 104, 108–9, 110–11, *111*, 112, *113*
matrix structure 95, 98, 104, 123–7
product structures 95
regional structures 95
requisite complexity 106, 110, 112
restructuring initiatives 2, 24, 66, 93–4, 99, 106, 178, 255, 275

right people/right things/right way 97, 105–31, 149, 232
roles and responsibilities 96, *96*, 102
simplification 105–31, 264
spans of control 47, 109–10, 111, *111*, 112, 113–14, 136
structure 96, *96*, 102
zero based approach 131–8, 197–8: activity clusters 134–5, 136–7; collaboration model 135–6, *135*; implementing 137–8; key activities/projects/ processes 133; spans of control 136; Stop/ Start/Continue exercise 133–4; strategic clarity 132; time use diagnosis 132–3
organizational complexity 9, 31, 92–139
banking sector 267, 273
case studies 98, 118, 128
costing 51
diagnosis questions 47
drivers 24, 31, 101–2, *102*, 104, 138
impacts of 34, *103–4*
pharmaceuticals sector 252, 260–1
simplification strategy: capability building 130–1; current design, simplifying 105–31, 264; decision-making, simplifying 115–23; duplications, removal of 129; job descriptions 129; matrix simplification 123–7; RACIs 130; role clarification 128, 129; zero based approach 131–8
strategy for change 105–39
symptoms 101
variations 94
outsourcing 198, 220, 237
over-engineering 62, 63, 83
processes 174, 180, *185*, 189
products/services 215, 219
over-intellectualizing 62, 83, 233

P&G 95
Panasonic 27
Pareto Analysis (80-20 rule) 166, 196, 198, 203, 236
people complexity 57–91
behaviors 58–63
case studies 58, 65–6, 81–2, 84
diagnosis 46, 88
drivers 31, 68–9, *69*: communications overload 31, 68, *69*; management behavior 31, 68, *69*; meetings 68, *69*
everyday complexity 83, 85
impact of 68–9, *69*
leaders *see* leadership
Maslow's hierarchy of needs 60–2, *61*
safety needs 61
self-actualization needs 62
self-esteem needs 61
simplification strategy 69–91: acting 72, 73, 83–7, 90; annual complexity reduction plans 86; clear and measurable objectives 72, 73, 83; communicating strategy 78, 87; cross-company programs 87; enabling people 71, 72, 82, 89, 90; engaging with people 71, 72, 74–80, 88–9, 90; individual level 73, 76–7; learning and changing by doing 72, 73, 84–5; major complexity problems 86; project teams 67, 86, 90; pull and/or push to change 70; raising awareness of 70; reducing headcount 79–80; reinforcing behaviors 72, 73, 86–7, 90; resistance to 79; rewards structure 79, 81, 87; sharing best practice 87; simplicity people program 54; systematic approach 70–3; team level 73, 76; toolkit 73–91, *88–9*; whole company level 73, 74

perfectionism 63, 233
performance measures
  see measures
performance–complexity
  matrix
  banking sector 17, 268–9,
    269
  insurance sector 280
  pharmaceuticals sector
    255, 255, 269
performance–complexity
  rankings 268, 268
performance–simplicity
  matrix 15–16, 16, 18
performers 21–2, 21, 269,
  278, 280, 286
personal complexity 43
  see also people
    complexity
PEST analysis 157–8
Petrobras 16
Pfizer 22, 23, 253, 254
pharmaceuticals sector
  21–4, 34–5, 177, 189–90,
  223, 226–7, 250–64
  complexity drivers 252,
    257–9, 258, 259
  external complexity 251,
    259–60
  GSI ranking 253–7, 253
  innovation process
    complexity 260
  organizational complexity
    252, 260–1
  performance–complexity
    matrix 255, 255, 269
  response to complexity
    challenge 23–4, 261–4
  strategic complexity 252,
    260
  technology-related
    complexity 252, 260
Philips 98
plan-do-check-act (PDCA)
  181
portfolio
  complexity tipping point
    209, 213, 227
  customer needs-driven
    215–16, 216
  innovation portfolio tool
    160, 160
  lean 65, 204, 208–9, 217,
    218
  proliferation 18, 213
  rationalizing 221–2, 223,
    231, 285
Potentials 131
price premiums 224

pricing systems 47
prioritization 55, 234, 235–8
  activity lists 235–8
  complexity problems
    40–1, 41
  pain/gain matrix 41, 41
  strategic priorities 27, 104
  value/urgency matrix
    236–8, 236, 237
problem avoidance 62
process complexity 28, 29,
  30, 31, 173–200
  banking sector 267, 274
  case studies 177, 183–4,
    189–90
  diagnosis questions 47
  drivers 31, 176, 185
  duplication 174, 186, 189,
    198
  overly-complex processes
    174–5, 176, 177
  simplification strategy
    184–200; elimination
    of redundant/
    unnecessary processes
    187; reshaping the
    process 197–9;
    standardization 181,
    187, 248; stock take of
    process complexity
    186–7; streamlining
    187–8, 190–200, 191,
    276; understanding the
    current process 192–7,
    193
  symptoms 184–5
  too many processes 174
process creep 176
process mapping 121, 248
process redesign 187–8,
  190–200
  documentation 199
  focus on pain and gain
    points 191, 196–7
  industry comparisons
    198–9
  piloting the new process
    199
  re-launch 199
  reshaping the process
    191, 197–9
  scope and design
    parameters 190, 191, 192
  shifting/outsourcing 198
  trade-offs 190
  understanding the current
    process 192–7, 193
  value drivers 194, 195
  zero based option 197–8

processes
  basic 175
  complexity drivers 177–9,
    178
  defining 175
  hierarchical 176
  key process identification
    166
  knowledge-based 51, 99,
    155, 179, 180, 181, 276
  machine-based 99, 179,
    180, 181
  non-core 198
  redundant 95, 154, 174,
    177
  strategic 175
  tactical 175
  transformational 176
  value of 175
  'work arounds' 184, 185
  see also business process
    re-engineering (BPR);
    over-engineering
product and service
  complexity
  case studies 208–9, 223
  drivers 31
  hidden costs 203–4, 205,
    225
  impacts 206–7
  insurance sector 279, 281
  simplification strategy
    209–27: contract
    manufacturers 226;
    cutting deeper 210,
    220–1; driving fixed
    costs down 210, 213–
    15; focusing on best
    products/services 210,
    221–3; harmonizing
    local variations 225;
    portfolio rationalization
    221–2, 223, 231, 285;
    reducing component
    complexity 226;
    simplicity-sells
    principle 223–5;
    simplifying product/
    service design 219–20,
    285; tail analysis and
    management 210–13,
    225–6, 226–7, 228;
    understanding the
    customer 210, 215–18,
    219–20; upstream
    and downstream
    complexity 209
product/service tail
  analysis 210–13, 211

cutting out tail customers 225
cutting your tail 210–11, 220, 225–6, 228
managing tail products 226–7
selling tail products to competitors 227
products and services 201–28
adding value 12, 226, 228
complexity diagnosis questions 46–7
cross-selling 270
diversification 24, 267
growth potential 220, 221
innovation 19
key product/service identification 165
launching 219, 227
new product/service launches 31, 32, 171, 203, 219, 220, 227
retaining poor performers 220–1
'special' products groups 226–7
see also innovation; portfolio
professional administrators, rise of 176
promotion process 79, 86
Prudential 17, 280
pruning 148, 197, 235

quantifying cost of complexity 50–3
activity based costing 51
cost vs. value creation 51
doing right things in the wrong way 52
major projects 53
management reports, costing 53
meeting costs 53, 239–40
non-value-adding activities 51, 52
organizational complexity 51
roughly right principle 50, 52
zero based costing 51

R&D see research and development (R&D)
RACIs (Responsible, Accountable, Consulted and Involved) 121, 125, 128, 130, 138
communicating 130

radical 130
ranking tool 166, 196
Reckett Benckiser 122
recruitment process 86, 105
reduce/clarify/standardize framework 55, 123, 235
redundant processes see legacy systems and processes
regulatory oversight 7–8, 266, 273, 274, 278, 282
regulatory risk 190
reinforcing simplicity principles 55, 71, 72, 73, 75, 86, 90
reinventing 62, 233
Renault 20
reporting see management reporting
research and development (R&D) 21, 23, 24, 26, 65, 98, 161, 177, 254
resource leveraging 151
resource wastefulness 33
restructuring initiatives 2, 24, 66, 93–4, 99, 106, 178, 255, 275
retail sector 18, 19–20, 84, 151, 202, 204, 208–9, 221
return on investment (ROI) 153
reverse budgeting 161
risk analysis 17
risk aversion 84, 128, 220, 275
risk management 8, 275
Roche 23, 253
role clarity 47, 102, 103, 264
roughly right principle 50
Royal Bank of Scotland (RBS) 16, 17, 18, 266, 270–1

Sanofi-Aventis 23
services see products and services
shareholder value, loss of 14
shifting/outsourcing 198, 220, 237
'Show It' exercises 141
sign-off processes 28, 52, 84, 101, 122, 147
Simple Success Keys 164–6, 165, 186
Simplicity 101 projects 41, 84–5
simplicity
beliefs 77

company value 74–5, 81–2, 84, 224
core simplicity principles 54, 55
defining 6
performance–simplicity matrix 15–16, 16, 18
personal benefits of 34, 78–9
simplicity index see Global Simplicity Index (GSI)
simplicity-sells principle 223–5
simplification strategy
core simplicity principles 54, 55
diagnosis results 54
everyday simplification ideas 54
major simplification projects 54
measurable complexity reduction objectives 54
simplicity people program 54
see also under everyday simplification; organizational complexity; people complexity; process complexity; product and service complexity; strategic complexity
simplifiers 20, 21, 278, 279–80, 285
'size of the prize' calculation 50–3
skills assessment survey 131
skills clusters 110, 113, 114, 115, 134, 135, 197
Sony 27, 67
sources of complexity see drivers of complexity; external complexity; internal complexity
spans of control 47, 109–10, 111, 111, 112, 136
CEOs 112, 136
optimization 109–10, 113–14
specialization 99
Spreadshirt 151
standardization 55, 105, 160, 235
decision-making 122, 123, 125–6
ingredients/components 226
processes 181, 187, 248

products/services 19, 151, 209, 213
Stars 131, 138
State Farm Insurance 279
Stop/Start/Continue tool 133–4, 161, *162*, 197
strategic complexity 8–9, 30–1, 140–72
  banking sector 267, 273
  cascade effect 149
  case studies 148, 154, 161
  complexity cross 150, *150*
  diagnosis questions 46
  drivers 24, 143–7: confused priorities 143, 147; initiative overload 143, 144, 147; overly-complex planning processes 143, 145, 147, 155; shifting goalposts 28, 143, 144, 147, 171
  impacts of *146*
  insurance sector 283
  pharmaceuticals sector 252, 260
  simplification strategy 145, 154–64: focus on external factors 155–6; revisiting and simplifying processes 155; simple strategy questions 156–7; Success Keys, identifying and prioritizing 164–6, *165*; tools 157–64
  symptoms *144*
strategy
  acid test of 149
  as simple rules 66, 151–3, 156: borderline rules 152; priority rules 152–3; source of complexity 153; stop rules 153
  clarity 106, 262
  communicating 167–71
  complexity driver 31, 141–2, 143–7, 153
  Complexity Impact Score (CIS) 32
  defining 142
  innovation 147
  international 147
  major projects, costing 53
  market 147
  measures 107–8
  mismatch with organization design 105

one-page summary 168, *169*, *170*
road testing 169
Simple Success Keys 164–6, *165*
strategic decision-making 30–1, 142, 172, 178, 262
strategic focus 21, 24, 100, 276, 285
tinkering with 62, 106
tools: 'how to win' checklist 162–4; innovation portfolio tool 160; situation analysis tools 157–8; Stop/Start/Continue tool 133–4, 161, *162*, 197; values and behaviors tool 162, *162*; visioning tool 158, *158*; 'where are we going to compete' tools 159–61
trade-offs 66, 151
viable 142–3
where to play and how to win 156–7, *157*
strugglers 17, 24–5, 27, 261
  banking 17
  individuals 131, 138
  insurance 278, 279, 280–1, 284–5, 286
  pharmaceuticals 261
Sumitomo 18, 279
supply chains 19, 118
  complexity diagnosis questions 46
  supplier relations 225
surveys
  complexity diagnosis survey 42
  Personal Simplicity Survey 76
  skills assessment 131
  360 surveys 76, 83, 90
SWOT analysis 158

Target 18
teams
  change agents 75
  complexity diagnosis 88
  cross-functional and cross-business 67, 98
  defensive and dysfunctional 68
  inter-group working, improving 115
  project teams 67, 86, 90
  strategic boundaries 67, 68
  support and training 76, 86

team culture 67, 68
technology-related complexity
  insurance sector 282, 285
  pharmaceuticals sector 252, 260
telecoms sector 2, 9, 16, 24–5, 26–7, 119, 203–4, 219, 224
Tesco 19
time-boxing 237
tinkering 62, 106, 174, 184
tipping point 10, 15
  banking sector 266, 268, 274
  people complexity 63, 71
  portfolio complexity 209, 213
Toshiba 27
Toyota 20, 194
trade-offs
  process redesign 190
  product/service trade-off analysis 219
  speed–accuracy trade-offs 119, *120*
  strategic 66, 151
Trader Joe's 208–9
'true cost' financial model 213

Unilever 95, 139, 218
unique consumer proposition 215, 221
upstream complexity 209

value chains 26, 100, 209, 226, 252, 262
value creation 194
value driver analysis 44–5, 194, *195*
value/urgency matrix 236–8, *236*, *237*
Vodafone 16, 75, 139, 224

Walgreens 18
Walmart 19, 139, 202
Welch, Jack 81, 82
Wickes 204
work diaries 51, 53
work–life balance 79, 232
write-off costs 214

Xerox 183–4

zero based option
  organization design 131–8, 197–8
  process design 197–8
Zurich 75, 224, 281